In the Shadow of Authoritarianism

In the Shadow of Authoritarianism

American Education in the Twentieth Century

Thomas D. Fallace

TEACHERS COLLEGE PRESS
TEACHERS COLLEGE | COLUMBIA UNIVERSITY
NEW YORK AND LONDON

Published by Teachers College Press, 1234 Amsterdam Avenue, New York, NY 10027

Cover design by Jeremy Fink.

Library of Congress Cataloging-in-Publication Data is available at loc.gov

ISBN 978-0-8077-5937-0 (paper)
ISBN 978-0-8077-7692-6 (ebook)

Printed on acid-free paper
Manufactured in the United States of America

25 24 23 22 21 20 19 18 8 7 6 5 4 3 2 1

Contents

Acknowledgments

The research for this book was generously funded by a grant from the Spencer Foundation and assigned release time from William Paterson University. I am very grateful for this support. Portions of the manuscript were previously published in "American Educators' Confrontation with Fascism," *Educational Researcher* by the American Educational Research Association and SAGE Press. I thank Christopher Phillips and Andrew Hartman, who both read the entire manuscript and provided very helpful feedback enabling me to clarify and strengthen my argument throughout. I built upon their previous research and benefitted greatly from their comments. I accepted most, but not all, of their advice, so I take full responsibility for any weaknesses or omissions. I thank Walter Parker for providing encouragement, conversation, and intellectual stimulation for the project, and the anonymous reviewers for feedback and making useful suggestions for additional sources. At William Paterson University, I thank Dean Candace Burns for her recognition and support of my research, and Joanna Doyle and Priscilla Stevens for helping me with the paperwork related to the grant. I thank librarians Yvonne Roux and M. Judy Matthew for tracking down and hauling over dozens of interlibrary loans. Finally, my wife, Victoria Fantozzi, read portions of the manuscript, while working on her own research, chairing her department, and raising our kids (with my help). After 14 years of marriage, I am more impressed by her with each passing year.

Introduction

How to Think, Not What to Think

Writing in 1949, historian Arthur Schlesinger, Jr., warned that the rise of authoritarianism across the globe represented "more than an internal crisis for democratic society. It signif[ied] an internal crisis for democratic man" because, according to Schlesinger, there was potentially "a Hitler, a Stalin in every breast."[1] For most of the 20th century, American educators lived in the shadow of ideological, political, cultural, and existential threats from abroad. Consequently, educators in the United States defined their approach to democratic education in contrast to what it was not: authoritarianism. *Authoritarian* was an adjective used repeatedly and consistently by U.S. scholars between World War I and the 1980s to depict the outlook of those regimes, groups, parties, and individuals characterized by social hierarchy, ideological homogeneity, and intolerance for dissent. Under authoritarianism, the individual was subservient to the collective party or state. Since the school was the nexus between the state and the individual, authoritarians approached the school as the primary means of transmitting its values and ideology to students. Consequently, authoritarian educators embraced propaganda and indoctrination and taught their students to be docile, obedient, intolerant, and compliant. Democratic educators, in contrast, deliberately avoided propaganda and indoctrination by teaching students to be open-minded, balanced, and skeptical. In democratic regimes, the state was subservient to the individual, not the other way around. At least, this is what most U.S. educators told themselves and one another repeatedly between World War I and the 1980s. During these years the description of authoritarianism shifted in response to evolving geopolitical realities—Prussianism, propaganda, collectivism, dictatorship, totalitarianism, the space race, mind control, and moral relativity—but the reaction by most leading American educators remained constant: The way to avoid the propaganda, intolerance, and indoctrination of authoritarian education was to teach students the dispositions of freedom and critical thinking. Democratic teachers taught students *how* to think, not *what* to think. Leading educators never really defined the idea of teaching how to think, not what to think with precision, yet the idea provided a malleable and powerful image around which U.S. educators of all political persuasions could rally, and did rally, for nearly 70 years.

Between World War I and the 1980s, most intellectuals and leading educational theorists in the United States viewed education as the key ingredient in the national, civic project to create a nation of free-thinking individuals. Those on both the political right and left defined democratic education as the deliberate avoidance of propaganda, indoctrination, and top-down authoritarian pedagogy and administration, often accusing one another of supporting these un-American ideas. Besides the brief embrace of indoctrination by some educational theorists during the Great Depression, American educators repeatedly defined *propaganda* and *indoctrination* as the opposite of *democratic education,* and championed the latter as the only approach to take in the United States For example, as the National Education Association (NEA) related in 1929: "The main purpose of propaganda is to teach *what to think*, while the guiding purpose of education is to teach *how to think*."[2] The same year, an education professor said: "The function of education is to acquaint the individual with a variety of opinions, doctrines, or courses of action so as to equip him intelligently to do his own thinking and to select his own courses of action." In contrast, the objective of authoritarian teaching was "to gain acceptance of a particular opinion, doctrine, or course of action under circumstances designed to curb the individual's freedom of action."[3] In 1935, the editors of the educational journal *Teachers College Record* made a similar distinction: "Indoctrination teaches what to think; education, how to think."[4] Writing in 1957, at the height of the Cold War, another education professor again insisted that to avoid authoritarian thinking, teachers must "help students how to think, not what to think."[5] Writing in 1961, two theorists of democratic education asserted that the greatest "danger for both the individual and the culture is the denial to any of the opportunity to develop the ability and inclination to think."[6] Further, as another educational researcher explained in 1976, "[t]o choose the democratic ideal for society is wholly to reject the conception of education as an instrument of rule; it is to surrender the idea of shaping or molding the mind of the pupil."[7]

The mantra of teaching students how to think, not what to think first emerged in the 1920s in response to the use of propaganda by the U.S. government during World War I. Educators' focus on the importance of thinking and open-mindedness in a democratic society was sincere, but it also provided an extremely useful and potent rhetoric for attacking their domestic political enemies. Looking back in 1966 over the previous decades, social studies educator James Shaver commented: "The red flag of indoctrination, with its implications of unthinking obedience, is often waved."[8] Indeed, as this study will demonstrate, educators waved the "red flag of indoctrination" repeatedly between 1916 and the 1980s in discussions over how to prepare future citizens in a democratic society. Between World War I and the 1980s, the terms *propaganda*, *indoctrination*, and *authoritarian* became common accusations employed by nearly all educational stakeholders seeking to dismiss the ideas of their opponents. Educational theorists argued over how to teach democratic citizens in a way that avoided indoctrination, while simultaneously (and paradoxically) strengthening allegiance to democratic ideals through the values of ideological skepticism, scientific thinking, and consensus building—dispositions and skills affiliated with teaching students how to think, instead of what to think.

During 1916, two major publications, Dewey's *Democracy and Education* and the NEA's *Social Studies in the Secondary Schools*, underscored the importance of citizenship education in a democracy. Both publications insisted that the existing history and civics curriculum was outdated and needed substantial reform in light of international and domestic events, such as industrialization, immigration, and world war. In 1983, two influential publications, the *Nation at Risk* report by the National Commission on Excellence in Education and E. D. Hirsch's article on "Cultural Literacy," repositioned the central importance of having schools transmit subject matter to students. These publications marked a key turning point away from the "how to think, not what to think" approach by making a case for rigorous national standards prescribing specific subject matter.

Between World War I and the 1980s, scholars and policymakers proposed and implemented waves of reforms to update the curriculum to better equip students to conduct themselves as democratic citizens in a world where democracy was perceived to be under constant domestic and foreign threat by authoritarianism. Furthermore, during these years, the American high school expanded from an institution serving the elite few to one that served the vast majority of adolescents. In 1919, only 31% of 14- to 17-year-olds were enrolled in high school. By 1980, enrollment had reached 90%. During these years, high school graduation rates exploded from 16% to 71%.[9] As a result, scholars and policymakers increasingly looked to the school as a way to respond to ideological and political threats in a global context because the school became an avenue to reach the vast majority of future U.S. citizens. The school also became a screen upon which educators and intellectuals projected their vision of what democracy ought to be. Even with the general consensus that democratic schools ought to teach how to think, not what to think, educators fiercely debated whether this implied that the curriculum should be based on the traditional liberal arts, the discussion of social issues, disciplined inquiry, or an exploration of students' values and morals. The consensus on teaching how to think, not what to think, held for 70 years because the vagueness of the concept allowed U.S. educators to debate exactly what this entailed, while still adhering to a general conviction that democratic education ought to diverge from authoritarian education.

American educators agreed that the survival of democracy rested, in part, on the curriculum of the U.S. schools. As a result, elite American educators believed that the curriculum had global implications. This is not to suggest that the rhetoric of reform reflected what was actually going on in the majority of U.S. classrooms at any given time. Local control, lack of ambitious and qualified teachers, the prevalence of textbook-centered teaching, resistance, and inertia made U.S. schools notoriously difficult to change. Thus, the rhetoric of "teaching how to think, not what to think" was often just that: rhetoric. However, as this book will demonstrate, several experiments did actually reach the classrooms of ambitious and engaged teachers, and changing course offerings and enrollments reflected slow but substantial change at the classroom level, although never to the extent described by both advocates and critics of student-centered education. My study is more about the story that educational elites told themselves than it is about what was actually going on in the average American classroom at any given time. Nevertheless, this story was extremely important to educational researchers and policymakers articulating a vision for the future of education in a democracy, and their ideas continue to inspire researchers and theorists today—the work of John Dewey being the most obvious example.

Regarding terminology, I use the deliberately broad term *democratic education* to describe the effort by leading public intellectuals, policymakers, professors of education, professors of humanities and social sciences, and classroom teachers to craft an educational experience that developed the knowledge, skills, and dispositions of citizenship in a democratic society. My focus is primarily on the content and theory of the curriculum, not on the institutional, administrative, legal, and political arrangements that made democratic education possible, although these elements are treated as important context. One of the essential traits of a good citizen was the ability to detect and resist propaganda and indoctrination, although the definitions of these terms were themselves constantly being debated and redefined. "An immense deal of actual indoctrination takes place in our schools and colleges, and must inevitably always take place," one contemporary commented in 1933. "When it does not please us, we call it propaganda; when it does please us, we call it education."[10] Leading educators defined *democratic education* dialectically against what they perceived to be the propaganda and indoctrination approaches of authoritarian regimes. The subjects of history, civics, and social studies have historically been at the center of civic education in the United States, but, at times, reformers also framed the subjects of English, math, and science in terms of how they could contribute to civic education. Further, the debate over democratic education expanded beyond the social studies into broader discussions over the purpose of schooling and the relationship between the curriculum and society.

My definition of *authoritarian* is likewise broad and follows the loose definition scholars employed between 1916 and the 1980s. The term *authoritarian* described a relationship between the individual and the state that was consistently used as a foil to democratic governance and life. Under authoritarian rule, the individual was subservient to the state, party, or ruling elite, while under democratic rule, the state or party was subservient to the individual. There was a coterminous economic element to the term *authoritarian* as well. Under authoritarian rule the economy was directed in part or completely by the state, whereas under democratic rule the state endorsed unfettered private ownership. In other words, under authoritarian rule the state chose winners and losers in both the ideological and economic marketplace, while in a democracy the state remained relatively neutral regarding issues of ideology and economics. Consequently, authoritarian leaders told students what to think, not how to think through propaganda and indoctrination, whereas under democratic rule students were, in theory, free to make their own ideological and economic choices about controversial issues.

Five authoritarian threats emerged between 1916 and the 1980s: Prussianism, communism, fascism, dictatorship, and totalitarianism. At first, American educators approached each of them with curiosity, but over time, as their authoritarian (and militaristic) tendencies grew, they were recast as existential threats to democracy. The first came from Prussia, the largest and most powerful region of Germany. In the 19th century, Prussian leader Otto von Bismarck implemented a series of top-down reforms that unified the 39 German states under Prussia. Bismarck crafted an industrialized, modernized, and imperialistic vision for Germany, and U.S. educators admired the forward-thinking reforms of Prussian education. However, when the United States entered World War I against Germany in 1917, American scholars cast "Prussianism" as an authoritarian ideology and denounced the Prussians' centralized approach to schooling and governance. The use of propaganda during the war by Prussia and the U.S. government inspired American educators to focus on teaching how to think as an antidote to domestic and foreign authoritarianism.

The second threat emerged during World War I, when the Russian Revolution brought the Bolshevik Party to power. Skeptics of communism pointed to the authoritarian aspects of the Bolsheviks, while others approached the Russian collectivist experiment with optimism. A dozen American educators even traveled to Soviet Russia to evaluate the Bolshevik labor schools in person. The third threat, fascism, emerged from Italy when Benito Mussolini marched on Rome and seized control of the nation in 1922, and in Germany when Adolf Hitler brought the Nazis to power in 1933. Americans initially approached Mussolini with curiosity, but they had no admiration for Hitler and feared his racist, nationalistic, and violent rhetoric. The fourth threat was a result of the reclassification of Hitler, Mussolini, and General Secretary of the Soviet Union Joseph Stalin as authoritarian "dictators" in the mid-1930s. Despite the ideological differences between communism and fascism, American scholars identified similarities in the absolute dictatorial powers of these three leaders, their regimes, and their educational systems. Finally, during the late 1930s, the fifth threat emerged when scholars conflated fascism and communism into the term *totalitarianism*, designating the complete economic and social immersion of the individual into the state. Identified as an approach beyond mere dictatorship, scholars considered totalitarianism an unprecedented orientation to social life, an approach made possible by the modern apparatus of industrialization, media, propaganda, surveillance, mind control, and schooling. This final threat—totalitarianism—extended from World War II to the 1980s. During this period, specific outcomes of the ideological battle against totalitarianism, such as the defection of "brainwashed" American soldiers to North Korea, the launching of the Soviet satellite *Sputnik*, and the domestic response to the Vietnam War, demanded that U.S. educators meet the authoritarian threat by teaching how to think, not what to think. Between 1916 and the 1980s, American educators applied the term *authoritarian* to all of these foreign threats, and they also applied the term to those domestic ideological and political threats that allegedly demonstrated authoritarian tendencies.

Of course, in reality, educators never really defined the sharp distinction between how to think and what to think. Most teachers would agree that students cannot think without having some subject matter in their heads to contemplate and, conversely, even the most textbook-driven teachers claim to develop the critical thinking of their students through discussion and essay questions. I suggest that many educators often used the phrase "how to think, not what to think" as a way to evade the inevitable political and ideological messiness of selecting specific topics to cover and omit in the curriculum. Not until World War II did some ambitious social studies educators really start to parse out the meaning of this phrase in a robust way by creating materials that fostered classroom discussion about controversial issues or discipline-specific inquiries.

By tracing the discussion and reactions of U.S. educators to authoritarianism between World War I and the 1980s—specifically, accusations and counteraccusations of propaganda, indoctrination, brainwashing, and moral relativity—I demonstrate how leading educators revised and reformed the rhetoric of democratic education in contrast to perceived domestic and foreign authoritarian threats. Anxieties over propaganda, indoctrination, and authoritarian methods reflected a world in which half of its inhabitants did not reside in democratic regimes, and in which foreign powers explicitly targeted the democratic way of life. Anxieties over these threats gave the American curriculum an overall sense of unity and purpose that has largely been missing from the educational scene since the 1980s. My book investigates a period when a major function of the school was civic and political because educators took seriously the threat of propaganda, indoctrination, and authoritarian thinking, and they agreed that schools could and should meet that threat. Despite their differences, U.S. educators had reached a consensus on the purpose of the American school as teaching how to think, not what to think, a consensus that was contingent upon the existence of authoritarian regimes as democracy's *other.* The debates over the curriculum were fierce, but all sides never wavered from the notion that the school was an important, perhaps *the most important*, institution in preserving and facilitating democratic life. With today's focus on college and career readiness, we have sadly strayed far from the American schools' historic purpose of fostering civic competency and developing democratic dispositions.

CHAPTER 1

In the Shadow of Prussianism

In 1916, William F. Russell, Dean of Teachers College, Columbia University, invited several leading scholars, including the nation's leading educational philosopher John Dewey, to consider the relationship between politics and public education during wartime. Most participants asserted the belief that the outbreak of World War I was largely a product of the Prussian school system and that U.S. schools ought to continue to develop in ways that diverged from the German example. Yet some recognized promise in Prussian schools' bureaucratic efficiency and sense of national purpose. This conflict—whether to diverge from or, to some degree, emulate the authoritarian schooling of foreign powers—would occupy American educators for the next 70 years as they responded to unprecedented ideological threats and cataclysmic events undreamt of in 1916. World War I offered the first opportunity to consider how American education emulated and/or diverged from the authoritarian education systems of its enemies.

Historian Charles Beard outlined the historical differences between the Prussian and U.S. societies and how their respective educational systems reflected these cultural and economic divergences. Beard concluded that, to keep the promise of American education alive, the schools would need to stay out of politics by focusing on shared culture and public life. "American citizenship is not merely citizenship of obedience," Beard averred. "It is a citizenship of strife and contention, of education and progress through conflict."[1] Educational historian Isaac Kandel argued the German education system fostered uniformity and control, and as a result, "the individual is suppressed and trained to become a cog in a political wheel."[2]

In his address "Organization of American Education" Dewey addressed the issue of how to better organize the American schools for a unified sense of purpose. He recognized that the United States would not be able to construct the kind of efficient "centralized and effective machinery which, in Germany, would take care of that need," even if it wanted to, because the U.S. schools were too decentralized, and Americans were too averse to taking orders from above. If Americans were to reform their schools, Dewey insisted, they would need to be convinced through the dissemination of "expert knowledge" and "expert ability." Dewey concluded: "I see no recourse but an organization of publicity to illuminate and direct public opinion" on issues of pedagogy and school administration. In other words, the way to improve education was more education, not more bureaucracy, centralization, and regulations. Dewey was vague about what he meant by "organization of publicity," as he was about many of his pedagogical prescriptions.[3] Nevertheless, Dewey was clear that he favored persuasion over compulsion, the dissemination of expert knowledge over centralized planning, and teaching how to think over teaching what to think. He saw little in the Prussian system to emulate, other than its shared sense of national purpose.

This critique of Prussian education between 1914 and 1918 represented a sharp rupture from the past. Prior to World War I, American educators had looked to Germany as a major source of educational ideas and ideals. Most of the leading U.S. scholars had studied in Germany and had immense admiration for its universities, secondary and elementary schools. However, as World War I began, American theorists of democratic education turned inward, away from Germany and toward the unique aspects of American society and culture. It was in the context of the war that leading educational theorists in the United States began to clarify their visions for education in a democracy. Specifically, Dewey, the most influential educational theorist of the first half of the 20th century, espoused an innovative vision for cultural pluralism, the comprehensive high school, and a student-centered approach to teaching that diverged from German philosophy and pedagogy.

Dewey had developed his ideas carefully over decades in his work at the University of Chicago, but the war provided a context that allowed him to sharpen his views on democratic education. In other words, the war enabled Dewey and his like-minded peers to define democratic education powerfully and potently in contrast to what it was not: Prussianism—a word that educators used vaguely to connote top-down bureaucratic reform, schooling differentiated by social class, teacher-centered instruction, and inculcation of loyalty to the state and war effort. As Dewey explained in *Democracy and Education*, "Under the influence of German thought in particular, education became a civic function and the civic function was identified with the realization of the ideal of the national state. The state was substituted for humanity; cosmopolitanism gave way to nationalism. To form the citizen, not the 'man' became the aim of education." As Dewey argued, since "a democratic society repudiates the principle of external authority," such as the kind of state education system in Germany, "it must find a substitute in voluntary disposition and interest." This disposition can be developed only through a democratic education that deliberately put students of different classes, religions, races, and ethnicities in the same school and class. Thus, Dewey clarified his own definition of democracy in relation to what it was not, as expressed in one of his most popular, influential, and enduring passages: "A democracy is more than a form of government; it is primarily a mode of associated living, of conjoined communicated experience."[4]

GERMAN INFLUENCE ON U.S. EDUCATION

Ever since the founding of the common school in the 19th century, U.S. educators had looked to Prussia and Germany for inspiration and ideas to improve its own schools. During the 19th century, England had no comprehensive public school system, and France offered a far less centralized and inconsistent education to its citizens.[5] Prussia was the first to establish a comprehensive, compulsory, centrally organized schooling and teacher education system, and American educators greatly admired this fact. As one scholar explained in 1918: "For the past seventy-five years America has knelt quite submissively before Germany, as the most educationally efficient nation in the world."[6] During a period in which "efficiency" stood for modern, advanced, and scientific, the Prussian schools were considered the best. For example, in the 1830s, the state of Ohio sent Calvin Ellis Stowe, Harriet Beecher Stowe's husband, to Europe to learn what he could from the Prussian schools. Stowe was impressed with the organization of their curriculum and how the Prussian teachers moved beyond mere rote learning to engage the students' higher faculties such as imagination and judgment. Stowe emphatically concluded: "[I]f it can be done in Prussia, I know it can be done in Ohio." In 1843, Massachusetts Secretary of Education Horace Mann likewise traveled to Prussia to study its schools. He too admired how the Prussian teachers helped students gain "precision in the expression of ideas" and encouraged them to "exercise their intellect." Mann concluded that, if Prussia could effectively construct a school system to support "arbitrary power," than "we surely can employ them for the support of republican institutions."[7] Henry Barnard, founder of the common schools of Connecticut and the first U.S. Commissioner of Education, also visited the Prussian schools in the 1850s and found much to admire. In 1860, Barnard related: "The very way in which children of different ranks of society are to be found mingled in the same school serves to show how superior the civilization of the lower orders in Germany is to that of the English peasants."[8] The earliest proponents of the common school admired the German system of public schooling and praised many of its pedagogical and administrative innovations. Yet they also recognized that Prussia was not a republic like the United States, and therefore the German ideas would need to be adapted to meet local conditions.

By midcentury, William Torrey Harris—the most important U.S. educational figure between Mann and Dewey—maintained U.S. educators' admiration for German ideas through his espousal of the idealism of German philosopher Georg Wilhelm Friedrich Hegel. Harris was a founding editor of the *Journal of Speculative Philosophy*, superintendent of public schools in St. Louis between 1868 and 1880, and U.S. Commissioner of Education between 1889 and 1906. In St. Louis, a community with 80% German ancestry, Harris implemented many German- and Prussian-inspired innovations, including kindergarten. He also advocated for the teaching of the German language in St. Louis schools and nationally. Beyond Hegel, the biggest philosophical influence on U.S. educators prior to Dewey was German philosopher Johann Friedrich Herbart. Herbart had tutored three Swiss boys in the late 18th century. Based on this experience, he constructed an innovative educational scheme, which was further developed by his German disciples Karl Volkmar Stoy, Tuiskon Ziller, and Wilhelm Rein. Ziller compiled the specific Herbartian steps of learning—analysis and/or explanation of facts; synthesis, assimilation of facts; and identification of the most important facts—as well as the applications of the learned principles. Through this process the content was not only learned, but "apperceived." German psychologist Wilhelm Wundt had recently popularized Herbart's term *apperception*—the idea of making one's experience clear in one's consciousness—through his own influential work.[9] By *apperception* the Herbartians meant that the facts had been incorporated into a psychic command-center of the mind, which controlled the organization and apperception of all subsequently acquired knowledge. These "apperceptive masses" guided the tastes and aided in the cultivation of the mind. Learning had not truly taken place until the content was associated with previously apperceived content and directed toward more complicated, difficult material. To make the internal apperception of material occur more naturally, according to Herbartians, content was externally arranged in relation to one another, through "correlation" or "concentration." Teachers were encouraged to explore the connections among the different disciplines and bodies of knowledge to present them in a correlated manner.[10] The Prussians had incorporated many Herbartian ideas in their own schools, and many German-trained scholars had brought these concepts back to the United States. In 1895, Charles De Garmo, Charles and Frank McMurry, and C. C. Van Liew founded the National Herbart Society. These scholars had studied the pedagogical and philosophical theories of Herbert in Germany, and when they returned to the United States, they began disseminating Herbart's ideas in educational journals, lectures, and textbooks.[11] For example, American educators had imported the idea of "home geography" from Prussian schools. Originating with the German idea of *Heimatkunde*, home geography explored how geographic concepts connected to the students' direct observations of local surroundings. Students left the school building to collect data on their immediate environs, an activity that experts considered hands-on and developmentally appropriate. The home geography fad gained in popularity at the turn of the century. As one professor of geography explained, "the teachers and educators of the country are coming rapidly to perceive that home geography must become the basis for later training, as has long been the habit in Germany."[12] One 1907 study discovered that 60% of schools it surveyed were teaching some form of home geography to its students.

Beyond geography, history was the subject most directly affiliated with the formation of citizens, and American historians furthered the effort to adapt Prussian ideas to U.S. schools through the writing of textbooks and recommendations of the committee reports such as those issued by the Committee of Ten (1894) and Committee of Seven (1899).[13] Most historians and social scientists concerned about the teaching of civics and history in the United States during the 1890s had studied at German universities, including historians Herbert Baxter Adams, Albert Bushnell Hart, John W. Burgess, and Charles Kendall Adams.[14] Influential historians who studied in the United States, such as Lucy Maynard Salmon and Woodrow Wilson, had done so under the mentorship of German-trained historians. Beyond these figures, pedagogical innovator Col. Francis W. Parker, civil rights advocate W.E.B. Du Bois, and psychologists William James and G. Stanley Hall had also studied in Germany. These scholars lauded Prussian schools and pedagogy, and they sought to import many of its innovations to the United States. In fact, the leading theory of historical development during the final decades of the 19th century—the institutional germ theory—venerated the German culture by arguing that the idea of American democracy originated with the Teutonic–Anglo-Saxon race.[15]

In an influential 1882 article, "The German Origin of New England Towns," Herbert Baxter Adams of Johns Hopkins University traced the idea of democracy to the "old English and Germanic ideas, brought over by Pilgrims and Puritans . . . ready to take root in the free soil of America."[16] Adams's theory not only affirmed the exceptionality of the United States, but suggested that the nation represented the perfection of latent potentials that originated in Europe, and specifically Germany. Popular American textbooks conveyed the Teutonic germ theory to students. "The political inheritance of modern Europe and America is derived mainly from three sources," one textbook explained, "Hebrew law, Roman law, and Teutonic customs and ideal of political life"; America was the final depository of these ideas. Another world history textbook explained how, unlike other European and non-European races, the Teutons, "had personal worth . . . because of their free independent spirit, of their unbounded capacity for growth, for culture, for accomplishment, the future time became theirs." As a result, the textbook suggested, the Teutons were the "only race of modernity and progress."[17]

The subject most affected by the German pedagogical influence was history. As Salmon asserted in 1891, discussions about the teaching of history were characterized by "the predominant influence of German ideas."[18] G. Stanley Hall likewise suggested that U.S. teachers had much to learn from the wisdom of German history instructors who had transcended the "purely colorless presentation of facts" that characterized the teaching of the topic in the U.S.[19]. Charles Kendall Adams boasted that "in Germany, history is a constituent part of the regular intellectual nourishment of the pupil during the whole of his preparatory work," and criticized schools in the United States for their failure to address the subject adequately.[20]

Although scholars offered some criticisms of Prussian pedagogy, administration, and philosophy, for the most part they considered the nation the pinnacle of culture and scholarship. Inspired by a sense of cultural inferiority, scholars sought out the German universities in droves, and brought the ideas they learned there back to U.S. shores. "Already in the [eighteen] nineties, our college professors and our artists were beginning to require the seal of European training to justify their existence," one scholar reflected. "We appropriated the German system of education."[21] Several innovations were specifically imported from Germany to the United States: the linking of abstract concepts to the students' immediate surroundings, the need to professionalize and train teachers more effectively, the need to move beyond rote learning by exercising the higher faculties of mind, and the need to align public schooling with the broader purposes of society and the state.

ANTI-PRUSSIANISM AND THE WORLD WAR

When World War I erupted in the summer of 1914, many scholars abandoned their admiration for German education because the nation was now viewed as an enemy and a threat to international peace and democratic ideas. "[W]hereas in the period from 1865 to 1914 efficiency was something to be admired and emulated," historian Christopher Lasch explained, "after 1914 it was something hateful; it came to be known as 'Prussian efficiency' and it became the duty of civilized people to destroy it."[22] Lasch exaggerates the degree to which intellectuals abandoned the pursuit of efficiency in the United States, but they certainly were careful to distinguish America efficiency from the excessively hierarchical and bureaucratic Prussian version. Educators who had once found much to emulate in German pedagogy and schooling either fell silent or attacked Prussian schools as narrow-minded, imperialistic, and excessively technocratic. For example, in 1909, education professor William Bagley admired how in a single century education had transformed Germany "from the weakest to the strongest power on the continent of Europe." Yet by 1918, Bagley considered Prussianism "a disease, a moral lesion which has cut away every sentiment of decency and humanity, which has eaten from the social mind the spiritual and moral values of life, which has glorified the material and left the brute supreme."[23] In fact, during the years leading up to World War I, educators in the United States self-consciously aimed at defining the U.S. system against the Prussian system of militarism, forced assimilation, and excessive bureaucratic efficiency. Prussia had become the *other* against which U.S. educators defined their own schools.

Leading educators in the United States, especially those with expertise in Germany culture, blamed the Prussian schoolmaster for fanning the flames of militarism. For example, in 1914, J. H. Phillips, superintendent of schools for Birmingham, Alabama, contrasted German education, which focused on "the national protection and expansion under national authority," with democratic education in the United States, which did "not seek to exploit the individual through the educational extension of the power and prestige of the State." When the United States entered the war in spring 1917, the anti-German rhetoric escalated. "[N]o schools in the world are such absolute failures as Germany's," one professor of education complained. "Instead of developing character, her education debases and destroys it." Paul Henry Hanus, the German-born Dean of Education at Harvard University, had even harsher critiques of German education. "The school system in Germany is planned to keep the masses of the people in dependence on the [upper] classes," he observed on his visits to the country. "The masses of the German people are stolid, doltish, and they are kept in that condition in the interest of the relatively small, selfish governing class."[24] Many U.S. scholars disavowed their earlier praise for the German education system and viewed the war as a direct result of Germany's schools.

Studies of German schools published during the war, such as the English translation (from French) of Victor H. Friedel's *The German School as War Nursery* and Thomas Alexander's *The Prussian Elementary Schools*, related how the Prussian schools had distorted German life and aimed German culture toward the imperialistic goals of the state. Friedel was director of the *Musée Pédagogique* in Paris, and Alexander was a professor of education at the George Peabody College for Teachers. Both argued that Prussian schools had played a major role in paving the way for German aggression. "The eagerness of the [German] pedagogues to seize public opinion from the first days of the war," Friedel related, "lies in their wish and in their duty to bring the mentality of the people to the concert pitch of Berlin." Friedel argued that the Prussian education system had left the German people without the intellectual, cultural, and political tools to challenge the nefarious goals of their leaders. As a result, Germans were not equipped to challenge any ideas or policies being issued by the state. Friedel alleged that the Germans were "unable to reach the necessary political maturity" to appreciate the "general principles of the civilization of our days."[25] As Michael E. Sadler wrote in the preface to Friedel's book, German education "has been one of the most powerful auxiliaries of the German Empire. And it has served the purpose of the existing economic regime."[26] Alexander's study of Prussian schools confirmed in slightly stronger language: "[T]he Prussian is to a large measure enslaved through the medium of his school" and "his learning, instead of making him his own master, forges the chain by which he is held in servitude."[27] That is, Prussian pedagogy aligned with Prussian administration in its focus on bureaucratic efficiency, social tracking, subservience, and nationalism.

Similarly, Gustavus Ohlinger, a captain in the U.S. army, related how "[d]ay by day [German students] were put through the mental goose step until their minds were fashioned to a single pattern and they were made into docile and efficient subjects." Ohlinger not only outlined the dangers of Prussianism abroad but also uncovered the "ascendency" of German ideas in U.S. schools. His book, *The German Conspiracy in American*

Education, traced how German Americans had allegedly collaborated with Prussian authorities to spread Prussian ideas throughout the United States through a "violent" effort to "graft" American culture upon a German stock. Reminding readers of the former scholarly fascination with Prussia, he argued that the war had proven the destructive nature of German ideas in the United States and revealed the ongoing conspiracy in the nation's schools.[28] Ohlinger argued for a complete purge of German ideas from American schools, asserting that the curriculum should turn back toward its English cultural roots.

With Prussia as its *other*, American educators agreed that "Prussianism" in education not only distorted the aims of schooling toward nationalism and efficiency but also directed pedagogy toward the values of subservience. If learning under "Prussianism" was passive and rote, then learning in a democracy ought to be active and critical. In an article on the pedagogy of Americanization in *Teachers College Record*, one teacher related how she had updated her instruction in light of her recent appreciation of how education in a democracy ought to differ from education under Prussianism. She no longer required students to conduct "individual recitation," a method she affiliated with Prussian education; she now required them to conduct "socialized recitation," an early version of class discussion she affiliated with democracy. She also changed the focus of her instruction during the war to emphasize patriotism and how "the ideals of democracy have taken their shape through the world." She related how "[h]istory, as conceived by the Prussian schools, has been taught so as to praise and exalt the Prussian State. It is important that history in the hands of American teachers should not become a sinister instrument of chauvinism."[29] Similarly, as Alexander explained in *The Prussian Elementary Schools*, in Prussia the schools were "molded to meet the needs of the state," but in the United States teachers ought to teach in accordance with the "democratic principles for which we are aiming and shape our educational policies towards that end."[30]

There were subtle differences in the assessments of the Prussian schools during the war years. Some scholars thought that Prussian efficiency ought to be avoided at all costs, and that the decentralized, heterogeneous nature of the U.S. system was a source of strength. Others admired many aspects of the Prussian system but thought that Prussian's bureaucratic innovations should be separated from its nationalist and imperialistic goals. That is, U.S. schools could and should emulate the professionalism and organizational innovations of the Prussians, but school leaders should aim these innovations toward the development of democratic dispositions, not toward authoritarianism and subservience. For example, Dean William Russell offered a laudatory history of how the Prussian schoolmaster helped create the great nation of Germany, which had just recently been seized by a militaristic caste. "And whether Germany goes down in defeat, humbled because of the arrogance of her military caste, or goes forward to the conquest of the world," Russell argued, "her mode of education will forever stand as an object lesson to every state that aspires to national unity and hopes for national greatness." Russell invited educators to look to the Prussian example as inspiration for the reform of education in the United States. Russell suggested an educational administration "that put the public good ahead of personal gain" and "appreciated reasonable law and secure voluntary obedience to constituted authority" would have a great advantage in the modern world.[31] In contrast, Charles Beard warned against the dangers of Russell's embrace of national unity and top-down reform. He responded that educators should not look to the German example as a model because "our fundamental policies of state are not fixed as in Prussia—at least before the Great War—and there is no single ruling class continuously in power."[32] The strength of the American system, Beard argued, was its ability to respond and absorb incremental political and cultural changes, which allowed schools not to be dominated by any particular sect (e.g. agrarians, businessmen, labor) or class, as was the case in Prussia.

THE AMERICANIZATION CAMPAIGN

The issue of the Prussian mindset during the war years was made more urgent by the flood of immigrants, including Germans, that entered the United States from Europe during the decades leading up to the conflict. In 1910, 2.5 million German-born (some naturalized, some not) people lived in the United States, with millions more first-generation children who spoke only German at home; 9.2 million Americans identified German as their first language, and there were over 500 German language publications in circulation prior to the war. After the United States entered the war in 1917, nativists and patriots aimed their ire at unassimilated Germans, producing many instances of anti-German violence.[33] Friedel's book had warned of unassimilated Germans in the United States who were vulnerable to German propaganda, and Ohlinger likewise warned of the ongoing influence of German propaganda in the schools aimed at undermining American interests.[34] After war was declared, President Wilson designated all male German citizens older than age 14 as "enemy aliens" who needed to surrender their firearms and stay at least half a mile away from all military installations. Many German-Americans were forced to swear allegiance to the United States, and thousands were detained.

In response to this anti-German sentiment, most American schools canceled and banned their German language instruction. The California State Board of Education identified German as "a language that disseminates the ideals of autocracy, brutality and hatred," and one overzealous Iowa politician declared, "ninety percent of all the men and women who teach the German language are traitors."[35] One pamphlet from the American Defense Society, entitled *Throw Out the German Language and All Disloyal Teachers*, declared that German was "not a fit language to teach clean and pure American boys and girls" because it reflected the values of "ruthless conquestadors [*sic*]."[36] The war and its 100% Americanism campaign inspired a spike in naturalizations, and night schools taught English to immigrants eager to appear assimilated. German language publications declined 75% by 1920, and enrollment in German language classes dropped from 24% in 1915 to only 1% in 1922.[37] "Instruction in the German language may be appropriate for the technician and the scientist," Ohlinger argued after the war, "but it should never again be permitted in the elementary and high schools."[38]

The anti-German sentiment that emerged during the war created a dilemma for the scientific racists who had been arguing on behalf of curtailing the immigration of less desirable groups from Southern and Eastern Europe because it pitted two visions of American democracy against one another—what historian Gary Gerstle called "civic nationalism" and "racial nationalism."[39] Civic nationalism was inclusive based on a common set of American ideals and goals, and racial nationalism was based on a set of perceived racial traits. Because Germans represented the best Teutonic racial stock, but were also considered to be potential threats to civic solidarity due to their alleged authoritarian tendencies, they represented a vexing problem for policymakers. In the short term, German immigrants experienced prejudice and violence during the war. Yet in the long term they benefitted from a scientific, social, and political community that valued their racial traits and cultural inheritance.

The efforts of racial nationalism had been rising since the turn of the century. William Z. Ripley supported the new focus on multiple White races in his popular 1899 book, *The Races of Europe*. Ripley drew upon the latest work of anthropologists to dismiss the "absurdity of the misnomer Caucasian, as applied to the blue-eyed and fair-headed Aryan race of Western Europe." In place of the single European origin theory, Ripley suggested that Europeans were composed of three major racial groups: Teutonics, Alpines, and Mediterraneans. The Teutons, according to Ripley, were of German and Northern European descent and were most responsible for forging the democratic institutions of Northern Europe and the United States. Ripley's racial distinctions were based on their cephalic index (shape of their head), a metric, Ripley argued, that was "one of the best available tests of race known." His conclusions, he insisted, were based upon "strictly scientific canons."[40] Ripley's distinction among European types provided a useful language for scientific racists who worried about the influx of immigrants who did not originate from the Teutonic stock.

For example, Madison Grant employed Ripley's three-race classification system in his book *The Passing of the Great Race*, published in 1916. Carl C. Brigham used Ripley's three races in his 1923 book, *A Study of American Intelligence*, based on tests administered on American servicemen during the war. These studies argued that immigrant races from Eastern and Southern Europe tended to have lower intelligence and higher likelihood of undesirable traits. The xenophobic fear of nondesirable groups predated the war and continued into the 1920s. In 1909, Stanford University professor of education Ellwood Cubberley argued "[t]hese southern and eastern Europeans are of a very different type from the north Europeans who preceded them." As Cubberley explained in his widely used textbook, *Changing Conceptions of Education*, "Illiterate, docile, lacking in self-reliance and initiative, and not possessing the Anglo-Teutonic conceptions of law, order, and government, their coming has served to dilute tremendously our national stock, and to corrupt our civic life."[41] Journalist George Creel, who headed the United States Committee on Public Information during the war (see Chapter 2), likewise worried about "certain fundamental differences between the Nordic stock and the Alpine and Mediterranean stocks" because the latter could allegedly not be easily absorbed into mainstream democratic life.[42] By 1914, 44 universities and colleges in the United States offered classes on scientific racism, or eugenics, and by 1928, 326 offered courses on the topic, which further fueled anti-immigrant sentiment.[43]

Immigrants were linked not only to lower intelligence and greater potential for crime but also to anti-American ideologies such as anarchism, communism, and authoritarianism. "You have it in your power," one U.S. Senator implored his colleagues, to "protect us against criminal agitators and red anarchists . . . to build a wall against bolshevism . . . to keep out of your country criminal hordes of Europe." Congress responded to these pleas with the immigration acts of 1917, 1918, 1921, and 1924, which curtailed immigration by 85% and virtually eliminated immigrants from Southern and Eastern Europe.[44] And yet, paradoxically, these restrictions still favored those of Nordic descent, including Germans. The war had demonstrated the fact that even those with the desirable Nordic stock could be corrupted by Prussianism. This underscored the importance of education in the forming of democratic citizens, and the central role of schools in shaping the national character.

In the context of these racist and xenophobic policies, educators took the lead in the effort to Americanize immigrant children and adults, and they explicitly used Prussia as the United States' *other*. As P. P. Claxton, head of the U.S. Bureau of Education, asserted in 1918, "Americanization can come only through teaching. We must win the mind and heart of the people for the country and its institutions and ideals. This cannot be done by force or compulsion. Americanism can never be obtained through the process of Prussianism."[45] Likewise, Royal Dixon, Vice President of the League of Foreign-born Citizens, warned against emulating the German system. "In the terrible name of efficiency, the thing for which Germany lost her soul," Dixon complained, many Americans were also catering "to the crass demands of the business world." Dixon urged U.S. teachers to focus less on students who were "technically proficient," and more on students who were "spiritually ardent."[46] This approach proved to be easier in theory than practice, and many believed that the Americanization campaign had gone too far. In 1920, Julius Drachsler, a professor from Smith College, expressed dismay at how the Americanization campaign seemed to emulate Prussianism. "It would seem the experience of Germany with Alsace-Loraine and East Prussia," he reasoned, ". . . would be a solemn warning to America that compulsion breeds stubbornness, and that stubbornness contains the seeds of conflict and of hatred."[47] Educators continued to use Prussian education as a foil to what they hoped Americanization could and should be.

Weighing in on these discussions, Dewey rejected Prussian pedagogy and administration, and he articulated a clear alternative to Prussianism in democratic pedagogy, Americanization, and vocational education. As the leading voice of educational reform between the 1890s and the 1950s, Dewey took the lead in constructing a more inclusive approach to Americanization, one that rejected the chauvinistic and top-down dictates of the Prussians. Like Claxton, Dixon, and Drachsler, Dewey recognized that assimilation in the United States needed to transcend mere indoctrination and economic socialization. Dewey also insisted that assimilating foreign-born workers from across the globe in a democratic manner represented a historically unique effort—it would need to be done thoughtfully and deliberately. To do so, Dewey constructed a new post-European, post-German cosmopolitanism to guide this pedagogical work, with the idea of teaching "how to think, not what to think" at its center.

THE AMERICANIZATION OF JOHN DEWEY

Dewey was raised in Vermont as an evangelical Congregationalist. He remained a member of the church and worked with Christian organizations through his early career at the University of Michigan and the University of Minnesota. Hegel had heavily influenced Dewey's earliest mentors, including H.A.P. Torrey, William T. Harris, and especially George Sylvester Morris. As a result, Dewey was initially attracted to Hegel's idealism because it accorded well with his religious faith and philosophical influences.[48] "Hegel's synthesis of subject and object, matter and spirit, the divine and the human, was," Dewey recalled, "no mere intellectual formula; it operated as an immense release, a liberation."[49] However, while in college and while earning his doctorate at Johns Hopkins University, Dewey was confronted with another major intellectual current of the time—scientific positivism. Sociologists such as Auguste Comte and Herbert Spencer refuted the idea of a spiritual or divine force guiding society. Drawing inspiration from Isaac Newton's laws of motion and later Charles Darwin's theory of natural selection, the positivists argued that the world was governed by transcendent biological and natural laws—laws indifferent to human cognition. Both the Hegelian and positivist views were historicist because both theories posited that the best way to study anything was to trace its historical development, and both challenged the Aristotelian concept that entities had a predetermined essence or latent potential in the intellectual realm that could be discovered independent of the experience of the material world. Instead, the empirical reality of history was the key to discovering knowledge. Both Hegel and Darwin agreed that to understand any entity, one must trace how it came into being. The belief in history-as-continuous-process-of-growth informed Dewey's early naturalistic philosophy and pedagogy.

As part of Dewey's appointment at the University of Chicago in 1894, he was expected to take the lead in the newly established department of pedagogy. Dewey was attracted by the opportunity to find a practical application for his philosophical ideas. Dewey's first book on education was *The Psychology of Number and Its Applications to Methods of Teaching Arithmetic*, co-authored with James McLellan, principal of the Ontario School of Pedagogy in Toronto. The study was the 33rd volume in the International Education series edited by William T. Harris, the U.S. Commissioner of Education. In a letter to Harris discussing the book, Dewey revealed: "It may interest you to know—what I shouldn't like to give away to the public—that I started first by trying to turn Hegel's logic over into psychology and then that into pedagogy," implying that Dewey had just barely moved beyond his Hegelianism when he began his career as an educational philosopher in 1894.[50] In 1896, Dewey established a laboratory school at the University of Chicago that helped catapult him to national and eventually international fame. Drawing on his findings at the lab school, Dewey published and spoke prolifically between 1896 and World War I by authoring the classic texts *Moral Principles Underlying Education* (1897), *School and Society* (1899), *The Child and the Curriculum* (1901), and *How We Think* (1910). By 1915, having moved to Columbia University in 1904, Dewey had reached such a level of influence that one contemporary declared: "Contemporary educational theory in America is dominated by America's foremost philosopher—John Dewey."[51]

Historians have not appreciated the extent to which Dewey's most famous works, such as *Democracy and Education*, were written and published in the shadow of Prussianism and World War I. Dewey reconsidered the significance of culture during the war because the conflict had thrust the issues of assimilation, nationalism, and Americanization to the forefront of the minds of most American policymakers, scholars, and teachers. Dewey argued that the war underscored a break from the intellectual roots of German thought in the United States. Dewey agreed with the critics cited above that the militarism of the Prussians was a direct consequence of their cultural, philosophical, and educational background. For Dewey, America's pluralistic culture stood in stark contrast to German monoculturalism and oppressive class structure. Further, he argued that, although the war necessitated the rapid acculturation of immigrants, the process should not emulate the Prussian model of forced assimilation to a single cultural type. Rather, the American process of acculturation had to reflect the exceptionality of the American experience.

Dewey and other leading intellectuals, such as Horace Kallen and Randolph Bourne, insisted that the cultures of the different immigrant groups had to be assimilated to one another rather than to one generic type.[52] Kallen was a German-born Jewish philosopher at the University of Wisconsin. In his essay "Democracy versus the Melting Pot," he suggested that Americans embrace their ethnic diversity to form a post-European cultural identity. Kallen contrasted his views with the culturally aggressive imperialism of Russia and Germany because Kallen did not want to see the United States adopt the same policy of forced assimilation. Instead, Kallen suggested, "'American civilization' may come to mean the perfection of 'European civilization,' the waste, the squalor, and the distress of Europe being eliminated—a multiplicity in a unity, an orchestration of mankind . . . so in society each ethnic group is the natural instrument, its spirit and culture are its theme and melody, and the harmony and dissonances and the discords of them all make the symphony of civilization."[53] Bourne was an independent scholar with a physical disability. In his essay "Trans-National America," Bourne similarly argued that assimilation to Anglo-Saxonism had failed, and that, in fact, Americans had formed a "unique social fabric" out of multiple ethnicities.[54] Both Kallen and Bourne contrasted their multiethnic vision with the forced assimilation of the Prussians. Dewey, Bourne, and Kallen argued that all immigrant groups had something to offer the transracial democratic culture, not just those with Anglo-Saxon and Teutonic roots.

The anti-German sentiments inspired by the war found their most scholarly and articulate voice in Dewey's *German Philosophy and Politics* and economist Thorstein Veblen's *Imperial Germany and the Industrial Revolution*. Both works, published in 1915, criticized the Germans' excessive emphasis on veneration of state and considered German imperialism as a natural outgrowth of its idealistic philosophy and bureaucratic efficiency.[55] In *Imperial Germany and the Industrial Revolution*, Veblen traced the emergence of German imperialism to an unnatural and vast disconnect between its rapid industrialization and its political and social ideals. Using English industrialization as a foil, Veblen concluded: "The case of Germany is unexampled among Western nations both as regards the abruptness, thoroughness and amplitude of its appropriation of . . . technology, and as regards the archaism of its cultural furniture."[56] Veblen and Dewey agreed that the rapid industrialization of the German state had distorted its culture by substituting philosophical idealism and bureaucratic efficiency for pluralistic evolution and democratic reform.

In *German Philosophy and Politics*, Dewey directly connected German politics to education. He traced the roots of contemporaneous German thought to Fichte, Hegel, and especially Kant. From these philosophers, Dewey argued, Germans inherited their dualistic allegiance to an internal idealistic life, and an externally ordered life characterized by "obedience, discipline, and subordination" as the "necessities of successful organization." Germans manifested these ideals, not only in militarism, but also in education. Dewey pointed out how "[h]igh schools and universities in German are . . . under the control of the state and part of state life," and "[p]hilosophy both directly and indirectly, plays an unusually large role in the training." Further, Dewey insisted that, in Germany, "[e]ducation is *the* means of the advancement of humanity toward realization of its divine perfection. Education is the work of the State." Thus, in Germany, the state was cast as "an essential moral Being charged with an indispensable moral function" of preparing students to be citizens defined by their duty to the state.

Dewey concluded *German Philosophy and Politics* by contrasting Germany with the United States, characterizing the latter as "interracial and international." He challenged Americans to embrace "the efficacy of human intercourse, irrespective of class, racial, geographic, and national limits."[57] Dewey reiterated the themes he had introduced in *German Philosophy and Politics* in his magnum opus *Democracy and Education*, published to glowing reviews in 1916, a year before the United States entered the war. One reader insisted that any educator who failed to read Dewey's latest text "will be little short of criminally negligent professionally," and another concluded that "it would be difficult to overstate [the book's] import and value for all students of education, philosophy, and society." As Dewey revealed to a friend, *Democracy and Education* was "the closest attempt I have made to sum up my entire philosophy."[58] Dewey's famous work summarized the philosophical and pedagogical ideas he had been addressing over the past 20 years. For this reason, *Democracy and Education* has become the one-stop read for many students and scholars looking for insight, not only into Dewey's philosophy and pedagogy, but also into the broader reform movement known as progressive education.

In addition to *Democracy and Education*, Dewey wrote an influential series of essays on culture and immigrants during the war. Although Dewey had always rejected Herbert Baxter Adams's germ theory narrative because it implied a static Germanic form of culture that only certain races could actualize, he nevertheless insisted on American post-European exceptionality. In other words, Dewey's definition of culture was contingent and transcended specific races and nations, yet he still placed American intellectual culture at the forefront of progress. In a 1916 essay, Dewey maintained that democracy would "fall to pieces" if schools did not do their part to assuage inherited "divisions of interests, class, and sectional ideas." Dewey outlined the kind of nationalism that should be fostered in the United States by carefully distinguishing his American brand of nationalism from the European. The American form, he explained, "was interracial and international in its makeup" and constituted a "unity created by drawing out and composing into a harmonious whole the best, the most characteristic which each contributing race and people has to offer." Dewey encouraged the mixing of cultures, but only so that the best traits from each could contribute to the greater, transracial fund of progress. "The way to deal with hyphenism [German-American, Jewish-American, and so on]," Dewey explained, ". . .

is to welcome it, but, to welcome it in the sense of extracting from each people its special good, so that it shall surrender into a common fund of wisdom and experience what it especially has to contribute. All of these surrenders and contributions taken together create the national spirit of America." Dewey reinforced his notion that the hyphen should "connect" rather than "separate" Americans from one another.[59]

In *Democracy and Education*, Dewey reiterated his support for the unified system of schooling, the coterminous nature of vocational and academic learning, and his vision for cultural pluralism. All three issues were housed in a critique of Germany philosophy and pedagogy. Dewey had the raw materials for these positions since the 1890s, but World War I pushed the issues to the forefront of his thinking. In the section on social efficiency in *Democracy and Education*, Dewey expanded his position on the role of vocational education in the curriculum. He prefaced his discussion by contrasting the culture and society of the United States with Germany. "In Europe, in the continental states particularly, the new idea of the importance of education for human welfare and progress was captured by national interests and harnessed to do work whose social aim was definitely narrow and exclusive," Dewey explained, ". . . and the result was a marked obscuring of the meaning of a social aim." Dewey suggested that education for nationalism had reached a peak at "the present time," inspiring nations to be in "incipient war with its neighbors." In contrast to what he was observing in Europe, Dewey offered a vision of democratic education in the United States that favored "participation in its good of all its members on equal terms" and fostered "interaction of the different forms of associated life."[60] Such a vision would not only reflect the values of democratic life, Dewey hoped, but would also nurture and create it.

Like Dewey, U.S. educators considered World War I as an opportunity for reform of the American curriculum to fulfill its democratic potential. As William L. Ettinger, the New York Superintendent of City Schools, expressed in an address to teachers in 1918: "As our schools are the most potent instrument in the development of national ideals, it would be strange indeed if this world crisis did not compel changes in our conception as to the value and function of education as a phase of industrial life." Ettinger considered the war to present a golden opportunity for reflection and growth on the civic purposes and outcomes of U.S. schools. "We are called upon to scrutinize anew our work in terms of our underlying theories," he continued, "in order that through reflection we may acquire that freshness of vision, that truthfulness of aim, and that purpose necessary to ensure the salvation of our democracy through the proper training of our future citizens."[61] Except for the vague reference to "truthfulness of aim," Dewey could have authored this passage himself. The fact that it was written by a lesser-known educator underscores the importance of the "crisis" of World War I to creating an environment conducive to the positive reception of Dewey's ideas on student-centered instruction, reflective inquiry, and cultural pluralism, and his focus on the knowledge, skills, and dispositions of citizens in a democratic society, even if the actual impact of these ideas on the curriculum was slow to sink in. Like Dewey, theorists of American education clarified what it meant to educate citizens in a democracy in contrast to what it was not: Prussianism.

American educators never precisely defined "Prussianism" during the war, but clearly it reflected a set of values they considered to be antithetical to democratic life: aristocratic rule, forced assimilation, schools segregated by class, a curriculum aimed toward subservience to the state, student passivity, a centralized top-down bureaucracy, and teaching students what to think. Thus, Prussianism served as a precursor to a popular term that educators would employ repeatedly over the next 70 years: authoritarianism. The Prussian schools represented a dialectical tool against which to define American education, with Dewey's *Democracy and Education* as the most articulate example of what democratic education could and should be. Although U.S. educators did not explicitly use the phrase "teaching how to think, not what to think," they had worked out the basic idea. Authoritarian regimes such as Germany filled the heads of their students with predetermined answers; in contrast, democratic regimes such as the United States taught their students to reach their own conclusions.

CHAPTER 2

In the Shadow of Propaganda

During the war, leading U.S. educators not only sought to clarify the goals and methods of democratic education in contrast to Prussia, but also responded to an additional unprecedented threat that potentially represented a form of domestic authoritarianism: wartime propaganda. Prior to World War I, scholars rarely used the term *propaganda*. When they did use the term, it referred mainly to conversion through religious, specifically Catholic, instruction. Consequently, since its inception, the term *propaganda* had unpleasant insinuations for the mostly Protestant scholarly elite in the United States. However, the term took on broader definition during and after the war. Defined by the NEA as "the systematic direction of effort to gain support for an opinion," critics pointed to the biased and one-sided nature of the materials produced by governments and regimes during the conflict, including the United States, and debated the role of propaganda in democracy and democratic education. The most common suggestion for addressing propaganda was to teach students how to think, not what to think.[1]

The term *propaganda* arose concurrently with a growing anxiety about the shaping, distortion, and dissemination of information to the general public between 1914 and 1918. Intellectuals first chided Germany for its use of propaganda to manipulate its people at home and abroad in support of war. For example, the term *propaganda* had appeared 20 times in Ohlinger's *The German Conspiracy in American Education* and 32 times in Friedel's *Prussian Schools as War Nursery*, which related how in German schools "eager patriots demand that children's history should be colored by propaganda."[2] After 1917, intellectuals blamed the foreign and domestic governments for using propaganda to distort and cloud the truth about the events of the Russian Revolution, and by the 1920s, critics blamed the U.S. government for its own use of propaganda to build support for the war. Concerns over propaganda peaked when a national scandal involving utility companies demonstrated the infiltration of pro-business propaganda in U.S. schools. As a result, the term *propaganda* not only entered the American consciousness but also engendered discussions over the role of advertising, public relations, mass communications, and schooling in the 1920s and beyond.

Concerns over propaganda increased in the years following the war, as intellectuals struggled to distinguish education from indoctrination and imposition. Fears of propaganda inspired many educators to define education as the ability to approach a controversial topic in a balanced way by teaching both sides of the issue and letting students decide for themselves. "Pupils must be trained to think for themselves, to weigh evidence, and to make decisions," one teacher from Michigan concluded. "[C]hildren must be trained to recognize propaganda and be prepared to view it in its proper light."[3] Thus, after World War I, teaching students how to think instead of what to think emerged as a common rebuttal to anxieties over propaganda in the schools and in society, and as an antidote to authoritarianism at home and abroad.

MOBILIZING STUDENTS FOR WAR

When the United States entered World War I in spring 1917, the Wilson administration organized the Committee of Public Information to unify the nation in support of the effort. Headed by journalist George Creel, the Committee identified education of youth and adults as a central component of fostering patriotism, silencing dissenters, and mobilizing the nation. Creel believed wholeheartedly in the "absolute justice of America's cause" in the war and "the absolute selflessness of America's aims" for entering it. As a result, Creel insisted that no other argument was needed for garnering support for the war beyond "the simple, straightforward presentation of facts."[4] Creel insisted that if the public was fully informed about the international events, then it would reach the same rational conclusions as leading experts and political leaders about the need to end its isolationism and win the war.

In cooperation with the NEA, the Committee on Public Information formed the National School Service and issued a series of pamphlets for distribution to U.S. schools. Under the editorial leadership of William Bagley of Teachers College, the pamphlets sought to "sternly [reveal] the methods and principles of Germany," while contrasting the Prussian regime with the "ideals of America." According to Creel, 75 million copies of these educational pamphlets were distributed to U.S. homes via 20 million students, in addition to other materials produced by local municipalities.[5] Further, local agencies opened up night schools for immigrants, and by 1918 nearly 30 states had organized state committees on Americanization. In addition, many states passed laws and policies to increase patriotism and support for the war. Numerous states, including New York, New Jersey, California, Louisiana, and Illinois, added military instruction and physical education to their high school curriculum.[6] As explained in Chapter 1, most school districts banned the teaching of the German language.

The Committee on Public Information placed the history and civics curriculum at the center of the effort to Americanize immigrants and instill patriotism in all American youth. Under the leadership of Creel, the Committee quickly authored wartime history and civic lessons and made them available to teachers, who were encouraged to "lay the foundations for an intelligent enthusiasm for the United States."[7] The initial reception of the Committee pamphlets sent to schools was positive. In fact, requests by teachers were so great that the Government Printing Office could not keep up and had to make arrangements with a large printing house to meet demand.[8] The Committee accompanied the campaign in U.S. schools with wartime posters encouraging thrift and sacrifice, patriotic pleas to engage in volunteer work to support soldiers, and speech competitions in support of the war.[9] Much of this material was aimed at school-age children.

Creel's effort to use the history curriculum for wartime preparation was supported directly by President Wilson. In particular, the president underscored the efforts to assimilate immigrants, foster patriotism, and create community. In 1917, Wilson issued a letter prefacing a pamphlet urging "teachers and other school officers [to] increase materially the time and attention devoted to instruction bearing directly on the problems of community and national life."[10] Further, in 1917, a panel of professional historians formed the National Board for Historical Service to issue a series of leaflets on what was being called "the Great War." The first leaflet, "Opportunities for History Teachers," supported U.S. involvement in the war and painted Germany as the sole aggressor. The Board historians suggested that throughout the curriculum, when approaching all historical topics, teachers should emphasize that one "stubborn fact of the past" was "that war may be necessary for the defense of vital principles."[11]

The next year, the National Board for Historical Service appointed a committee, which included Albert McKinley, editor of the *History Teacher Magazine*, to issue a more comprehensive pamphlet titled "Outline of an Emergency Course of Instruction on the War." The pamphlets were first advertised in McKinley's magazine. Creel was uncertain how to reach teachers in the highly decentralized U.S. school system, so he advertised directly to them through the publication. The advertising campaign in *History Teacher Magazine* successfully created demand for the wartime pamphlets, but also inadvertently linked advertising with government and business propaganda from that point forward.[12]

The "Outline of an Emergency Course of Instruction on War" pamphlet demanded that the general topic of war "should form an integral part of the course of study in every grade of our public schools." This resource offered more comprehensive and specific recommendations on how the curriculum could be directed toward the war. In addition, the Outline suggested ways that young children could help, such as "Save pennies for thrift stamps," "Eat less things the soldiers and people of the allied countries need," and "Do not waste Food and Water." Regarding the reasons "Why Germany Wanted War," the historians listed the German "belief that war is a necessity in the evolution of nations," the "Idea of her divine mission to spread German *Kultur*," and the "belief that war is the most profitable business a nation can engage in." Overall, the pamphlet explained, teachers ought to emphasize the ideas of "*patriotism*, *heroism*, and *sacrifice*."[13]

Prior to the war, an effort had been underway by educational reformers to revise the history curriculum by placing more emphasize on recent history, organizing materials in a more relevant way, and reorienting subject matter away from rote memorization toward critical thinking and the consideration of social problems. To this end, the NEA issued an influential report, *The Social Studies in Secondary Schools*, in 1916, which one historian identified as "the birth certificate of the field" of social studies education.[14] Indeed, the report introduced the term *social studies* in reference to the teaching of history and social sciences in the schools, recommended two new interdisciplinary classes—Community Civics for 8th grade and Problems of Democracy for 12th grade—and emphasized the need for more recent and relevant history. By the 1930s, about a third of all high schools implemented the recommendations of the social studies report. To the extent that it was adopted, the new social studies scope and sequence replaced the recommended 4 years of history as outlined by the 1899 American Historical Association's Committee of Seven.[15]

Present-day historians have decried the Committee on Social Studies report as the beginning of the end of the 4-year history sequence in U.S. high schools, which had been the norm prior to 1916.[16]They blame Dewey and like-minded reformers such as historian James Harvey Robinson for the alleged dumbing down of the history curriculum with student-centered ideas of utilitarianism, interdisciplinary study, and an excessive emphasis on relevance. However, these critiques fail to contextualize the social studies report in curriculum revisions of the war. During the war, President Wilson—himself a former professor of history—and the historians of the National Board for Historical Service supported the very same reforms as the social studies report. In 1918, President Wilson explained how the reforms suggested by the Board were not a "plea . . . appropriate merely to the period of the war," but rather "a plea for a realization in public education of new emphasis which the war has given to the ideals of democracy."[17] Like the Committee on Social Studies, the National Board emphasized the need to study "the recent past . . . which most deeply concerns us in the present national and international relations" and the fact that the "historical curriculum, in order to be useful, must be practical." In addition to an emphasis on current events, the Board emphasized critical thinking, such as the "ability to weigh evidence, to criticize statements from the standpoint of good faith and accuracy, and to distinguish between assertion, opinion, and proof."[18] This focus on teaching how to think, as discussed in Chapter 1, allegedly stood in contrast to the kind of teacher-centered schooling that was taking place in Germany. As one of the wartime pamphlets explained, the German schools were "nurseries of autocracy" where students were taught to be "efficient, docile, and contented."[19] In contrast, U.S. schools were decentralized, democratic, and humane, and students were allegedly taught critical thinking and intelligent patriotism.

The emphasis on relevance, utility, and citizenship espoused by the National Board for Historical Service and the social studies committee received further support by the NEA's influential *Cardinal Principles of Secondary Education* (1918) report, which sought to update the high school curriculum in light of increased enrollments and the latest developments in pedagogical theory. The 1916 social studies report was a preliminary part of the *Cardinal Principles*, so the latter included citizenship as one of its seven objectives—along with health, command of fundamental processes, worthy home membership, vocation, worthy use of leisure, and ethical character. Under citizenship, the *Cardinal Principles* report related how schools ought to give students "a basis for understanding international problems" and a "comprehension of the ideals of American democracy." In accordance with the work of the Committee on Public Information, the report insisted that "loyalty" to democracy should be a prominent aim of civic education."[20]

Wilson, Creel, and the Committee on Public Information had housed the rapid mobilization for war in idealistic rhetoric and disseminated it quickly to U.S. schools. The materials produced by the Committee had the full support of the NEA and capitalized on many of the curriculum trends suggested by leading social studies theorists such as critical thinking, thematic organization of content, relevance, and functionality of knowledge. However, later critics of the wartime pamphlets focused specifically on the biased nature of its materials. This raised many issues about federal overreach, academic freedom, the use of government-backed media, the role of schools in wartime preparation, advertising in schools, and the cooperation among the business elites and the government. Although Creel denied that the Wilson administration was engaged in propaganda—because he was disseminating truth, not lies—many failed to see the distinction because the selection of certain facts, at the expense of others, enabled the government to endorse a particular interpretation of the event. Creel could not successfully divorce his wartime pamphlets from the term *propaganda*, especially after numerous critics and scholars employed the term to depict his effort.

PROPAGANDA ANXIETY ARISES

Once the war ended, Congress quickly disbanded the Committee on Public Information in anticipation of a possible backlash against the group. By 1920 the backlash had arrived. Despite Creel's claims that these wartime pamphlets simply reported the facts, critics detected bias in the materials. The most direct attack on the Committee's wartime materials emerged from a group of business leaders calling itself the National Industrial Conference Board, which labeled the pamphlets "insidious propaganda." The Board focused specifically on the "Lessons in Community and National Life" pamphlet issued in 1918, accusing the Wilson administration of disseminating materials "of a distinctly propagandist character which has no proper place in a schoolbook" by endorsing the "eight hour day, old age pensions, social insurance, trade unionism, the minimum wage, and similar issues." The tone of the materials, the Board asserted, were anti-employer. Such one-sided accounts, the critique continued, would lead to "the development of incorrect and dogmatic habits of thought" and showed little "respect for the scientific method of treatment and the principles of true education."[21] The businessmen insisted that the democratic way to teach American students was to present a balanced account of labor relations and then let students decide for themselves. The National Industrial Conference Board housed its rhetoric in democratic principles by equating bias and one-sidedness with Prussian indoctrination and by equating balance, neutrality, and science with democratic thinking. Students should be taught how to think, not what to think.

In a more subtle critique called "Propaganda in the Schools," historian Charles Beard questioned the one-sidedness of a pamphlet disseminated locally to New York City teachers because it advocated universal service "as a settled national policy" and offered a highly biased and simplistic account of the Russian Revolution.[22] For Beard, the tendency to assert certainty of facts in areas of political and scholarly dispute meant that the materials reflected a particular viewpoint. For Beard, *propaganda* was the forwarding of only one side of a contentious issue by conveying that position as if it were established fact.

Coverage of the events of the Russian Revolution during World War I reinforced growing concerns about the dangers of propaganda and bias common in the period. As the Russian state unraveled over 1917 and 1918, policymakers and the press worked with incomplete, biased, and distorted evidence. Allied leaders argued over whether the Revolution was a positive or negative development for the war effort. Some considered the Russian uprising as a democratic sign of the masses throwing off the chains of monarchical oppression, while others painted the event as a German plot to undermine the Allied cause because the Russians had been fighting alongside the Allies before they withdrew from the conflict. Either way, everyone agreed that the facts had been muddied by Russian and Allied propaganda, which tended to be believed or refuted based on one's preexisting views on the event.[23]

The materials of the Committee on Public Information reflected the uncertain reaction to the Russian Revolution during the war. The pamphlets first expressed sympathy for the cause by making a comparison to the American Revolution. In 1917, the *Outline for History Teachers* pamphlet suggested that "[o]ur War of Independence may help us to appreciate the problems of the new Russian Republic, because it was fought by a government, or governments, still in progress of organization." In August 1918, in an *Outline for an Emergency Course of Instruction on the War* pamphlet, the Committee related the simple facts: "A revolution in Russia deposed the Czar; the new government makes peace with Germany; Germany takes control of large part of Russia."[24] However, by October of that year, the Committee had changed course and issued a pamphlet called *The German-Bolshevik Conspiracy*, based on a recently acquired set of documents by Edgar Sisson, a member of the Committee. The pamphlet claimed that "present heads of the Bolshevik Government—Lenin, Trotsky and their Associates—are German agents." The Committee pamphlet related how the National Board for Historical Service had authenticated Sisson's controversial documents. However, several journalists and later historians believed that Sisson's documents were forgeries.[25] As a result, the Committee's handling of the Russian Revolution further undermined the claims of objectivity of the U.S. Government and its use of propaganda in the war. As journalists Walter Lippman and Charles Merz observed in their review of coverage of the Russian Revolution in the *New York Times* between 1917 and 1920: "In the large, the news about Russia is a case of seeing not what was, but what men wished to see. . . . The chief censor and the chief propagandist were hope and fear in the minds of the reporters and editors."[26] If the Committee had been biased in their assessment of the Russian Revolution, it was simply following the contours of the press, which had been equally misled, biased, and confused. As late as 1928, scholars complained of "being fed lies and propaganda about Russia" and being "flooded with propaganda of all shades" about the communist experiment.[27]

In 1920, Creel published his own account of the work he had done with the Committee on Public Information, entitled *How We Advertised America*. Creel's account of how the Committee unified and mobilized the nation to victory in the war was both defensive and boastful. Just as the National Industrial Conference Board had done, Creel contrasted the U.S. approach to information with the German approach, insisting that democratic nations disseminated truth, while authoritarian nations disseminated lies; the former was education, the latter was propaganda. "We did not call it propaganda, for that word, in German hands, had come to be associated with deceit and corruption," Creel explained. "Our effort was educational and informative throughout, for we had such confidence in our case as to feel no other argument was needed than the simple, straightforward presentation of facts." Guy Stanton Ford, the chairman of the National Board for Historical Service, offered a similar defensiveness the same year. Responding to accusations that his board had not been transparent, the historian asserted that it had been "one of the most unique experiments a democracy ever made in the field of education" and "one of the most effective efforts any government made during the war to put propaganda on a level with truth telling."[28] Apparently, Ford was not on the same page as Creel regarding the use of the term *propaganda*, which Ford freely employed, as long as the term was aligned with truth. Cynics and critics denied that the facts of the Committee on Public Information had been as unbiased as Creel and Ford asserted, and they sought remedies to ensure that schools were reporting the most balanced, useful, and up-to-date facts.

POSTWAR DISILLUSIONMENT

By 1920, reflection on the unprecedented destruction and death of the war, the disappointment of the Treaty of Versailles, and the enormous gap between the wartime rhetoric (e.g., "war to end all wars" and "making the world safe for democracy") and the actual outcome of the war left most intellectuals with a deep sense of cynicism and regret. The war had not spread democracy; it had merely upheld European imperialism and rewarded the victors with spoils. As the editors of the *Dial* sadly concluded in 1918: "America has won the war; America has lost the peace, the object for which she fought."[29] In addition to the disappointment in the postwar negotiations, there was a sense that the patriotic urge during the war had been too intense, and as a result, academic freedom had been unjustly compromised. Several high-profile professors such as Beard, H. L. Dana, and James McKeen Cattell of Columbia University had either resigned or were fired during the war because of their refusal to pledge their absolute loyalty to the war effort.

Numerous intellectuals were particularly disappointed with President Wilson's failure to follow through on the promises he had housed in democratic rhetoric. For example, Max Eastman, a leading disciple of Dewey, had praised Wilson during the war for his "poise and fluency of mind," but after the war Eastman explained how he had been too gullible and had been "made a fool of." Historian Carl Becker likewise aimed his anger at himself, incredulous that he "could have been naive enough to suppose . . .that Wilson could have ever accomplish those ideals." The young theologian Reinhold Niebuhr wondered if he could "ever again believe anything" after comparing the "solemn pretensions of statesmen with the cynically conceived secret treaties."[30] A 1922 book entitled *Disenchantment* stated the postwar mood clearly: "There had been an illogical hope in 1914 . . . that could move mountains," but less than a decade later, that hope "seems to be scarcely able to shift an anthill."[31] As a result of postwar disillusionment, scholars linked the Committee on Public Information's wartime propaganda to the overall sense that the public had been duped into supporting U.S. involvement in the conflict. For example, looking back at its work in 1927, Charles and Mary Beard concluded: "Never before in our history had such a campaign of education been organized; never before had American citizens realized how irresistibly a modern government could impose its views upon the whole nation."[32]

Further anxiety erupted in the United States following the realization that the Russian Revolution would not fail. A labor strike in Seattle in January 1919 launched a short-lived Red Scare. That year, African American educator Carter Woodson declared: "[A] better understanding of the races is now necessary to maintain that conservatism to prevent this country from being torn asunder by Socialism and Bolshevism."[33] Woodson optimistically hoped that improved understanding of Black history would lead to better cooperation among races in the United States; he justified his view by appealing to growing fears of communism. Looking back at the Red Scare, another educator reflected how "the thick clouds of anti-war suffering and despair reflected to the ends of the earth the fearsome glare of the Russian revolution." He insisted that the Russian "menace was real, not psychological" because "to our surprise and dismay, Russian Bolshevism did not collapse as we had expected it to."[34] Many scholars considered a satisfied and stable middle class as the best antidote to communist propaganda and socialist revolution. The war had put an end to some of the more ambitious reform initiatives of the Progressive Era, as political and social conservatism swept across the postwar political landscape. Many social scientists withdrew from their attempts at social reform and sought merely to describe the world objectively rather than try to transform it.[35]

Further, postwar disillusionment led to an emphasis on the contents of textbooks, which were believed to have contributed to the outbreak of the conflict. During the war, the National Board for Historical Service pointed out: "War history was considered objectionable not only because there was too much of it relatively, but also because it seemed to be so presented as to stimulate the war spirit, perpetuating popular prejudices and suggesting to each succeeding generation that kind of patriotism which consists largely of hatred for some other nation."[36] One 1925 study of textbooks in France, Germany, Japan, and the United States confirmed that nations distorted the facts of the past for their own purposes. In other words, the schools had been used, not only by the Germans but by all participants in the Great War, to pave the road to war by preaching nationalism and one-sided accounts of major events. "We find that children of different countries are taught opposite attitudes toward the same historical events," the study concluded. "We find our own textbooks not only contrasting with those of our late enemies, but differing widely among themselves." The study demonstrated that claims of objectivity and neutrality had been a farce because "committees of public information in every country utilized such unrepresentative truths during the war, and they have now been embodied in more permanent form in textbooks, because few have been interested to challenge them."[37] The fact that democratic governments misrepresented the facts in the same manner as authoritarian regimes was disturbing enough. But that such accounts were aimed at children became a major cause of concern.

Furthermore, Upton Sinclair, famous socialist and muckraking author of *The Jungle*, argued that the war had revealed the elitist nature of the U.S. government, its close ties to the business community, and its grip on the public schools. Earlier, Sinclair had enthusiastically supported the war, because, as he later reflected, "I thought that Woodrow Wilson really meant his golden, glowing words."[38] However, after the war, he too felt betrayed and disillusioned, and so he turned his critical eye to the nation's schools. "Our education system is not a public service, but an instrument of special privilege," Sinclair insisted. "[I]ts purpose is not to further the welfare, but merely to keep America capitalist.'" Disgusted by U.S. involvement in the conflict, in which "we spent some thirty billion of treasure, and a hundred thousand young lives to put down the German autocracy," Sinclair concluded that, in reality, what the United States had done was extend the authority of "the Money Trust." In his 1923 exposé of the schools, *The Goose-Step*, Sinclair invited readers "to see if I am not right in my contention that what we did, when we thought we were banishing [German autocracy] from the world, was to bring it to our own land, and put ourselves under its sway—our thinking, and more dreadful yet, the teaching of our younger generation." Sinclair's attack was not aimed specifically at the materials produced by the Committee on Public Information, but rather at the "interlocking directories" led by the "plutocratic empire" of bankers, University presidents, school board presidents, superintendents, and textbook authors.[39] Few intellectuals were as conspiratorial as Sinclair, yet most were convinced that the ease and speed with which Wilson mobilized the nation for war and the crackdown on dissent revealed some underlying flaws with democracy and progressivism.

Journalist Walter Lippmann, who had worked for the Committee on Public Information, reached an equally cynical conclusion after the war in his book *Public Opinion*. Lippman offered a sober analysis of the "[g]overnment's propaganda during the war." He explained how propaganda occurs when "a group of men, who can prevent independent access to the event, arrange the news of it to suit their purpose." Lippman identified the importance of censorship to a successful propaganda campaign, because "[i]n order to conduct a propaganda there must be some barrier between the public and the event." However, Lippman was not criticizing Creel and the Committee on Public Information for the successful propaganda campaign during the war; rather, he was critiquing American politicians and citizens for their ability to be manipulated so easily. In other words, propaganda was not the problem; propaganda was the symptom of a larger willful ignorance on the part of the general public to grasp the complexity of the international scene. "For it is clear enough that under certain conditions men respond as powerfully to fictions as they do to realities," Lippman insisted, "and that in many cases they help to create the very fictions to which they respond." To remedy this problem, Lippman did not put his faith in a reformed and improved schooling to better educate the citizenry, as Dewey and his like-minded educational reformers had done in the 1910s. Instead Lippmann proposed an "independent organization for making the unseen facts intelligible to those who have to make the decisions." Lippman suggested that these experts "accumulate a body of data which political science can turn into generalization, and build up for the schools into a conceptual picture of the world. When that picture takes form, civic education can become a preparation for dealing with an unseen environment."[40] Lippman's elitist proposal for an intermediary group of experts between the public and its leaders ran directly counter to the democratic rhetoric that had fueled the progressive reforms and war effort, but it accurately captured the sober mood of the postwar years.

Further skepticism emerged during the war when John Dewey's former protégé, Randolph Bourne, attacked the philosopher for his qualified support of America's role in the conflict. Bourne, a pacifist, argued that Dewey's articles pledging conditional support for the war had demonstrated the "inadequacy of his pragmatism as a philosophy of life in this emergency." Bourne suggested that Dewey's pragmatism was fundamentally a philosophy of means, and therefore could be easily directed toward any objective, good or bad, including war. Bourne charged that Dewey and most U.S. intellectuals had gotten caught up in the slow, steady, incremental campaign for intervention in Europe. As a result, they had lost sight of their longstanding ideals. Although Bourne's attack did not address propaganda directly, it did further suggest that a steady, directed, and emotional effort at harnessing public opinion could sway not only the public but its leading intellectuals as well.[41]

Dewey and Kallen's vision was part of cultural pluralism in a post-European exceptionalism that made it seem as if the United States was the final stage of sociocultural development. That is, the United States represented the final and highest stage of culture on the universal global scale. This arrogant rationale gave the war a sense of purpose because progressives believed that the post-European U.S. democracy represented the desired future of the entire world. The United States was simply pushing history along in the right direction through its military intervention. Bourne recognized the hypocrisy in the logic of imposing of democratic ideals through war. He also recognized the ability of the few to impose their views on the many through the modern tools of persuasion. Whereas education was supposed to be a substitute for war, in reality, education had become part of the justification for war because propaganda had become part of the wartime apparatus. Bourne considered the progressive rationale for war to be a betrayal of the progressives' faith in education as a means of social betterment.

By the mid-1920s, propaganda analysis became a formal area of study, as social scientists offered objective readings of the materials and methods of mass persuasion. The publication of Harold Lasswell's 1927 study *Propaganda Technique in the World War* represented a major turning point in the study of propaganda and crested a wave of scholarship on the topic. In fact, a bibliographic review of work on propaganda identified over a thousand studies on the topic published between 1919 and 1934. Lasswell's groundbreaking book sought to clarify and explain the "ominous clang" of propaganda, for citizens who "are puzzled, uneasy, or vexed at the unknown cunning which seems to have duped and degraded them."[42] By studying the use of propaganda by both the Allies and enemies in the war, Lasswell introduced a level of objectivity and analytic sophistication to the topic characteristic of the time. Like Lippman, Lasswell did not necessarily attack the use of propaganda by the United States. Rather, he considered propaganda to be a somewhat inevitable outcome of the development of mass media, a largely ignorant public, and an increasingly complex world. He also provided an important distinction between education and propaganda that put deliberation at the core of the difference. "Deliberation implies the search for the solution of a besetting problem with no desire to prejudice a particular solution in advance, Laswell explained. "The propagandist is very much concerned about how a specific solution is to be evoked and 'put over.'"[43]

Lasswell concluded that any discussion of a topic that conveyed a predetermined solution could be considered propaganda. By this definition, virtually any textbook or curriculum could be defined as propaganda. Consequently, the only way to avoid propaganda in a school setting was to engage in deliberation, a position first proposed by Dewey (see Chapter 3). In fact, Laswell considered himself to be a Dewey disciple, writing that his approach to social policy was a "contemporary adaptation of the general approach . . . recommended by John Dewey and his colleagues in the development of American pragmatism," lending some posthumous validity to Bourne's accusations about the reinforcing nature of pragmatism, propaganda, and mobilization for the war.[44]

EDUCATORS AGAINST PROPAGANDA

A 1920 editorial in *The Review* entitled "Propaganda and Education" lamented how during the war the press had passed along opinions as facts, many of which found their way into U.S. schools. The author suggested that, moving forward, both schools and the press needed to clarify their aims in presenting information first as "ascertainable facts," then transparently apply expert judgment, discussion, and debate to those facts. "True education of public opinion is through candid discussion and argument," the author insisted. "This, naturally, is not the aim of advertising, nor is it the aim of propaganda."[45] During the 1920s, numerous scholars shared their own concerns over propaganda in schools and looked to education as both the root of the problem and the best solution to counteract what would come to be known by the end of the decade as "the propaganda menace."[46]

As early as 1919, New York State historian James Sullivan identified the problem of propaganda in schools and linked it to issues of academic freedom. Sullivan identified two camps on the issue: those who believed that "a teacher should have his own particular views on any subject and use his position as a teacher to exploit these views and impress them upon the upon the youth" and those who believed "one should avoid in the classroom all mention of any subject which might be conducive to a discussion of present day problems and thus involve the teacher in the temptation of becoming a propagandist for his own particular view." Sullivan suggested a middle position. He averred that teachers needed to address important controversial issues in the classroom, but they also needed to be careful to "present both sides."[47] Sullivan's argument was subtle, but he recognized the dangers of teaching a particular topic in a way that potentially turned it into propaganda for a cause. However, subsequent scholars simply chose to present a common-sense distinction between propaganda and education, as Lasswell had done. As educational researcher Wayne Soper wrote in 1922: "The function of education is to acquaint the individual with a variety of opinions, doctrines, or courses of action so as to equip him intelligently to do his own thinking and to select his own courses of action." In contrast, the objective of propaganda is "to gain acceptance of a particular opinion, doctrine, or course of action under circumstances designed to curb the individual's freedom of action."[48] He concluded that schools were not the place for propaganda.

Before and during the war, leading curriculum reformers were mostly occupied with revising the content of curriculum to make it more relevant and up to date. But after the war, curriculum theorists began to explore the idea that the only way to avoid propaganda or imposition was to teach a variety of positions on an issue. Propaganda anxiety thus inspired a discussion over education in a democracy, as educators sought to define education against what it was not, or at least not supposed to be. For example, in an essay about how to limit or control propaganda, one concerned psychologist offered the following distinction: "Propaganda differs from 'education' with which it is purposely confused, in that in the case of the former the aim is to spread one doctrine, whereas in the case of the latter the aim is to extend a knowledge of the facts as far as known."[49]

The conditions, context, and precise definition of *propaganda* were difficult to pin down, but scholars agreed that propaganda had a distorted, perverted, or distant relationship with the facts. Propaganda taught students what to think. Discussions of propaganda were often conflated with concerns about advertising, swindling schemes, sales pitches, interest-group politics, and political partisanship. Nevertheless, educators agreed that none of these things—propaganda, advertising, partisan politics—belonged in the schools, especially because children were so trusting and vulnerable. Propaganda anxiety arose alongside the ascendancy of mass media, interest-group politics, and advertising, making it difficult to decipher where one began and the other ended.

Concerns that business interests had infiltrated the schools were confirmed in November 1928 when the U.S. Federal Trade Commission investigated methods employed by a coordinated group of public utility companies (referred to as "the power trust") and found them guilty of spending "hundreds of thousands of dollars annually to bias the judgment of students, at nearly all ages from the kindergarten to the PhD candidate, on the relative merits of public and private ownership." During the 1920s, a group of privately owned public utility companies had paid teachers, professors, editors, and journalists to convey pro-public utility information to students and readers. In addition, the utility companies conducted internal reviews of popular textbooks, which they then used to lobby publishers and local and state school boards to have books revised or removed. All of this was done in secret.

Educators were appalled. The NEA called the power trust scandal a "crime against youth," and the American Federation of Teachers dubbed it "the greatest crime against civilization."[50] One writer concluded: "Possibly there has never been in our history a more gigantic and insidious attack on our public schools."[51] Marlen Pew, the editor of the newspaper *Editor and Publisher*, called the power trust scandal "the most audacious attempt ever made to corrupt the newspaper press of this country with propaganda calculated to make the people blindly accept private ownership without a fair debate."[52] Books such as *High Power Propaganda* (1928), *The Propaganda Menace* (1933), *The Power Fight* (1932), *Confessions of the Power Trust* (1932), and *Education and Organized Interests in America* (1935) traced the controversy and connected it to the broader issues of advertising, political lobbying, and interest-group politics in the United States.[53]

In response to the power trust scandal, the NEA launched a formal investigation into propaganda in the schools, and several local groups formed Save-Our-Schools Committees. Dewey served as vice chairman of the New York Save-Our-Schools chapter. As early as 1918, Dewey cynically wondered "whether the word 'news' is not destined to be replaced by the word 'propaganda'" because "propaganda disguised as the distribution of news is the cheapest and most effective way of developing the required tone of public sentiment."[54] In his visits to Japan and China between 1917 and 1919, Dewey recorded numerous uses of propaganda by these regimes to sway the views of its people. However, it was during Dewey's visit to the Soviet Union in the fall of 1928 that he observed firsthand the potential power of using the schools for propaganda purposes. In fact, as the power trust scandal came to light, Dewey was publishing a series of articles in *The New Republic* on his visit, where he observed the "omnipresence of propaganda" in the Russian schools.[55] Although Dewey objected to the use of propaganda in a democracy—as his vice chairmanship of the Save-Our-Schools Committee of New York demonstrated—he did not denounce it outright. In fact, he expressed a sense of awe and admiration at the Russian example, having been partially persuaded by the rhetoric of his hosts. "[I]n Russia, the propaganda is in behalf of a burning public faith," Dewey observed. "[T]heir sincerity is beyond question. To them the end for which propaganda is employed is not a private or even a class gain, but is the universal good of universal humanity. In consequence propaganda is education and education is propaganda."[56] Dewey would later regret these words on the "sincerity" of the Soviet leadership as the true nature of Soviet Union revealed itself in the late 1930s. However, even if Dewey conditionally endorsed propaganda for the "universal good," he clearly opposed the use of propaganda in the schools for private or group interests. In fact, Dewey's writings on propaganda had inspired Lumley to write *The Propaganda Menace*.[57]

In the wake of the power trust scandal, propaganda anxiety in education had reached its peak. In June 1928, a national Save-Our-Schools committee met in Washington, DC, with representatives from 25 states. As a result, the group organized a formal investigation and issued its findings in 1929. The Committee on Propaganda in the Schools listed seven reasons why propaganda was a potential problem: first, because of the "antagonism between education and propaganda as to attitude, method and purpose"; second, because children were more vulnerable than adults; third, because U.S. schools were so decentralized and more easily influenced by local and provincial forces (rather than the common good); fourth, because public schools were common schools and should not reflect the interest of a single class, religion, or political group; fifth, because of the "importance of keeping the school close to . . . the needs of practical life"; sixth, because the curriculum is already overcrowded; and seventh, because the "the school owes a duty to society to train citizens who understand propaganda and can cope with it."[58] In light of the power trust scandal, the NEA report defined *propaganda* rather broadly, not only as political partisanship in addressing controversial issues but as any influence by advertisers, corporations, or interest groups on school curriculum.

The Committee surveyed hundreds of schools for evidence of outside influence on the curriculum. It discovered that most schools across the nation had indeed been solicited by outside groups, but most were able to recognize and resist the requests. Forty-five percent of respondents reported that their school board had specifically considered and discussed "the propaganda question," with large urban districts reporting greater concern than smaller cities. Several states had issued guidelines on how to deal with outside pressures and solicitations from interest groups and businesses. Drawing on its survey, the Committee issued recommendations for school boards and superintendents to review new materials for propaganda. Ultimately, the NEA was consistent with the statements of the educational theorists mentioned above that propaganda did not belong in schools because education differed from propaganda in regards to its relationship to the facts and its role in maintaining public trust. "The propagandist's mind is made up on a particular subject," the Committee concluded. "He seeks to inculcate one viewpoint. The teacher's mind is open on all subjects. He seeks to present all viewpoints."[59] William Carr, research director of the NEA, concluded that avoiding the influence of propaganda was impossible, so teachers ought to address it directly. "An army of propagandists is knocking at the school door," Carr explained. "[T]heir weapons . . .[are] the heavy artillery . . . of state legislative prescriptions" and "the shotgun" of textbooks. Because propaganda was an unavoidable "condition of modern life," Carr continued, teachers must "assume responsibility for training citizens who understand propaganda and who can cope with it."[60] In accordance with the Committee on Propaganda report, Carr reiterated that the job of teachers was to instruct students how to think, not what to think, but he added that teaching about propaganda needed to be part of that process.

The focus on utility, relevance, and social issues during World War I placed the social studies curriculum on a collision course with some of the less savory aspects of modern democratic life—specifically, propaganda as a form of domestic authoritarianism. By the decade's end, leading theorists of democratic education from the NEA to Lasswell to Dewey agreed that the best antidote to the increased use of propaganda was not to avoid it but rather to face the threat head-on by embracing deliberation and debate. Despite the overall sense of postwar disillusionment and detachment that characterized liberals and progressives in the 1920s, a faith in democratic education as the avoidance of propaganda via the thoughtful consideration of controversial issues slowly gained strength over the course of the decade. It would be another 2 decades before this vision of social studies as reflective deliberation was fully articulated, but the seeds of the idea can be traced to the postwar concerns about propaganda of the 1920s.[61]

Further, the propaganda anxiety of the 1920s raised the issue of subjectivity in historical inquiry to a national and conspicuous level. Prior to the war, pragmatic philosophers such as Dewey and William James had pointed to the relative and contingent nature of social science research, and new historians such as James Harvey Robinson had applied their naturalistic approach to the writing and analysis of history.[62] However, the Committee on Public Information, the National Board for Historical Service, and their support of propaganda during the war underscored how context and purpose could dramatically impact newspapers, textbooks, and the writing of history, even when the authors self-consciously aimed to report only the facts. Publically and privately, journalists and professional historians expressed their misgivings about the accuracy of the accounts written by the National Board during the war, which cast doubt on all claims of historical objectivity.[63]

Most importantly, concerns about propaganda of the 1920s forced U.S. educators to define more clearly how democratic education differed from education under Prussia, at home and abroad. Both critics and defenders of the Committee on Public Information's wartime materials housed their arguments in rhetoric about how U.S. schools and curriculum diverged, or at least how they ought to diverge, from authoritarian Prussia. A real democratic education, scholars, intellectuals, and educators agreed, provided a balanced account of an event and let students decide for themselves through thoughtful analysis of the facts. A decade later, the NEA concurred by succinctly concluding: "The main purpose of propaganda is to teach *what to think*, while the guiding purpose of education is to teach *how to think*."[64]

CHAPTER 3

In the Shadow of Collectivism

Many educators in the 1920s agreed that future citizens in a democracy needed to be taught how to think, not what to think. By doing so, students could avoid the pervasive influence of propaganda. Suggestions such as teaching both sides of the issue, avoiding controversial topics, and allowing students to take their own positions on controversial topics were not only supposed antidotes to domestic propaganda, they also provided students with intellectual tools to combat foreign propaganda from communists and fascists. The surprising emergence of Soviet Russia, the domestic Red Scare of 1919–1920, and the rise of fascism in Italy in the 1920s underscored the existence of competing political, social, and educational systems on the global stage. Once the immediate fear of a communist-socialist uprising in the United States abated, American educators continued to observe Russian and Italian education with keen interest. When the U.S. economy collapsed at the end of the decade, the Russian and fascist experiments became particularly relevant because both ideologies embraced collectivism over individualism, and both ideologies employed centralized planning over *laissez faire* economics. Some of the leading voices in progressive education temporarily abandoned the consensus on teaching students how to think between 1930 and 1935, as they debated the merits of a radical curriculum explicitly aimed at indoctrination toward collectivism.

AMERICAN EDUCATORS ON SOVIET RUSSIA

After the Bolsheviks withdrew from the war and solidified their control of the Russian government in 1917, they made formal schooling a central component of their effort to forge Russia into a collectivist society. At first, the Bolsheviks encouraged cutting-edge pedagogical experimentation, local initiative, and bottom-up reform. As a result, several Russian educators cited and implemented the child-centered ideas of American progressive educators. As Russian educator Albert Pinkevitch recalled in 1929: "We have found in the work of American pedagogues . . . a rich source of materials," and he singled out the work of Dewey, William Heard Kilpatrick, and Edward Thorndike as particular influences.[1] Kilpatrick had risen to prominence in the United States because of the project method, an interdisciplinary, hands-on pedagogical approach to content. Thorndike had pioneered the use of objective testing based on his empirically derived laws of learning. Drawing on these innovations, the Bolsheviks ambitiously pursued education for all their citizens through labor schools that were universal, coeducational, secular, practical, and collaboratively designed. The Bolsheviks' effort to establish universal preschool put them at the vanguard of educational reform in this area.[2]

However, postwar Russia was vast, mostly rural, and populous, was recovering from revolution, famine, and civil war, and had a pre-war illiteracy rate estimated at nearly 80%. The task of creating a revolutionary educational infrastructure was daunting, and so the early spirit of experimentation had mixed results. The Russian-born Leo Pasvolsky cynically concluded after his assessment in 1921 that "it is safe to assert that the Russian communism, whatever its claims of theory, has not during its three years' experiment, made any contribution to the world's store of knowledge in the domain of education."[3] A visitor in 1922 similarly concluded that the early educational reforms had been a failure because bureaucracy, red tape, inefficiency, and low enrollment plagued Russian schools. The reforms were further undermined by the poor economic conditions and the obstructions of the teacher unions, which refused to work with the Bolshevik regime. "These schools had no textbooks, no pencils, and the children were sitting in their hats and ragged coats," the visitor reported. "The teachers, lean, pale and pitiable-looking, exhausted individuals, in shabby clothes told me that they were receiving hardly anything materially or spiritually."[4] Another visitor to Moscow in 1924 reported how he observed "teachers of good will . . . sadly overworked and bewildered." The Russian schools, the visitor continued, were filled with "flocks of children learning nothing of fundamental value, and precociously, ludicrously 'political.'" He recognized the earnestness of the Russian educators for their "visionary theories put into practice with boundless energy," but he ultimately dismissed their efforts as a "tragi-comedy."[5]

The same year, socialist writer Scott Nearing visited Russia for 2 months and reported continued experimentation and disorganization in the schools. Nearing quoted a Russian educator who cynically reported: "There is no educational system in Russia today . . . the general educational system is in hopeless chaos." Nearing recognized more hope and optimism than his Russian host. He confirmed that Russian schools were inconsistent, underfunded, and disorganized, but he enthusiastically proclaimed that Russian education was a "battleground . . . against ignorance, using all the weapons that the modern educational world had invented and forged for the purpose."[6] Nearing concluded that the Soviet Union was the most important educational laboratory in the world, and invited American educators to study it closer and with more scientific interest. By the end of the 1920s, America's leading educators, including Dewey, and George S. Counts, took Nearing's advice and made the long trip to Russia to assess the experiment firsthand.

Dewey visited Russia in 1928 and published his reports in the *New Republic* and as a book the next year.[7] He noted "an immense amount of indoctrination and propaganda in the schools," but he hoped that their approach would eventually lead to "the awaking of initiative and power of independent judgment."[8] He was particularly won over by the sincerity and unleashed ambitions of the Russian people. Likewise, Kilpatrick, whose project method was very popular with Russian teachers in the 1920s, praised the Russians' "outstandingly ambitious enterprise."[9] He observed that "no school system in history has been more thoroughly and consistently made to work into the social and political program of the state . . . every item is planned to further the Soviet plan of society."[10] Lucy Wilson, a principal at South Philadelphia High School, recognized that the Russian education system was "still inadequate, at least quantitatively, to its great and self-recognized needs," but was nevertheless impressed during her visit with how in "the last ten years, Soviet Russia has fundamentally reorganized her entire educational system" and, as a result, had "made remarkable material gains."[11] By the end of the 1920s, Dewey, Kilpatrick, and Wilson were impressed with the Russians' spirit of experimentation and their unified sense of purpose. They hoped that the Russian experiment would develop along more democratic lines once the schools and collectivist society were fully established. Beyond these qualified endorsements, the most prolific and enthusiastic American writer on education in Soviet Russia was George S. Counts.

Counts was a quantitative researcher and sociologist whose studies of high schools and school boards in the 1920s demonstrated how the education system reflected the stratified, conservative politics of American society. Counts used these studies to critique what he considered to be the undemocratic, class-structured nature of American schools. Counts concluded with statistical evidence that, rather than challenging and disrupting social and economic hierarchies, American schools actually reflected and reinforced the inequalities of American society.[12] Before he ever visited Soviet Russia, Counts had envisioned the American school as an engine of social reform aimed at challenging economic inequality. In 1923, he urged U.S. secondary schools to be "intelligently organized and administered with a view to promoting" the "larger interests" of "social welfare."[13] After professorships at several universities, Counts arrived at Teachers College in 1927 as associate director of the International Institute. In this capacity, he first visited Soviet Russia for 3 months in 1927. He returned in 1929 and drove a truck across the country for 7 months.[14] Based on this extensive research, he authored several articles and two books—*A Ford Crosses Soviet Russia* and *The Soviet Challenge to America*. He also facilitated the translation and publication of Russian educational materials for an English-speaking audience.[15] Counts's *The Soviet Challenge to America* was an assessment of Russian's first Five-Year Plan and how it related to the economic woes of the United States during the Great Depression.

Under the leadership of General Secretary Joseph Stalin, the Soviet Union launched its first Five-Year Plan in October 1928. The Plan included radical programs of agricultural collectivization, rapid industrialization toward ambitious public goals, and renewed emphasis on education and propaganda through centralized planning and top-down reforms. Russians were taught not only *through* the Five-Year Plan, they were also explicitly taught *about* the Five-Year Plan and how it related to the goals of the party. The Five-Year Plan capped off an impressive assault on Russian illiteracy that, according to Russian sources, increased literacy from 12% to 92% in less than 2 decades. American educators were impressed with this rapid progress and attributed it to centralized planning. One scholar recognized the "liquidation of illiteracy" as "the biggest achievement to date of the Soviet system."[16] Another visitor remarked: "The honest observer must acknowledge that the improvement achieved in a short space of time is so remarkable as to warrant a belief in the ultimate fulfillment of the Communist ideals."[17] Yet another commented: "[T]he Soviet system is only fifteen years old. One wonders how in such a short time they could organize the small details of their schools so consistently with their social philosophy."[18]

Counts was likewise impressed by the progress of the Russian schools. He admitted that there were problems in Soviet Russia with the "restriction of individual freedom," but, like Dewey, Kilpatrick, and Wilson, he was nevertheless impressed by the Russians' "driving passion for human betterment." He agreed that the Soviet educational experiment "should provide genuine stimulus for the mind" and was inspired by the Russians' optimism, "which contrast strangely with the widespread cynicism of the United States."[19] Mocking the continued enthusiasm for aimless *laissez faire* capitalism in the United States, Counts predicted that "we shall find that the society which endeavors to plan its future has a tremendous advantage over the society which entrusts its future to the fates."[20] Counts invited his fellow educators to look closely at the Russian experiment, especially "the organization of the curriculum about nature, labor, and society, and the large emphasis upon useful labor."[21] Subsequent visitors to the Soviet Union during and after the Five-Year Plan were also impressed by the growth of the Soviet schools. "Not only were there more schools, better and more equipment and apparatus, more educational knowledge (much of it untried theory)," Beatrice King related, "but there were now young Communist teachers to train further new teachers."[22]

By 1931, Russian teachers had completely disavowed (by decree) the progressive methods imported from the United States, such as Kilpatrick's project method, and revised the curriculum to align with the industrial goals of the second Five-Year Plan. This about-face on American educational ideas inspired the ridicule of Teachers College professor William Bagley, who was skeptical that Soviet Russia had anything to offer American educators. Bagley gleefully reported how "our American educational pilgrims to the land of the Soviets have been giving us false reports."[23] In contrast,

King still found much to admire in Russian education. While she admitted that many educators, such as Bagley, considered the abandonment of student-centered ideas to be a retrogressive step, she insisted that, "the fundamentals of Soviet education are the same as they were in the beginning. It is still Communist education, and will remain so as long as the Revolution lasts."[24] Overall, visitors to Russian schools during and after the Five-Year Plan recognized merit in the ways that Russian education transcended mere schooling to incorporate museums, night schools, clubs, and youth groups, and invited American educators to consider these innovations as potential ideas for to American schools.

Not all visitors, however, were that optimistic. Following Dewey's lead, some observers were disturbed by the Russians' embrace of propaganda and indoctrination. "The school is 'politicized' in the broadest sense of the term," one professor of Russian language observed on his visit, "There is frank and active indoctrination of Marxism-Leninism as the only scientific method of analyzing social phenomenon."[25] Education professor Philip W. L. Cox was also disturbed by "the sweeping paternalism and superimposition of uniformity of attitudes which characterize the Russian state-controlled education." He concluded that "the spirit of tolerance and the respect for the individual expression" was a better educational approach for democracies to maintain than the authoritarianism of the communists. For Cox, the major and significant difference between democratic and communist approaches to education was epistemological; the Russians dangerously claimed to know the truth and transmit it to its citizens through indoctrination and propaganda, but in democratic education "no man pretends to know truth in any final sense of the word."[26]

In contrast, Counts defended the indoctrination of Soviet Russia. He accused capitalists of being unconscious victims of their own indoctrination. "Having been *indoctrinated* with the idea that any attempt to mold the child according to pattern is essentially sinful," he countered, the capitalist "sees the children inhabiting one-sixth part of the land surface of the globe being subjected to this very process." However, Counts continued, had a capitalist clique suddenly seized control of Soviet Russia and began indoctrinating the Russians in the "sacredness of property and essential soundness of parliamentary institutions, there would be little protest from the Western democracies."[27] In his own visits to Soviet Russia, another observer agreed with Counts that Westerners were indoctrinated in capitalist ways, which inhibited their ability to view Russian education in an unbiased way. "[W]e are bound to face the fact that much of our objection to the drastic utilitarianism of Soviet values of education arises from what the Bolshevik calls an incurably *bourgeois* point of view," the scholar argued. "It is only after we have allowed for the prejudices in regard to education that are necessarily engendered in a capitalist society that we can proceed to criticize the educational prejudices of communist society."[28] As Lumley asked in his book *The Propaganda Menace*: "In Russia the children are drilled in lessons which arouse uncritical admiration of revolutionary heroes; but what are some American patriots trying to do?" Lumley insisted that both Russians and Americans are taught "isms," but concluded that "to stuff the minds of the young with any ism is to put an obstacle in the way of clear and critical thinking later."[29] Counts and Lumley questioned whether Soviet schools were really that different from Western schools in their transmission of specific facts aligned with a particular ideology. That is, both communist and democratic regimes indoctrinated their students with ideals; the communists were just more self-conscious and open about it. Counts and Lumley argued that while the communists embraced a commitment to the common cause, democracies hid their latent commitments behind appeals to balance and objectivity.

In the opening chapter to *The Educational Frontier*, a volume of essays published in 1933 by a group of professors at Teachers College, Boyd Bode also praised the accomplishments of Soviet Russia and its Five-Year Plan. "If we could establish a social program, in the manner of Russia," Bode explained, "our educational problems would largely disappear." However, Bode also criticized the authoritarian methods of the dictatorship, reasoning that "[w]hen the cause of human rights becomes a dogma, it gradually ceases to be humane . . . when we begin to operate with fixed principles, there is trouble."[30] While distinguishing the democratic United States from authoritarian Russia, U.S. educators nevertheless envied the Russian's sense of purpose, collectivist ideals, and the direct connection between long-term economic planning and schools.

Over the 20 years of observing Russian education from the Russian Revolution to the Five-Year Plan, U.S. educators witnessed a complete reversal in the flow of educational ideas on pedagogy and schooling. In the 1920s, the Russians sought to import American methods such as Kilpatrick's project method in order to quickly modernize their schools and society with the latest techniques. However, by the early 1930s, the Russians had wholly rejected American ideas, and elite U.S. educators looked to the Russians for what could be achieved through centralized planning and national commitment to a common vision. Counts in particular drew on his experiences in Soviet Russia to construct a radical critique of American society and education. He insisted that with "the passing of the old agrarian order and the coming of the industrial civilization we will be forced eventually to turn our attention to a number of very fundamental questions which today we are inclined to ignore."[31]

AMERICAN EDUCATORS ON FASCIST ITALY

The rise of collectivist Soviet Russia was only one side of the collectivist coin. The other was fascism. Unlike the communism of Soviet Russia, which demanded strict adherence to the self-evident truths of Marxism-Leninism, fascist regimes in Italy embraced the relativity of knowledge. Unlike the communists, fascists did not look outside themselves for justification; rather, they generated the most useful truths by themselves and for themselves. Truth, for fascists, did not transcend the state; truth was constructed, disseminated, and maintained by the state. Despite this difference, both communism and fascism rejected the idea of teaching students how to think, not what to think, as both approaches professed to know the only acceptable answers to all questions. Both communism and fascism employed propaganda, indoctrination, and authoritarian methods, as both sides required social solidarity as a precondition for political success. Both ideologies valued the collective over the individual.

In October 1922, Benito Mussolini (a.k.a. *Il Duce*) and his fascist supporters marched on Rome and seized control of the Italian government. The fascists reformed the Italian education system by firing socialist teachers, restoring the teaching of Roman Catholic faith in elementary schools, encouraging the proliferation and oversight of private schools, and removing much of the preexisting bureaucracy that allegedly stunted innovation. Upon the fascist takeover, some patriotic and Catholic groups in the United States were glad to see Mussolini stand up to the socialists and communists, and declared solidarity with the fascist cause. For example, the American Legion boasted: "Do not forget that the Fascisti are to Italy what the American Legion is to the United States," and American Catholics were glad to see the revival of religious education.[32] Many American liberals were also open-minded about fascist Italy because of its collectivist and experimental ideals. Specifically, Charles Beard, Sidney Hook, and Horace Kallen were initially impressed by Mussolini's ability to forge nationalistic solidarity in overcoming economic uncertainty through centralized planning.[33]

Just as they had done with the Russian Revolution, liberal U.S. educators approached the centralized reforms of Italian fascism with cautious optimism. As one American visitor to Italy reported in 1925: "There is no doubt . . . that the reforms already made represented a decided step in advance."[34] Five years later, another American educator praised Italian educational reform as "organic" and "free from various local fads and fancies that are prone to weaken scattered and independent changes." Another visitor reported on the "excellence of the work" he observed in Italy, which he attributed to the "devotion and intensity of purpose of the educational leaders with whom he talked" and "to the vital, energetic spirit in every classroom visited."[35] Six years later, another visitor conveyed: "The aims of the revision of the entire educational system may still be far from accomplishment, but it can readily be seen that a great stride has been made into the future."[36] Observers made connections between the ambitious reforms in Italy and Soviet Russia. "The fascist revolution is not unlike the Communist revolution," Kallen asserted in 1927. "Each should have the freest opportunity once it has made a start."[37] As Dewey and John Childs wrote in 1933: "Russia and Italy both present us with patterns of planned societies. We agree profoundly that society requires planning."[38] In contrast, the more conservative Dean William F. Russell of Teachers College was more circumspect. He visited Italy in 1927 and related how it was impossible not to appreciate the "efficiency of the [Italian] government." However, he also warned: "[A]nyone who sees the way in which the entire fortunes of the country are in the hands of a benevolent dictator trembles for the future."[39] As they had been with Soviet Russia, progressive scholars in the 1920s were impressed by how the Italians had confronted and overcome the aimless drift of *laissez faire* capitalism, but were disturbed by fascists' use of propaganda, indoctrination, and authoritarian methods.

Under the leadership of the Minister of Education, Giovanni Gentile, the Italian fascists implemented a series of reforms in the Education Act of 1923, such as making public schools more selective, implementing rigorous examinations, imposing oversight on independent schools, and increasing discipline in teacher education. Gentile endorsed an approach to pedagogy that sought to collapse false dualisms of work/play, theory/practice, thought/action, and individual/state.[40] As Gentile later explained, he used "all the instruments of propaganda and education . . . to make the thought and will of the Duce the thought and will of the masses" because "[f]ascism sets itself in trying to bring the whole mass of the people, beginning with little children, inside the fold of the Party."[41] As an American admirer of Gentile's neoidealism explained, "freedom is essential to spiritual activity, and spiritual activity, or the spirit in action, is Gentile's definition of education."[42] In the odd logic of the author, freedom was achieved through the spiritual surrender of the self to the goals of the state.

Mussolini further explained the purpose of Gentile's educational reforms in his autobiography, which was excerpted in the American publication *High School Journal* in 1933. "I was the son of a school-mistress," Mussolini explained. "I myself was taught in the elementary and secondary schools. I knew, therefore, the school problem. Because of that, I wanted to bring it to concrete conclusion." He praised the work of Gentile, insisting that the reforms were the result of his orders. Mussolini was particularly proud of throwing "on the scrap heap the democratic conception which considered a state school as an institution for everyone—a basket into which treasure and waste were piled together." Mussolini considered such egalitarian thinking that characterized the American high school as weak and inefficient. The fascist reforms to education, according to Mussolini, imposed a new "discipline to which everyone must submit" by infusing "schools with broad humanistic currents in which our history and our tradition are so rich." As the dictator boasted: "Fascism put a stop to all this [weakness] by making discipline supreme, discipline both for the high and for the low, particularly for those who had the high duty of teaching order and discipline and of maintaining the highest concepts of human service in the various schools of the regime."[43] By aligning discipline with culture and purpose, Mussolini and Gentile's education vision appealed to many Americans who saw U.S. schools as aimless, relativistic, and lacking in rigor.

Gentile's pedagogical theory with its cooperative approach to learning, its linking of schooling to social solidarity and reform, and its attack on theory/practice dualism sounded a lot like the pedagogy of Dewey, although the Italian did not directly cite the American pragmatists as an influence. However, Mussolini did directly cite pragmatic philosopher William James as an early influence on his thinking, leading many Americans to reconsider the connection between fascism, relativity, and pragmatism. As Harvard political scientist William Y. Elliot argued in 1926: "The observers who have commented on Fascism have agreed upon one thing at least—that its method is essentially pragmatic. . . . Fascism has come to mean in the popular imagination just the application of pragmatism to politics."[44] Following the lead of Elliot, both critics and admirers tried to connect the dots between the Italian dictator and James. For example, in 1928, political scientist William Kilborne Stewart speculated on the connection between Mussolini and James, concluding that: "James's exposition of pragmatism was at the same time a polemic against absolutism in thinking. Mussolini's public utterances are full of this sense of relativity. He discards fixed principles and pre-established categories."[45] Since both Mussolini and James rejected *a priori* argument and embraced the philosophy of "what works," Stewart argued, they shared a common outlook. As Hook likewise observed, "Mussolini is nearer to pragmatism than any other creed."[46]

Despite their limitations, education in Soviet Russia and fascist Italy appealed to some liberal and radical American educators because of their willingness to directly link schooling to public programs of social and economic reform. In a 1926 *New York Times* profile of Gentile, the paper reported that pedagogy in Italy "puts group interests above individual liberty," an idea that appealed more and more to progressive educators in the late 1920s and early 1930s.[47] While U.S. politicians seemed wedded to *laissez faire* capitalism, observers argued, Stalin and Mussolini were willing to try out collectivist ideas. In the case of Soviet Russia, Marxist theory dictated that the dictatorship of the proletariat was meant to be temporary, but in the future control of the country would be handed back to the people. This enabled admirers of education in Soviet Russia to overlook the Communists' curtailment of personal freedoms.[48] In the case of fascist Italy, some American educators admired Mussolini's willingness to try bold new economic, pedagogical, and social strategies, regardless of ideology. In both Russia and Italy, education under these authoritarian regimes taught students what to think, not how to think, employing indoctrination and propaganda to do so. However, admirers pointed out, such an approach was necessary to bring about the kind of massive social reforms the failing economy required.

EDUCATION FOR SOCIAL PLANNING

As Teachers College professor R. Bruce Raup explained in 1933, the Russian schools had been a "stimulus" to discussions of a planned economy in the United States, but he continued, "even without Russia our own conditions would have brought it about."[49] The conditions to which he referred were those of the Great Depression, which marked a major turning point in the ongoing debate over indoctrination, collectivism, social planning, and the role of schooling in society among the educational elites at Teachers College, who by the 1930s had attained leadership positions in the Progressive Education Association.[50] When the U.S. stock market crashed in October 1929, unemployment rapidly increased from 4 million in 1930 to 8 million in 1931, and eventually to 12 million in 1932. Half-hearted attempts at fixing the economy by President Hoover made things worse. Millions of Americans, and most intellectuals, interpreted the free-falling economy and the failure of political leaders to fix it as a sign that *laissez faire* capitalism was no longer effective. As the *New Republic* reported in 1931: "[T]he morale of business is shaken; the old recipes of 'rugged individualism' and controlled competition are seen on every hand to be insufficient."[51] Counts described the extent and impact of the Great Depression in his foreword to *The Soviet Challenge to America*: "The economic depression which, as I write these lines, continues to hold the entire Western world in its grip, depriving millions of men of employment and bringing misery to vast populations, has revealed grave weaknesses in the contemporary industrial order and has turned the minds of economists and statesmen everywhere to the question of social planning."[52] For many who were already skeptical of *laissez faire* capitalism, the ideology of the business elites had been completely discounted by the economic catastrophe. "How well we remember the arrogance with which business vaunted itself before October 1929," one professor of education recalled. "How often we were exhorted to learn from business management how to conduct schools."[53] Counts too seemed to revel in the crestfallen business community, recounting how "[d]uring the days of prosperity we were told through every agency of propaganda that authentic giants ruled the economic order."[54] He believed that the economic situation demanded the kind of collectivist reform for which he had been advocating for a decade.

By the 1930s, Counts and his peers, such as historian Charles Beard and curriculum theorists Harold Rugg and John Childs, embraced the idea that the road to authentic democracy was a citizenry informed about the present realities of social and economic life. They also agreed that schools could and should be engines of social reform and reconstruction. However, they diverged from leading liberal educators, such as Dewey, in the belief that teachers ought to be disinterested arbitrators in the classroom focused on open-ended discussions of social and economic problems. Instead, the new brand of radical progressives made an ideological commitment to collectivism and social planning. The radicals envisioned the school as a place where students would learn about the harsh reality of the current socioeconomic situation, be taught specific political and social goals for the future and learn how to make that future a reality. They argued that the time for open-ended inquiry and discussion had come to an end; when it came to the issue of social planning, students ought to be told exactly what to think.

Beard was a popular and prolific historian whose 1913 revisionist classic, *An Economic Interpretation of the Constitution of the United States*, depicted the founding fathers as politically and socially conservative. After resigning from Columbia University, he essentially lived off the royalties of his immensely popular textbooks and worked as a public intellectual and independent scholar. In the early 1930s, Beard took a leadership role in educational reform by authoring major components of the American Historical Association's Commission on Social Studies reports, through which he espoused the inevitability of collectivism in American life. Beard endorsed a "rapid transition from an economy based on individual enterprise and competition for private gain to an economy essentially cooperative and integrated in character and dependent . . . on careful planning and co-ordination of production and consumption."[55] Beard was not an unknown outsider when he wrote these words in 1934; he was one of the most popular and prestigious scholars in the nation. By 1934 he had served as director of the New York Bureau of Municipal Research, president of the American Political Science Association, and president of the American Historical Association.[56]

Rugg shared Beard's social outlook, but he had a much closer relationship to classrooms and practitioners. Rugg was part of a new breed of curriculum theorists who sought to construct the curriculum through "scientific" means.[57] The use of quantitative methods and the selection of teaching materials based on social utility were two of the defining features of the scientific study of curriculum. "The very great progress which has been made in the last ten years in making curriculum has been due first to the tendency to adopt the point of view of social utility in selecting the items which are making up the curriculum in any subject," one professor of education explained in 1919, "and secondly, [to] the use of scientific methods in searching out items."[58] By "scientific" methods, the author meant quantitative methods using a transparent and repeatable methodology, which most of the previous educational research had failed to do. Accordingly, Rugg had dismissed the 1916 Committee on Social Studies report as "armchair philosophy" because its recommendations had "not been based upon investigation, measurement of results attained in current instruction, objective determination of desirable content, or upon experimentation."[59] After co-authoring an analysis of child-centered education in 1928, Rugg wrote a series of best-selling pamphlets and textbooks based on over 800 generalizations collected from his analysis of over 60 works of scholars he dubbed "frontier thinkers," such as Dewey and Beard.[60] Drawing on this scientific analysis of the frontier thinkers, Rugg's texts organized their content around social issues and problems, and presented students with rationales for the reform of American society. His texts were adopted by thousands of schools across the country and were read by millions of students. Some estimates suggest that nearly half of all middle school students in the United States were using Rugg's textbooks by the late 1930s.

John Childs had joined the faculty at Teachers College in 1931 and published his dissertation as a book, *Education and the Philosophy of Experimentalism*. Drawing heavily on the work of Dewey and James, Childs argued that educators ought to focus on "creative intelligence," "purposeful activity," and "no fixed goals" because these were aims uniquely appropriate for life in a democracy. He endorsed an educational focus on learning how to think because democratic life required "the continuous process of social reconstruction."[61] Childs's book did not openly endorse economic collectivism, nor did he embrace indoctrination. However, Childs must have been heavily influenced by Counts and Beard because only a few years later he would defend both of these positions. He abandoned his espousal of "no fixed goals" and embraced the direct teaching of collectivism to students.

By the early 1930s, Counts, Beard, Rugg, and Childs agreed that schools ought to be aimed explicitly at reforming the social order through indoctrination. Counts argued that the schools ought to help build a new social order that was "highly socialized, coordinated and planned."[62] Beard insisted that schools ought to teach "the subordination of personal ambition and greed to common plans and purposes."[63] Childs argued: "[D]emocracy is no longer compatible with our historic laissez-faire profit system [so] . . . the educational task is the construction of a planning society."[64] Rugg related how "private ownership and personal competition interrupt the operation of the system and withhold much of it from use" and dismissed "concepts such as expansion, scarcity, laissez faire, and private ownership and control of basic industries and utilities" as "useless language.[65] These scholars agreed that objectivity was impossible and that attempts to be objective were actually serving the forces of conservatism, unfettered capitalism, and the status quo.

Further, the radicals directly attacked the mantra of the 1920s of teaching students how to think, not what to think. As Teachers College professor Jesse Newlon explained, the idea of "teaching to think, but not what to think" reflected an educational "myth" that "teachers should be political neutrals."[66] However, Newlon argued, such neutrality was impossible because the dire economic conditions demanded a commitment to a particular economic and social vision. Newlon's colleague R. Bruce Raup agreed. "The stress on 'all sides fairly' is really a good thing gone wrong," Raup explained, because teachers had erroneously allowed this neutral approach "to become a substitute for good choice and decision." Denouncing the NEA's 1929 report on propaganda in the schools as too conservative, Raup insisted that there was a third option between embracing propaganda and employing objective open-mindedness. The third option was participating in the "process of generating and regenerating the aims, principles, and policies by which we manage living together." Dismissing the politically neutral "how to think, not what to think" approach further, Raup concluded: "Fair mindedness is a condition of doing this [i.e., social planning] well, not a substitute for doing this at all."[67]

The collectivists argued that the existing school curriculum still emphasized the outdated 19th-century values of the individualist, *laissez faire* agrarian past, but should be focusing on the cosmopolitan, urban, collectivist future. To have the curriculum keep pace with the modern world, educators needed a specific vision toward which to direct students, and that vision was collectivist in nature. In his controversial *Conclusions and Recommendations* of the AHA Commission on Social Studies, Beard asserted that "[c]umulative evidence supports the conclusion that . . . the age of individualism and laissez faire in economy and government is closing and that a new age of collectivism is emerging."[68] Beard's AHA report was quoted and echoed in the opening pages of the new journal *Social Frontier*, launched at Teachers College in October 1934. The first issue of *Social Frontier* declared "that the age of individualism in economy is closing and that an age marked by close investigation of social life and by collective planning and control is opening."[69]

In contrast to Dewey, the collectivists placed little emphasis on the ability of students to weigh evidence and arrive at their own conclusions. For example, in the foreword to his magnum opus, *Foundations for American Education*, Rugg aspired "to let my mind conclude what the facts of life conclude."[70] Likewise, in the *Nature of the Social Sciences*, Beard considered historical knowledge to be a "collection of facts, verified, authenticated, and generally agreed upon."[71] Both Rugg and Beard approached the creation and identification of "facts" as mostly unproblematic and obvious. Their approach to pedagogy and society merely involved choosing the most appropriate facts that best aligned with a better, more collectivist future. Progress, for Rugg and Beard, was simply a matter of replacing outdated knowledge with new knowledge—that is, replacing facts that served the status quo with facts that better served what they considered to be the inevitable collectivist future. Counts, Beard, and Rugg focused on proper content, not on the process of thinking. That is, they focused on what to think, not how to think. Dewey, in contrast, kept the focus on teaching how to think front and center. Counts famously sparked the debate in his 1932 address to the Progressive Education Association, "Dare the Schools Build a New Social Order," in which he notoriously implored educators to "become less frightened . . . of imposition and indoctrination."[72] Counts' proclamation kicked off a debate in the pages of *Social Frontier* that pitted moderate progressive educators such as Dewey and his former student Boyd Bode against radical collectivists such as Counts and Childs.

In a 1933 article in the *Teachers College Record*, professor of education Thomas Briggs supported Counts in his position that propaganda was inevitable and that Americans ought to embrace it. After all, the Europeans had been successfully using propaganda in their schools for decades with spectacular results: "We see and marvel at the results in other nations; but because they are Germany, Italy, and Russia, with ideals far different from ours, we are foolishly afraid of the same means. But be assured that democracy needs an integrated people, too."[73] Bode, a professor of education at Ohio State University, disagreed. In the 1930s, Bode was the leading voice of moderation in the discussion over the role of indoctrination in the schools. He believed that movement toward central planning by the government was desirable, but he was opposed to the alleged "conditioning" suggested by the radical collectivists because such an approach was "the negation of democracy." Like Dewey, Bode endorsed the ongoing deliberation, instead of a preestablished set of goals. Bode concluded: "We must aim at a democratic social order and we must avoid indoctrination."[74] Childs rebutted: "[A]ll education necessarily moves within some framework of things deemed necessary, possible and desirable," and therefore the school cannot aid in progress unless it conveys a "preferred social order."[75]

Counts, Childs, Rugg, and Dewey were all professors at Columbia University in New York. Starting in 1927, these educators had started meeting informally to debate the merits of an educational system aligned with a planned economy. In a 1932 letter to Horace Kallen, Dewey outlined what was at stake with this group:

> There is a question quite acute with some younger men in education which has at least tangible bearing on our theme. Can there be social planning of a concrete sort which will not necessarily react upon education? And if it will react, how will it be secured? Will not education be bound up with propaganda if there is to be any unified aim, instead of mere drift?[76]

Kallen responded to Dewey that he doubted "whether teaching and indoctrination could ever be anything but synonymous"; therefore, if indoctrination had to occur, then teachers should indoctrinate students with the themes of "freedom and individuality."[77] Dewey voiced a similar position, but he clung to his belief that indoctrination could be avoided if the curriculum was approached through open-ended inquiry. Dewey retained his commitment to democratic socialism as an outcome, but he reiterated his moderate pedagogical position on open-ended discussion.

Dewey agreed with the radical collectivists that impartiality was impossible, and he opposed "the amount of indoctrination for a reactionary social order that now goes on in schools."[78] By reactionary social order, Dewey specified the influence of conservative groups in the 1920s such as the Ku Klux Klan, Daughters of the American Revolution, and American Legion; religious fundamentalists; and the War Department, which had led to local textbook revision, mandated loyalty oaths, banning of teacher unions, compulsory military training, and the protection of Bible reading in the schools.[79] Despite his rejection of reactionary politics, Dewey disagreed with Counts and Childs that "schools can in any literal sense be the builders of a new social order."[80] He proposed a realistic survey of current conditions, but he opposed direct indoctrination. Thus Dewey considered both conservatism of the current system and the radical collectivism proposed by Counts, Rugg, and Childs as forms of indoctrination, and espoused a middle ground based on reflective inquiry, discussion, and deliberation.

If democratic education was not approached through reflective inquiry, Dewey explained in an essay on the social studies, it was "likely to became either accumulations of bodies of special factual information, or, in the hands of zealous teachers, to be organs of indoctrination in the sense of propaganda for a special social end, accepted enthusiastically, perhaps, but still dogmatically."[81] Dewey recognized little distinction between approaches that reflected the ideals of the status quo and those that sought to reconstruct society through indoctrination and propaganda if both approaches presented their narratives in a dogmatic manner. In 1938, Dewey specifically endorsed "methods of investigation and free cooperative discussion" as antidotes to indoctrination.[82] He recognized a distinction between teaching toward "a plann*ed* society" and teaching toward a "*continuously* plann*ing* society." The former required "fixed blue-prints," while the latter required "release of intelligence through the widest form of cooperative give-and-take."[83]

This high-profile debate occupied the pages of *Social Frontier*, *Teachers College Record*, and the meetings of the Progressive Education Association. Most educators rejected indoctrination and aligned with Dewey and Bode. For example, in 1937, the Progressive Education Association rejected an offer to combine its journal *Progressive Education* with *Social Frontier*, due to the radicalism of the latter. Furthermore, essays in *Social Frontier* and *Teachers College Record* by leading educational theorists rejected the kind of indoctrination espoused by Counts, Beard, and Childs. Even the *Teachers College Record* Editorial Board eventually took a direct position against indoctrination.[84] Beyond this, Charles Merriam, a political scientist at the University of Chicago and member of the Commission on the Social Studies, refused to endorse Beard's embrace of collectivism in *Conclusions and Recommendations*. Another member of the Commission who also refused to sign the report dismissed Beard's rhetoric as "Utopian yearning."[85] The radical collectivist ideas of Beard, Counts, Rugg, and Childs were provocative, but ultimately they were not persuasive or particularly influential.

While the circumstances of continued domestic and global depression initially made collectivism seem appealing in the early 1930s, international events ultimately made collectivism seem dangerous and irresponsible by the end of the decade. Both radicals and moderates envisioned a more democratic society, but the radical collectivists defined democracy in partial emulation of foreign regimes that were turning into dictatorships, while moderates defined democracy in contrast to those foreign dictatorships. Both placed their intellectual bets on the anticipated economic and social outcomes of foreign collectivism. In other words, it was not purely logic and reason, but, more importantly, international events that shaped the debate over the role of indoctrination in democratic education.

Historians have written extensively about this episode, but the impact of the indoctrination debate on the practice of teachers was minimal.[86] Rugg's popular textbooks took on a slightly more radical tone over the course of the early 1930s, but his issue-based approach to the curriculum predated the indoctrination debate by a decade, and Rugg scaled back some of his collectivist rhetoric later in the decade. The content of Rugg's pamphlets and textbooks were based on his scientific analysis of the frontier thinkers in the 1920s, and were only partially influenced by the ideas of Counts, Childs, and Beard.[87] The liberals, such as Dewey, who argued on behalf of open-ended inquiry and deliberation—learning how to think, not what to think—ultimately won the argument against those who favored indoctrination, especially as the geopolitical reality made collectivism a less savory option later in the decade. Nevertheless, the discussions about the unavoidability of indoctrination in education introduced by Counts, Beard, and Childs anticipated similar claims made by intellectuals and educators in the 1960s.

CHAPTER 4

In the Shadow of Dictatorship

In the 1920s and early 1930s, U.S. educators lumped communism and fascism together as "collectivist" approaches to government and education, and they looked to Soviet Russia and fascist Italy for inspiration. However, by the mid-1930s, some began distinguishing communists from fascists because the two had squared off against each other in European legislatures, and, in theory, the ideologies differed over fundamental issues, including economics, nationalism, racism, and imperialism. By 1935, those sympathetic to Marxism-communism dismissed fascism as an imperialist-capitalist movement opposed to international economic justice. Other more moderate voices lumped communism and fascism together as "dictatorships." The rise of the Nazi party in Germany in the 1930s pushed most scholars in the United States to adopt the latter view.[1] As a result, between 1935 and 1939, leading educators abandoned their earlier appreciation for collectivist approaches to government and schooling. This reorientation took place against the backdrop of attacks on naturalistic philosophy by critics who identified similarities between the moral relativism of naturalists and the ideologies of dictatorship, as well as continued efforts to teach U.S. students to combat propaganda. By the end of the turbulent 1930s, leading educators, led by Dewey and Counts, began to revise, and even repudiate, the collectivist ideas they had endorsed earlier in the decade. The binge and purge of collectivist ideology in the 1930s led American educators to reaffirm their commitment to teaching students how to think, not what to think, as an antidote to authoritarian education.

COLLECTIVISM RECONSIDERED

As a result of dramatic political events in Europe, the social, cultural and ideological landscape of radicalism in the United States shifted significantly over the course of the 1930s, inspiring a reappraisal and eventual rejection of collectivism as an objective in education. In 1931, Stalin issued a decree banning any references to American pedagogy, and removed several Russian educators, including those who had hosted the Americans in the 1920s, from power. For example, Counts' friend, Russian professor of education Albert Pinkevitch, was sent to a forced labor camp, where he soon died. Further, between 1935 and 1938, Stalin launched a series of brutal purges (known as the Moscow trials) against his political enemies that disturbed and divided American intellectuals sympathetic to communism. In particular, the generation of leaders who had engineered the Bolshevik Revolution was eventually murdered by Stalin's regime.[2] Further, in 1933 the Nazi Party seized control of the German *Reichstag* and established dictatorial powers for Nazi leader Adolf Hitler, whose alarming use of overt racism and militarism differed from Mussolini's less radical version of fascism. In March of 1935, Hitler declared that Germany was renouncing the Treaty of Versailles and rearming its military, and in October of that year Mussolini led an invasion of Ethiopia, ignoring the protests and sanctions of the League of Nations. The next year, Mussolini and Hitler established the Rome-Berlin axis.

In Germany, Hitler outlawed discussion and dissent in school and mandated the state-authored curriculum, which included lessons on race biology and the superiority of the Aryan race. Unlike the earlier praise for Gentile's educational reforms in Italy, American educators recognized nothing positive in Hitler's approach to schooling. In his appraisal of the Italian and German education under fascism, Philip W. L. Cox dismissed fascist approaches as indoctrination and social control. He saw little in the Italian approach to education worthy of emulation in the United States.[3] The same year, Isaac Kandel, professor of education at Teachers College and associate at the International Institute, identified similarities between the regimes of Italy, Nazi Germany, and Communist Russia as reflected in their approaches to schooling. Identifying these regimes as "totalitarian," Kandel distinguished education "for enlightenment" in democracies from "education as a coercive, controlling force (propaganda and indoctrination in every sense of the word)" in totalitarian regimes. The latter entailed "the ultimate subordination of all individuals to the will and guidance of the state as represented and expressed by a dictator or by a party." He argued that totalitarian regimes collapsed formal and informal education to forge a "cult of emotions," treated state ideology as a religion, and vested all their power in a single leader or party. Kandel denounced the values of totalitarianism and worried that the focus on "the mechanics of educational administration, organization, and practice" in the United States was threatening the health of democracy at home. He implored educators to embrace the values of "independence, tolerance, freedom of thought, and freedom of expression," as antidotes to totalitarian thinking.[4]

Similarly, Thomas Woody linked the educational approaches of Soviet Russia, fascist Italy, and Nazi Germany. He traced the roots of totalitarian education to Prussia, because the Prussians were allegedly the first to establish the "complete ideological groundwork for totalitarian education which 20th century nations, due to concatenation of events, had variously translated into reality." He identified five elements of modern totalitarian education: aristocratic rule, anti-pluralism, anti-rationalism, collectivism, and activism. Aristocratic rule referred to the exclusive administration by those who declared themselves to be the most fit. Anti-pluralism referred to "rooting out of old divided loyalties and stifling their expression." Anti-rationalism referred to the belief that "[t]here is no universal truth; man is incapable of such objectivism." Collectivism referred to rejection of the individual and his or her rights. He defined activism as encouraging "only controlled activity, limited to the attainment of goals that have been predetermined." The totalitarian state was maintained, Woody continued, "by the denial of freedom for investigation and expression on the part of teacher and learner; and through the absolute domination of minds through state-controlled cinema, radio, and press."[5] Although Woody did not explicitly make a case for democratic education in the essay, the implication was that these elements ought to be rejected by democratic nations. The conflation of Soviet Russia with fascist Italy and Nazi Germany overlooked substantial ideological differences among the regimes, but the concept of totalitarianism nevertheless created a convenient foil against which democratic educators could refine their own goals.

By 1937, even Rugg noted similarities between Nazi Germany and Soviet Russia. In the updated edition of his textbook *Changing Governments and Changing Cultures*, he related that "[i]t is important to note, that each of these governments—both the Fascist and the communist—is a dictatorship." Rugg opened the book with profiles of "terror" of "the Russian dictators," "Hitler's Nazis," and "Mussolini and the Fascists." He related how the Bolsheviks "exiled tens of thousands, and executed not less than 50,000 of their enemies in the first years of their seizure of government."[6] Rugg's chapter on Soviet Russia was hopeful that the nation would move in a more democratic direction in light of some recent reforms, but he was highly critical of the past actions of Stalin and the Communist Party. Anticipating the coming world war, he identified several "danger spots" where international conflict was likely to break out.

In 1938, 2 years before he was assassinated, the exiled Russian revolutionary Leon Trotsky explained the corruption of the Bolshevik cause in an essay published in *Social Frontier*. As he reported: "Twenty years after the revolution the Soviet state had become the most centralized, the most despotic, and the most bloody apparatus of violence and coercion." Trotsky recognized Stalin's "indubitable" success in raising literacy rates through his education reforms, but these new skills were moot because Russians "have been deprived of the right of expressing their opinions and interests in print," the press served "only the bureaucracy," and the textbooks conveyed "nothing but falsifications" supporting the "personal absolutism of Stalin." The Moscow trials, according to Trotsky, represented "the most gigantic falsification in human history," and he compared Stalin's dictatorship to Hitler's.[7] The Hitler-Stalin comparison demonstrated the growing fears among some early skeptics that, despite its rhetoric about global economic justice, the Soviet Union was turning into an oppressive dictatorship indistinguishable from fascism.

Dewey had never fully embraced the collectivist rhetoric espoused by Counts and Childs, and he was a consistent critic of Marxism. Nevertheless, he had praised Soviet schools and embraced some of the collectivist rhetoric of the early 1930s. By the mid-1930s, Dewey was leading the charge against communism at home and abroad. Dewey had seen the duplicity of Stalin's Communist Party firsthand when he led an investigation into the charges brought against Trotsky in 1937. Dewey disagreed with Trotsky's dogmatic Marxism, but he believed that the exiled leader had not been given a fair trial by Stalin's regime. After an investigation that brought Dewey to Mexico to interview the former Bolshevik in person, the American Committee for the Defense of Leon Trotsky concluded that Trotsky and his son were not guilty of Stalin's charges against them. Dewey denounced Stalin in the press, insisting that "we must stop looking to the Soviet Union as a model for solving our own economic difficulties and as a source of defense for democracy against fascism," a position unpopular with socialists at the time.[8] Just as Kandel had done, Dewey adopted the conflation of Nazism and communism into the term *totalitarianism*, which was used by most scholars as a foil to the democratic way of life.[9] Dewey admitted that his earlier cautious optimism for the Soviet Union in 1928 had been misplaced. "Conditions in totalitarian countries have brought home the fact, not sufficiently realized by critics, myself included," he explained, "that the forms which still exist [in democracies] encourage freedom of discussion, criticism and voluntary associations, and thereby set a gulf between a country having suffrage and popular representation and a country having dictatorships, whether right or left."[10] The communists rejected open-ended inquiry, which had consistently been at the heart of Dewey's philosophy and pedagogy. As a result, Dewey never subscribed to the close-minded ideological commitment of his more radical peers. Dewey's moderate position in the debate over indoctrination was vindicated when the dictatorial nature of the Communists was revealed in the final years of the 1930s. Nevertheless, he admitted he had been partially fooled by the communist propaganda earlier in the decade.

Dewey was very critical of domestic communism as well. Upon observing the obdurate behavior of the Communist Party in Local No. 5 of the American Federation of Teachers in New York City, Dewey concluded, "[t]he greatest enemy to the organization of teachers in connection with the labor movement is in my opinion the activities of the CP in trying to use the organization." He privately attacked the communist clique as "partisan . . . lying . . . [and] stupid," and helped launch a splinter union called the New York Teachers Guild.[11] Dewey resented the irrationality and rigidity of the communists and their willingness to destroy sympathetic figures and institutions that did not follow their exacting lead. Similarly, historian and former communist sympathizer Richard Hofstadter reflected in 1939 how he "used to sneer when I read that communism was a substitute religion, but I don't anymore," because he had witnessed firsthand "the simpering dogmatic religious-minded" tactics of the Party. By the end of the decade Hofstadter had abandoned his sympathies for collectivism and embraced the values of "freedom of individual intellectual inquiry, scientific attitude of mind, [and] respect for the facts," attributes not respected by the communists.[12]

However, the biggest conversion came from Counts, formerly Soviet Russia's most enthusiastic educational champion. After his third visit to Russia in 1936, Counts complained that "the Soviet leadership had turned against me."[13] In 1937 he included an updated assessment of Soviet Russia in his book *The Prospects of American Democracy*, in which he explained "how the Communist Party repudiated political democracy completely and established, almost from the beginning, a rigid dictatorship," a harsh indictment missing from his earlier accounts of Soviet Russia from the early 1930s. "Seizing political and military power," Counts continued, the Communist Party in Russia "gained control of the institutions of government, abolished civil liberties, converted the courts into revolutionary organs, conducted an unremitting struggle against all enemies, [and] molded the entire apparatus to its purposes." In a complete rebuttal of his 1931 book, *The Soviet Challenge to America*, Counts concluded "that America will follow a very different course, and . . . all who look to Russia as an example to be copied will be subject sooner or later to severe disillusionment." In a repudiation of his earlier invitation for American teachers to build a new social order, Counts insisted, "the power of the school is severely limited" and "that life is the great educator."[14]

Over the course of the 1930s, life had indeed educated and humbled Counts; it had taught him to denounce utopian visions and unyielding ideological commitments, and to appreciate the bourgeois values of democracy, including individualism, open-ended inquiry, and consensus-building. By the end of the decade, Counts joined Dewey and Hook in rooting out communists from the American Federation of Teachers, which Counts successfully did after being elected president of the organization in 1939. In a 1941 article for the *Social Frontier*, which had changed its name to *The Frontiers of Democracy* in 1939, Counts revisited the positions he had espoused in the first issue of the journal. While he still pledged his support for the position that all men were created equal, he had learned three things since 1934. First, Counts admitted that he had underappreciated the role of military force in social oppression and change and overemphasized the influence of property and wealth. "The rise and course of the dictatorships in Europe, whether Communist or fascist," Counts explained "demonstrate that the power of the machine gun can be far more decisive and oppressive than the power of property and that the latter is by no means always prior or superior to the former." Second, he underappreciated the necessity of maintaining the democratic process at all times. He learned that indoctrination, propaganda, and authoritarian methods should never be employed, even if their use was in route to a more democratic outcome. "The use of undemocratic means to achieve democratic ends," he concluded, "can only lead to disaster." Finally, Counts appreciated the importance of individual rights. "Democracy, to be successful, must rest upon the integrity of the individual," he wrote in repudiation of his previous praise for collective action and social planning. "It requires the wide acceptance of the so-called 'bourgeois virtues.'" Ultimately, Counts explicitly repudiated his earlier praise for the Soviet's "rigid dictatorship," contrasting it with the "honesty, fair-mindedness, restraint and scientific spirit" of democratic life.[15] Further, in their 1943 book *America, Russia, and The Communist Party in the Post-war War*, Counts and his co-author John Childs implored the Soviet Union to "abandon slavish adherence to a nineteenth-century system of revolutionary dogma" because the Russians could no longer assume "the early collapse of capitalist democracies" or the "doctrine of world-wide upheaval following the peculiar pattern of the Russian Revolution."[16] While still committed to a more equitable society, Counts no longer dismissed the merits of bourgeois values such as representative government, incremental change, individualism, compromise, and open-ended inquiry.

Any remaining sympathy for Stalin and collectivism ended abruptly in August 1939 when the Russians announced they had signed a nonaggression agreement with the Nazis. The Soviet-Nazi Pact was the ultimate betrayal to American socialists still looking to Russia to stand up to fascism. The Pact marked an unequivocal and sudden end to sympathy for Soviet Russia and its collectivist ideals. As theologian Reinhold Niebuhr reflected: "What [Russia] has done as the fatherland of socialism, to which millions . . . in this very nation have given their devotion, is despicable." The betrayal, he continued, represented "a bitter blow" to those who looked to Russia for inspiration and hope.[17] Sociologist Robert Lynd wrote to his colleague, "[T]he Soviet move hit me back of the ears like a lead pipe."[18] Similarly, writer Norman Holmes Pearson commented: "What the Nazi-Soviet Pact represented, diplomatically speaking, was *Realpolitik*, but what it represented ideologically was the denial of the primacy of morality in politics."[19]

Indeed, throughout the 1930s, U.S. collectivists had taken the moral high ground in their pursuit of social and economic justice in the United States and the world. But the Nazi-Soviet alliance made such a position unviable because the agreement exposed Stalin as a ruthless, self-interested dictator willing to abandon the morals of the global cause to save his own regime. Walter Lippman expressed an even harsher conclusion following the Nazi-Soviet Pact: "To have realized that the present Russian government repudiates the principles of truth and justice must, I think, eventually lead to the realization that this is not a corruption of, but the inevitable consequences of, the ideals of communism."[20] Looking back at a decade of propaganda, indoctrination, intolerance, terror, and one-party rule in Soviet Russia, fascist Italy, and Nazi Germany, it became clear that all three systems had more in common than the radical collectivists wanted initially to admit. Right before their eyes, Stalin had distorted the truth and used authoritarian methods against his own people, but radicals told themselves that such policies were temporary tools employed toward a greater collectivist future; the radical collectivists told themselves that at least the communists were not racist, nationalistic, and imperialist like the fascists. However, by 1939 this distinction no longer held up, especially when the Russians occupied the eastern part of Poland as part of their agreement with the Nazis. Even President Roosevelt, in a 1940 article in the *New York Times*, lamented that he had hoped that "Russia would work out its own problems and their government would eventually become a peace-loving, popular government with free ballot," but by 1940 he had to "face the fact" that Soviet Russia "is run by a dictatorship as absolute as any other dictatorship in the world."[21]

NATURALISM UNDER ATTACK

The radical collectivists of the 1930s who had praised Soviet Russia drew on a naturalistic approach to knowledge in their critiques of U.S. society and education.[22] For example, Counts embraced the contingent nature of knowledge, arguing that "[c]omplete impartiality is utterly impossible."[23] As Beard explained, social sciences can "present systems, trends, probabilities, and alternatives, but they cannot declare purposes or make choices . . . they do not issue commands . . . [t]hey cannot declare ends; they are means to ends."[24] Likewise, Rugg insisted, "concepts are finders of scientific laws, not mere summarizers of them," and he rejected the "idea that truth is something 'out there' . . . established by 'history,'" because such an approach exhibited "deep contempt for the contemporary."[25] In the early 1930s, the radicals argued that the contingent and evolving nature of knowledge made commitment to a particular social order necessary. They believed that benefits could be gained by a purposeful curriculum aligned explicitly with social, economic, and political goals.

During the 1930s, some scholars viewed naturalism as a direct threat to absolute values, and they blamed progressive educators for their role in spreading moral relativism through U.S. schools and society. For example, in 1938, Geoffrey O'Connell traced the "crime wave and the other social evils of divorce, relaxed moral standards, and intellectual agnosticism" to "the decline in Christianity due to the growth of naturalism in American life and education." For several decades, O'Connell argued, "such indoctrination has been under way" in American schools, but the momentum had allegedly increased in recent years. O'Connell linked naturalism to socialism, communism, and fascism because all of these doctrines rejected the primacy of God over man and embraced relativity over transcendent truth.[26] Naturalistic education, another critic insisted in 1934, "leaves the mind free to follow any principle or no principle, any destiny or no destiny, it takes its own origin for granted and cares not whither it tends," making it compatible with authoritarianism.[27] In 1938, another critic accused Dewey, Kilpatrick, and Rugg of propagating doctrines that "inevitably undermine American institutions and prepare the advent in the United States of atheistic totalitarianism."[28] The critics of naturalism equated civilization with the discovery and application of absolute values revealed through premodern and religious texts. Both Marxism and naturalism, critics argued, necessarily sought to dismiss the wisdom of the past and worked to disrupt existing social and intellectual hierarchies. Critics of naturalism linked progressive education with a relativistic philosophy that undermined moral absolutism and teacher authority, leading, they argued, to the corruption of civilization itself.

The debate between naturalists and absolutists took place against the backdrop of growing fears over the rise of authoritarian ideologies and regimes in Europe. As a result, leading progressive educators linked fascism with reactionary politics, pro-business values, and patriotism in the United States. In return, right-leaning critics cast progressive educators as alleged communists, socialists, and Marxists. Both sides accused the other of espousing ideas that led to dictatorship and authoritarianism. These cross-accusations erupted in 1935 during an incident in which the Hearst newspapers sent a fake, red-baiting letter to several progressive educators, including Counts, Kilpatrick, and John Washburne of Syracuse University. The authors of the Hearst letter posed as prospective students inquiring about communist organizations they could potentially join if they attended the targeted universities. Upon discovering the origins of these fake letters, the educators were irate and linked such tactics to fascism. "If William Hearst succeeds in his efforts," Counts exclaimed, "he will reduce the American Universities and schools to the ignominious condition of the German schools and universities under Hitler." Counts pondered: "Is this the beginning of a nationwide Fascist campaign to destroy our basic American freedoms?" Kilpatrick similarly linked the attack on the freedom of speech to "the destruction of intelligent democracy and the enthronement of some demagogic fascism."[29]

Despite this inflammatory rhetoric, Kilpatrick doubted that authoritarianism, whether fascist or Communist, could really be implemented in the United States. "We have no proletariat in the European sense, so we cannot have a dictatorship of the proletariat," Kilpatrick speculated. "Nor is it easy to take Fascism as a serious proposal. No Mussolini could maintain dictatorial power in this country."[30] Yet, some educators recognized similarities between the United States and Europe in their irrational embrace of nativism, racism, and nationalism during a time of economic uncertainty. For example, R. Bruce Raup recognized the similarities between fascism and the reactionary politics of nationalism. "Anyone who has watched the reaction of Germany from its social democracy to that frame of mind which made possible Hitler's Third Reich," Raup explained, "knows how powerful is the pull-back of an old culture when the new way ahead becomes dark and difficult."[31] Similarly, Phillip W. L. Cox considered the prospects of both communism and fascism in America, concluding that "some form of fascism is not improbable in this country," but "no informed and rational American has any belief that communism will triumph in the United States."[32] Generally, progressive and collectivist educators dismissed concerns about domestic communism but worried about the potential inroads of fascism, while patriotic and pro-business groups dismissed concerns about domestic fascism but worried about the potential inroads of communism.

By the mid-1930s, even those who had once expressed optimism about Mussolini's collectivist experiment in Italy began to express their doubts. For example, Horace Kallen, who had once praised the reforms in Italy, now recognized fascism as a political dead end. However, he still championed naturalistic philosophy as the approach most compatible with democracy and defended naturalism against the criticism that the philosophy had paved the way for fascism. In an article for *Social Frontier*, he attacked Sidney Hook and William Elliot by name because both scholars had linked the naturalistic philosophy of James and Dewey to Mussolini. Kallen presented his case for divorcing the ideas of James from the fascist dictator. He reported that an interview he had conducted with Mussolini revealed that the dictator had only a superficial knowledge of the work of James. When he asked *Il Duce* about which texts of James he found most influential, Mussolini responded with disgust at the question. "If Mussolini owes anything to William James," Kallen concluded, "he owes it to a William James he never met and not a word of whose work he had ever read, except the word 'pragmatism.'" Kallen suggested that Mussolini's citing of James in the 1920s was merely an attempt to win sympathy from American intellectuals. Kallen further dismissed the logic behind Elliot's attempt to link pragmatism to fascism, writing: "Thinking of this kind seems the pattern: *A man walks on two legs; a bird walks on two legs; therefore a man is a bird.*"[33] Kallen argued pragmatism differed from fascism because it deliberately sought out conflicting voices and was based on unfettered, open-ended inquiry, not the official doctrines of the state, party, or dictator.

Others took a more nuanced approach to the connection between pragmatism/naturalism and fascism. For example, philosopher I. Donsky admitted that the epistemology of fascism "reminds us of Pragmatism." However, he continued, "there is a striking difference between the epistemologies of Pragmatism and of dictatorship" because "[p]ragmatism holds truth to be relative to practice, but does not hold it to be absolute at the same time. Pragmatism does not assume, like dictatorship, the absolute value of the relative truth."[34] That is, pragmatists accepted that all conclusions were conditional and contingent. Unlike fascists, pragmatists appropriately treated their own conclusions as open to revision by inviting deliberation and revision. Dictators, in contrast, invented their own truths by deliberately excluding and outlawing deliberation and revision. Thus, the act of open and transparent deliberation and revision was what separated democracy from dictatorship, and naturalism from dogmatism.

In 1938, Boyd Bode attempted to get ahead of the growing criticism of progressive education, naturalism, and its link to moral relativism in his book *Progressive Education at the Crossroads*. Bode clarified the official—and what he depicted as moderate—positions of Dewey, Rugg, and Kilpatrick on issues such as naturalistic epistemology, student interest, needs, growth, and the role of subject matter in education. Bode characterized progressive education as wholly compatible with democratic life, which he contrasted with the absolutism of the Nazis and communists. "The youth of Russia, so we are told, are aflamed to maintain and promote communism against the wicked designs of capitalism," Bode explained. "In Germany[,] Nazism seems to have become a youth movement." Progressive education, in contrast, rejected the existence of a fixed body of absolute values and content by introducing students to open-ended thinking and democratic reasoning. Bode argued: "A democratic program of education must necessarily rest on the perception that democracy is a challenge to all forms of absolutism."[35] References to the work of Counts, Childs, and radical collectivists were conspicuously absent because Bode was trying to rescue progressive education from the radicalism and extreme child-centeredness that had come to characterize it in the early 1930s. However, the damage had already been done.

With the economy improving due to the war and the collectivist rhetoric of radicals discounted by the Nazi-Soviet Pact, pro-business and patriotic groups fought to win back the esteem they had lost during the 1930s. Since Rugg had the most immediate and conspicuous impact on the actual curriculum through his popular textbooks, it was he who took the brunt of the anti-progressive education backlash in the 1940s, when pro-business and patriotic groups publicly attacked his texts. By 1944, the sales of Rugg's popular textbook series *Man and His Changing Society* had dropped 90% from their peak in 1938. However, critics of Rugg did not target his naturalistic philosophy. Instead they attacked what they considered to be the anti-American and anti-capitalist views of his books.[36]

Attacks on Rugg's textbooks began in Washington, DC, in the mid-1930s. By the 1940s, attacks had erupted in Englewood and Mountain Lakes, New Jersey; Garden City and Binghamton, New York; Cedar Rapids, Iowa; Rapid City, North Dakota; Philadelphia, Atlanta, and San Francisco. The debate received national press coverage from the *New York Times* and *Time* magazine. Many of the patriotic and pro-business critics who attacked Rugg had never even read his textbooks but were nevertheless appalled by his affiliation with collectivist thinking at Teachers College and convinced by the accusations of other groups who had reviewed them. Objective, bipartisan reviews of Rugg's texts reported that they contained only a minimal amount of collectivist rhetoric, certainly not enough to actually sway the political and social views of students. For example, the American Committee for Democracy and Intellectual Freedom invited several scholars to review Rugg's texts in their area of expertise, and they found them to be relatively balanced.[37] Nevertheless, by the 1940s the majority of school districts using his texts chose to adopt other texts because the economic focus of his books seemed out of step with the ideological battle against totalitarianism. Rugg's inclusion of the terms "collectivist" and "social planning" reflected a commitment to a specific political and social outcome. As

Rugg had said in his textbook *An Introduction to Problems of American Life*, society was entering a "new age of social planning" because the old system had "brought about an enormous waste in every outstanding brand of industry."[38] Such language was acceptable to most in the early 1930s, but after the Moscow trials and the Soviet-Nazi Pact, this was no longer the case. Learning from the Rugg controversy, Paul Hanna and James Quillen of Stanford University removed any references to "social planning" from drafts of their new textbook series. As a result, Hanna and Quillen's apolitical texts largely displaced Rugg's books in American schools in the 1940s.[39]

During the controversy, both Rugg and his opponents cast each other as propagandists for a particular social agenda during a time when propaganda was code for dictatorship and authoritarianism. Both sides appealed to the general public by accusing the other side of employing the propaganda, indoctrination, and other methods of authoritarian regimes. Specifically, pro-business critics accused Rugg of being a secret Marxist and socialist; Rugg countered that his critics were surreptitiously controlled by reactionary and pro-fascist interests. Neither side considered teaching students "how to think, not what to think," even though this is what many wanted, especially during the war. For example, one set of parents in San Francisco explained during the Rugg textbook controversy: "We want [our daughter] to grow up able to make her own decisions, rather than being forced to abide by those of her elders. . . . Such freedom of decision is the essence of democracy." A San Francisco teacher agreed, writing: "Intelligent democracy demands that our children face all of the facts, not just the facts on one side of current issues. . . . Our children must at all cost learn to think for themselves."[40] The National Association of Manufacturers similarly hoped to preserve "the freedom of discussion in schools" by presenting "controversial issues . . . in the proper balance" and accused Rugg's textbooks of providing only one side of the story.[41] Even Kilpatrick had endorsed the idea that a student "face the problems for himself and for himself . . . think them through to his own conclusions."[42] Nevertheless, both Rugg and his patriotic and pro-business adversaries chose ideological commitment over ideological neutrality, as both sides considered neutrality to be too dangerous in a world of authoritarian dictators.

Between 1939 and 1941, pro-business groups repeatedly attacked Rugg for being a propagandist and indoctrinator for socialist ideas. For example, the Advertising Federation of America charged Rugg with "anti-advertising propaganda," Merwin K. Hart of the New York State Economic Council insisted that Rugg "wanted to indoctrinate the pupil with collectivist ideas and to make school teachers indoctrinators of new social doctrines," and the *National Republic* magazine accused Rugg of "Marxian propaganda" for "class war" and "class hatred."[43] The Guardians of American Education accused Rugg of employing "subtle" techniques "with gentle language and pedagogic smile," leading unsuspecting students through the "successive stages of indoctrination," and B. C. Forbes insisted that Rugg's textbooks were filled with "the kind of propaganda championed by Communists."[44]

Rugg rebutted that the members of the American Legion were "authoritarians who are trying to censor American Schools."[45] Rugg contextualized his ongoing textbook controversy in 30 years of "wave[s] of censorship" that had "rolled up on the schools," including the efforts of "propaganda organizations" such as the Patriotic League for the Preservation of American History and the "witch-hunting" activities of the American Legion in the 1920s and 1930s.[46] Teachers College professor Jesse Newlon called the critics' effort to censor Rugg "one of the most sinister developments in the history of American education." Newlon implored teachers to recognize "the fascist tendencies in certain sections of big business, in certain chauvinistic 'patriotic' organizations, and in other homegrown reactionary groups." He asked that teachers guard their curriculum choices against reactionary forces because "this is the realm in which propaganda most dangerously operates," leading to "totalitarianism."[47]

When Rugg took over editorship of *The Frontiers of Democracy* in 1943, he continued to espouse his radical views by maintaining his counterattack against the American Legion through an ideological commitment to social and economic reform. "*Frontiers* will not be neutral. On every issue it will take sides," he insisted. "[I]t will strike to let light in on the ugly and menacing forces and make plain the alternative courses of action."[48] However, with the ideological climate moving in a more centrist direction by 1943, Rugg's overt rejection of neutrality was out of step with the presiding mood of leading educators such as Counts and Dewey. As a result, the Progressive Education Association, which had taken over control of the journal a few years earlier, decided to discontinue the *The Frontiers of Democracy* in 1944, over the objections of Rugg.

Despite his subtle shift toward to the center, during the late 1930s Dewey continued to be attacked by anti-naturalists as well. While working through a secular framework, University of Chicago president Robert M. Hutchins further critiqued the philosophy and pedagogy of Dewey and his like-minded educational reformers by linking the ideas of naturalism with fascism. With the adoption of Dewey's naturalism, Hutchins suggested, the "journey from the man of good will to Hitler is complete" because "fascism is a consequence of the absence of philosophy."[49] Hutchins defined philosophy as the search for metaphysical truth contained in the Great Books of the Western canon. Hutchins's like-minded colleague Mortimer Adler also blamed Dewey for the purging of prescribed liberal arts content from the schools. Adler proposed a "fundamental educational reform below the level of the university" to restore the abandoned "common tradition" and "common heritage of learning" that Dewey and his naturalist allies had allegedly displaced through their reforms, which left the nation open to relativistic encroachment by fascists.[50] Hutchins and Adler blamed Dewey for introducing and implementing relativism in American schools. In return, naturalists aligned Hutchins's approach with fascism because it was based on philosophical absolutism and fixed first principles.

Dewey insisted that the absolutism of Hutchins and Adler was supportive of dictatorship and authoritarianism because "any scheme based on the existence of ultimate first principles, with their dependent hierarchy of subsidiary principles, does not escape authoritarianism by calling the principles 'truths.'" Dewey suggested that the absolutist philosophy of Hutchins was "akin to the distrust of freedom and the consequent appeal to some fixed authority that is now overrunning the world."[51] He explained how any elitist attempt by the few to formulate fixed principles and goals for the many, no matter how well meaning, would ultimately undermine the processes and values of democracy. For Dewey, democratic means was as important as democratic ends when formulating curriculum and educational outcomes.

In 1944, Dewey and his naturalistic peers responded further to Hutchins with a collection of papers, *The Authoritarian Attempt to Capture Education*, which aimed to "resist the method of authority and the forces of authoritarianism in whatever guise they show themselves." The naturalistic leanings of the authors were on full display. As Jerome Nathanson, leader of the New York Society of Ethical Culture, explained in the preface to the book, the authors of the volume "are not dogmatic in their insistence on any one truth or any set of truths. They believe that all truths, whatever their origin, are established by the scientific method."[52] By emulating the scientific method, the philosophy of the naturalists accumulated and revised truth through experience and interaction, not through alignment with preexisting principles and dogmas. In contrast, Hutchins and Adler wanted schools to establish and disseminate transcendent truths to all students because such truths were foundational to civilization. An understanding of the transcendent, Hutchins argued, would protect civilization against the relativism of authoritarian dictators. The philosophical absolutism of Hutchins, the naturalists countered, was anti-scientific, outdated, and dangerous. As philosopher Charles W. Morris explained in his chapter, "The dogmatic attitude is democratically sterile, since it subordinates growth to attainment, open-minded flexibility to fearsome defensiveness, creativity to security."[53] Dogmatism of any kind, the naturalists insisted, was undemocratic because it appealed to a fixed set of principles instead of seeking out collective reform, adjustment, and growth.

The contributors to *The Authoritarian Attempt to Capture Education* were specifically responding to Hutchins's dualistic proposal to sever knowledge completely from any utilitarian and functional use by making it purely intellectual. In the introductory chapter to the book, "The Democratic Faith and Education," Dewey defended the arguments he first made during World War I that vocational and academic education should be coterminous, and dismissed the proposals of "President Hutchins to cut vocational training off from any contact with what is liberating." Such an approach, Dewey insisted, was "a denial of democracy." Dewey pledged his allegiance to the "vital principles of the scientific method," through which "science, education, and democratic cause meet as one."[54]

During the war years, debates among absolutists and naturalists filtered down to teachers in New York City as professional associations solidified along religious, philosophical, and ethnic lines. The mostly Irish Catholic, conservative teachers formed the Teachers Alliance of New York and American Education Association, while the mostly Jewish, progressive teachers formed the Teachers Union and Teachers Guild. The conservative Catholic associations supported the teaching of absolute values and attacked the relativism of progressive education, which they linked to the alleged communism of the Jewish teacher unions. Progressive critics countered that the Association was anti-Semitic and pro-fascist. In 1939, the Association president declared that battle over the curriculum, and its underlying dispute over absolute and relativistic values in the schools, represented nothing less than a "war of ideas."[55]

The debate between the absolutists and naturalists, conservatives and progressives, was never fully resolved. However, focusing solely on the dispute obscures the underlying consensus on which both sides agreed: Democratic education ought to be defined in contrast to the epistemology and educational techniques of totalitarianism. The question was figuring out exactly how to go about doing this. Whereas in the 1920s and early 1930s some educators had admired fascism for its collectivist ambitions and spirit of experimentation, by 1935 educators aligned fascism solely with propaganda and indoctrination. Totalitarianism had become the *other* against which democratic education defined itself for the next 25 years. In the postwar years, naturalists and absolutists continued to argue over whether students ought to be taught how to discover transcendent, apolitical truths, as suggested by Hutchins, or taught critical thinking, open-mindedness, and cultural adjustment, as suggested by Dewey. Because fascists paradoxically espoused "the absolute value of the relative truth," both absolutists and relativists saw the ideas of their opponents reflected in the evils of totalitarianism.[56] Although all could agree that totalitarianism needed to be rejected, few could agree on whether that meant embracing or rejecting absolute values in democracy and democratic schools.

The embrace of science at the end of the decade signaled the return by leading scholars and educators of the politically neutral approach of the 1920s.[57] By the end of the 1930s, the professors at Teachers College had seen their optimism for collectivism upended by international events. For some who had lived through the postwar disillusionment of the 1920s, such as Dewey, this was the second round of disappointment. Dewey responded to the first in the 1920s by moving in a slightly more student-centered direction. Dewey had been forward looking and optimistic in his embrace of teaching of social issues in the classroom, when most other liberals were skeptical of further empowering the masses. In the 1930s, Dewey's continued commitment to open-ended inquiry and rejection of predetermined goals cast him as a moderate when compared to his more radical peers such as Beard, Counts, and Rugg. Dewey responded to this second disillusionment by reaffirming his commitment to open-ended inquiry and teaching how to think, not what to think. By the 1940s, when he was in his 80s and the ideological landscape moved to the center, his ideas aligned perfectly with leading liberal American intellectuals and educators who looked to science as a model for democratic thought. Dewey's open-ended inquiry approach to pedagogy also aligned with the second wave of propaganda education.

PROPAGANDA ANALYSIS

After World War I, fears of propaganda in the United States led many educators and social scientists to suggest the need for teaching students how to detect and resist propaganda. The power trust scandal of 1928 confirmed the fears of many educators that pro-business forces had influenced the curriculum in surreptitious and undemocratic ways. Progressive educators had two responses to the power trust scandal. Radical collectivists such as Beard, Counts, Childs, Rugg, and Raup argued that, because the curriculum clearly reflected the values of the business elites, students needed to be presented with a counternarrative in support of social planning. Since the alleged objectivity of the curriculum was a farce, students ought to be indoctrinated with a particular social vision for the common good as a countermeasure to the inculcation of *laissez faire* ideology that was, and had been, taking place in U.S. schools. Raup's *Education and Organized Interest in America* explicitly made this argument. However, the more moderate NEA continued to espouse the ideologically neutral approach of teaching students "how to think, not what to think," although this phrase continued to be vague and open to interpretation. The NEA was not necessarily embracing the discussion of controversial issues; rather, they supported the balanced and apolitical presentation of facts from both sides to avoid any controversy altogether, as if this were possible.

Both the radical collectivists and moderates supported teaching about propaganda, but the radicals endorsed ideological commitment, while the moderates endorsed ideological neutrality. In the early 1930s, the collectivists diverted attention away from the moderate position, but by the late 1930s the pendulum began to swing back toward the moderate "teaching how to think" approach. The explicit use of propaganda by Stalin, Mussolini, and especially Hitler in the years leading up to World War II underscored the importance of teaching students to recognize and analyze propaganda. As one educator explained in 1938: "The life of democracy itself in the midst of a world of aggressive totalitarian dictatorships depends upon the ability of the ordinary citizen to discriminate amid the whirl and confusion of propaganda."[58] Further, as another educator explained, propaganda in the modern world was unavoidable, so students needed the tools to distinguish the destructive from the constructive propaganda. "As a people we stand probably as never before in the center of propagandas—bad, good, and indifferent, domestic and imported—Democracy cannot shut them off as dictatorship can, and instantly does. Propaganda must function constructively in and among them or else it must fail."[59] Between 1937 and 1941, propaganda analysis reached its peak, with the use of propaganda by European dictators a primary justification for addressing the topic.

The interest in propaganda education both reflected and was supported by the founding of the Institute for Propaganda Analysis at Teachers College in 1937. Teachers College professor Clyde Miller directed the Institute, and it lasted for 5 years before losing its funding during the war. During its brief and controversial existence, the Institute disseminated monthly bulletins to its nearly 6,000 subscribers, including hundreds of schools across the nation.[60] The Institute also published books on key topics such as *The Fine Art of Propaganda: A Study of Father Coughlin's Speeches* (1939) and *War Propaganda and the United States* (1940).[61] Although propaganda analysis seemed like an uncontroversial idea in theory, it proved to be controversial in practice, especially as World War II approached.

The Institute published its first issue of its *Propaganda Analysis* bulletin in November 1937 to an enthusiastic audience hungry for analysis of current events. The first issue, "How to Detect Propaganda," identified seven devices commonly used by propagandists. The first device was *name-calling* in which the propagandist inaccurately applies names such as "fascist" or "Communist" to the opponent. The second device was *glittering generalities*, in which the propagandist identifies his program with the use of "virtue words" such as truth, justice, or freedom. The third device was *transfer*, in which "the propagandist carries over the authority, sanction, and prestige of something we respect and revere [often church and nation] to something he would have us accept." The fourth device was *testimonial*, in which the propagandist uses a statement from someone recognized as a trusted public authority. The fifth device was *plain folks*, in which elites posed as ordinary folks. The sixth device was *card stacking*, in which the propagandist used "under-emphasis and over-emphasis to dodge issues and evade facts." The seventh device was *bandwagon*, in which the propagandist tries to make the reader "follow the crowd to accept the propagandist's program en masse."[62]

Miller's seven propaganda devices received wide attention in the press, and he was praised for the clarity and simplicity of his presentation. Teachers in particular appreciated the seven devices and cited them in their work with students.[63] However, it was unclear what methodology Miller had used to generate the devices, and/or in what ways he had drawn on the robust literature on propaganda. Further, it was likewise unclear that Miller's devices really applied solely to propaganda and not to all persuasive speech, advertising, public relations, and politics. Certainly, Dewey, Counts, Kilpatrick, and Rugg were guilty of these devices in their debates over the

American curriculum, although few (at Teachers College, at least) would have dubbed their rigorous defense of naturalism and progressive education as propaganda. In addition, the seven devices seemed to focus more on style than substance. In other words, the devices could help identify a message as propaganda, but they did not necessarily help determine the validity of the message itself. In fact, only one of the seven—card stacking—actually applied to the relationship between the propaganda, evidence, and the truth.

In support of the Institute, the 1937 Yearbook of the National Council for the Social Studies Teachers was devoted to propaganda analysis.[64] Beyond the subject of social studies, English and even math teachers from around the country implemented units on propaganda analysis.[65] These teachers appreciated the usefulness of Miller's seven devices as a pedagogical tool and expressed their appreciation of the importance of propaganda analysis as a response to totalitarian threats. For example, one teacher related how "[p]ropaganda analysis is one of the indispensable tools of citizenship."[66] Another concluded: "[S]ince democracy depends upon . . . an enlightened citizenship, never in the history of our country has it been more important for high school boys and girls to be trained to recognize and evaluate propaganda."[67] However, once implemented, propaganda analysis proved to be more complicated than originally conceived.

For instance, based on his experiences with propaganda analysis, one teacher recognized that teachers needed to strike a balance between excessive cynicism and open-minded skepticism; too much of the former could actually cause students to be more vulnerable to propaganda, not less.[68] Two other teachers at Horace Mann High School for Girls had this very problem, reporting that how their students "began to think everything was propaganda, and to act accordingly" led to "excessive cynicism and a hypercritical attitude."[69] In a 1941 article in *Public Opinion Quarterly*, another teacher related how, based on his experience teaching propaganda analysis to high school and college-age students, he too discovered that "an extremely high, if not menacing, degree of cynicism develops" among students. However, even more problematic was that some students preferred that some governmental authority step in and establish the truth on behalf of citizens. Thus, the teacher said, propaganda analysis was having a counterproductive effect by frustrating students and inadvertently providing justification for authoritarian leadership to step in and establish truth on their behalf. He recommended a more comprehensive revision of the curriculum beyond propaganda analysis toward a broad overview and analysis of the structures of U.S. society.[70] Further, one empirical study on the propaganda analysis curriculum found that the intervention did not necessarily leave a lasting impact on students, as the experimental group did not demonstrate a statistically significant difference from the control group in their ability to resist propaganda after a 2-week period. The study reinforced the proposal for a more comprehensive approach to critical thinking, beyond "a study of 'tricks' of the propagandist" as espoused by the Institute for Propaganda Analysis.[71]

These comments on the limits of propaganda analysis inspired a direct response from Clyde Miller, who doubted the accusation that students were demanding authoritarianism as a response to propaganda analysis. He defended his approach by citing numerous examples of teachers who had used his program successfully to combat cynicism. In fact, one teacher at Clayton High School in Missouri reported how he had effectively implemented Miller's program, explaining that the "teacher who works through the final stages will find the common attitude of cynicism will give way to healthy, but reasonable skepticism."[72] However, all of Miller's evidence was anecdotal.

Despite Miller's defense, the tide was turning against propaganda analysis by fall 1941. When Americans began aiding the European Allies in the war, the vague definition of propaganda offered by the Institute for Propaganda Analysis—"the expression of opinion or action by individuals or groups deliberately designed to influence opinions or actions of other individuals . . . with reference to predetermined ends"—became less convincing.[73] Ultimately, when the stakes were raised by fascist aggression during the war and the future of democracy was in peril, most Americans were willing to accept the use of the seven propaganda devices if they were employed toward a just and noble cause: the preservation of democracy. After all, was it really propaganda to suggest that Hitler was maniacal, evil, and driven by a desire for world domination?

By 1941, the Institute's neutral approach to propaganda analysis undermined its own mission to preserve democracy by attacking the patriotic and morale-boosting messages of President Roosevelt. Some accused the Institute of being anti-war and biased against the Roosevelt administration by, as one contemporary complained, falsely giving "the impression that Roosevelt is as big a liar as Hitler." In 1941, Kilpatrick resigned from the Board of Directors because he had been "troubled by what has seemed to be on the part of some of the Institute writers a disposition to discuss controversial issues not in a scientific manner and spirit, but with some apparent bias." Later that year, the publisher Harcourt Brace rejected the next book-length study by the Institute because "the whole drift of public opinion for the near future will be away from the critical examination of propaganda" due to the fact that "propaganda is not to be analyzed but it to be acted upon in one way or another." By October of 1941, the Institute for Propaganda Analysis lost its funding and closed down, fearing that its "analyses could be misused for undesirable purposes by persons opposing the government efforts" in the war.[74]

One of the problems for the Institute was that the term *propaganda* continued to be used loosely throughout the 1930s and 1940s without any clear definition emerging. Scholars often employed the term to dismiss any position with which they disagreed. For example, in a 1940 article for *Frontier of Democracy*, anthropologist Margaret Mead used the term *propaganda* to dismiss the claims of biological racists at home and abroad.[75] Likewise, both Rugg and his patriotic/pro-business critics accused each other of propaganda in their fights over Rugg's textbooks. It was this vague use of the term that contributed to the fall of propaganda analysis as a curriculum approach, giving credence to one scholar's quip: "An immense deal of actual indoctrination takes place in our schools and colleges, and must inevitably always take place . . . [w]hen it does not please us, we call it propaganda; when it does please us, we call it education."[76] While some scholars argued that propaganda was inherently sensationalistic, nefarious, and untrue, others considered propaganda to be an unavoidable aspect of modern life that could be used for good. A mostly unrecognized epistemological issue embedded in this controversy was how to distinguish the true from untrue, facts from values, evidence from interpretations, and media from the message.

Scholars identified another issue plagued by the inability to define propaganda with precision: How was propaganda different from education? During the 1920s, scholars considered the distinction between education and propaganda to be fairly obvious, but by the late 1930s they offered more nuanced analyses. One of the more thoughtful responses to the issue appeared in 1935, at the height of the indoctrination debate discussed in the previous chapter. Carroll Woody, a political scientist at the University of Chicago, identified 10 ways that propaganda differed from education. Woody's distinctions were aimed as much at radical collectivists like Beard, Counts, and Rugg as they were at foreign dictators. First, Woody explained, education was aimed at children, while propaganda was aimed at adults. Second, education took place in schools, while propaganda took place out of school. Third, "[e]ducation is teaching things that are true; propaganda is teaching things that are false." Fourth, education focused on desirable facts, while propaganda focused on undesirable facts. Fifth, "[e]ducation is rational; propaganda is irrational." Sixth, education is aimed at the common good, while propaganda is aimed at benefitting one particular group. Seventh, education is controlled by educators, while propaganda is controlled by outsiders. Eighth, "[e]ducation consists in transmitting the social inheritance; propaganda consists in indoctrinating those who are taught with a desire to alter the social system." Ninth, education avoided controversy, while propaganda took sides on controversial issues. And finally, tenth, "the function of education is to reduce or to eliminate the effectiveness of propaganda."[77] Woody's distinctions between education and propaganda hinged on the principles that a curriculum could and should be politically neutral, that facts were easily and transparently established, and that education for children was different from education for adults. His rather blunt distinctions between truth and falsity, and rational and irrational, razed some complicated epistemological ground regarding who ought to decide what was true and rational, but he nevertheless put forth a precise definition of propaganda, something the Institute for Propaganda Analysis was unwilling to do.

In a 1939 essay, Kilpatrick addressed this epistemological issue surrounding propaganda directly. Both indoctrination and propaganda, he argued, shared a common authoritarian approach to truth as obvious and undisputed. In contrast, his naturalistic approach to pedagogy embraced the open-ended nature of knowledge, which was a more democratic and accurate approach to scientific inquiry. By drawing on a Deweyan approach to truth as warranted assertion, Kilpatrick defined education in opposition to indoctrination. Unlike Woody, Kilpatrick denied that universal truths could be objectively established and transmitted. In fact, education ought to aim at the embrace of this epistemological uncertainly, not seek to avoid it. "If teaching is the kind to build prejudices, we count it wrong and call it indoctrination," Kilpatrick explained. "If the teaching is of the kind to foster open-minded study, both as a means for present independent choice and as the most useful future attitude, we count the teaching proper and call it education." Contrasting education in a democracy with the indoctrination under "Hitler in Germany, Mussolini in Italy, Stalin in Russia," Kilpatrick concluded schools should approach students "not to make them converts to my cause, but to foster independent thinking and decision on the part of all whom I touch, independent it may be, even to the rejecting of my cause."[78] Thus, Kilpatrick once again framed open-ended inquiry in terms of its contrast to education under authoritarian regimes.

Thus, by the time the United States entered World War II, leading progressive educators had completely abandoned the indoctrination idea of the early 1930s because the approach was too similar to education under authoritarianism and dictatorship. However, the rise and fall of propaganda analysis demonstrated that equipping students with the tools of knee-jerk skepticism through a crash course on propaganda was not necessarily effective either. As a result, wartime and postwar educators tried to steer between the Scylla of authoritarian indoctrination/propaganda and the Charybdis of knee-jerk skepticism. What educators had learned in the interwar years was that phrases such as "teaching both sides of the issue" and teaching "how to think, not what to think" needed to be fleshed out to a much greater degree, even if there was general consensus over the efficacy of these ideas.

Bruce Lannes Smith's critique of Miller's propaganda analysis marked the transition toward a more robust understanding of the "how to think" approach. After expressing his experiences in how propaganda analysis had bred cynicism in his students, Smith outlined a more comprehensive approach he called the "science of democracy . . . a clear, concise, empirical analysis of our social structure." He also insisted that the social studies teacher must move beyond an understanding of social structure to the study of "personality problems," including an investigation into students' "mental hygiene," because "no human being who deeply understands the problem of his own mental and biological hygiene will ever become a menace to society."[79] Smith's framework was largely inchoate, but he introduced some ideas and vocabulary that would be explored in much greater depth during the postwar years, such as "science," "personality problems" and "mental hygiene." Smith's article marked a pivot away from using schools as tools for collective social reform toward an effort to preserve democracy through developing the hearts and minds of individual students.

THE PARADOX OF RACE

The rise of fascism in Europe not only pushed the issues of propaganda to the forefront of educators' thinking, it also drew attention to theories of biological racism. The Nazis mercilessly persecuted European Jews by using an erroneous, exaggerated, and outdated theory of racial superiority. In 1938, the American Anthropological Association passed a resolution stating, "Anthropology provides no scientific basis for discrimination against any people on the ground of racial superiority, religious affiliation, or linguistic heritage" because the "psychological and cultural connotations [of race], if they exist, have not been ascertained by science."[80] Leading progressive educators such as Dewey and William Heard Kilpatrick echoed this position.[81] Nevertheless, psychometricians such as Lewis Terman continued to pursue the idea that intelligence was hereditary and in some way tied to race. As late as 1940, Terman dismissed many of the studies that pointed to the power of education, environment, and culture on intelligence "as biased and uncritical."[82]

The use of racial theory by the Nazis to persecute European Jews and others inspired most U.S. educators to abandon innate and biological explanations of racial difference by the end of World War II. Earlier proponents of scientific racism, such as Charles Ellwood and Carl C. Brigham, repudiated their earlier support for eugenics. The argument against integration of Blacks shifted from biological to cultural justification. That is, rather than argue that Blacks were biologically destined to social inferiority, leading social scientists argued that African Americans lacked the educational, sociological, and cultural attributes to contribute to American society on equal terms. Eventually, racial scholars argued, if Blacks continued to progress, they would be able to assimilate, but that time was considered to be far in the future. Even anthropologist Ruth Benedict, who in the 1930s fought scientific racism as vigilantly as anyone of her generation, claimed that "great numbers of negroes are not ready for full citizenship."[83] Yet, overall, the war provided a small step forward for the civil rights of African Americans.

One professor of education anticipated the impact the war would have on race relations as Americans realized that "we are making common cause with dark races of Africa and the East." He thought that American Whites were poorly prepared "with their traditional attitudes and beliefs on race questions, to cope with the probable consequences of that fact."[84] Another professor of education also predicted that "the principles of democracy will undergo a severe test in the treatment of ethnic and minority groups, including those associated with the enemies, those associated with our allies and the American negro."[85] Civil rights leader W.E.B. Du Bois recognized the irony of President's Roosevelt's four freedoms—freedom of speech, freedom of religion, freedom from want, and freedom from fear—and its inapplicability to African Americans. "The continuing failure of war philosophers to mention the race and Color Line," Du Bois wrote, "continues to be a matter of distress to racial philosophers." In a section of an article entitled "The Nazi and the Negro," Du Bois documented the oppressive Nazi treatment of European Negroes, an aspect of Nazi racial ideology and policy rarely addressed. Yet Du Bois also pointed to Allied hypocrisy by documenting numerous cases of Allied oppression of racial minorities at home and abroad, despite the Allied rhetoric about fighting for democracy and freedom in Europe.[86]

The skepticism that Du Bois expressed about race relations was not necessarily reflective of other Black educators, who expressed patriotic fervor during the war and argued that, despite the problems of the color line in the United States, Blacks were much better off under democratic rule than under totalitarianism. "The world is now at a crossroads, the signposts point one way to democracy, and the other way to dictatorship," one African American educator agued in 1941. "We believe in democracy and should be pointing our pupils along this highway by word and by deed."[87] The U.S. Office of Education specifically fostered this patriotic sentiment. In 1942, the Senior Specialist in the Education of Negroes, Ambrose Caliver, sent a letter to principals of Negro high schools contrasting the treatment of African Americans to Jews under Hitler. "[I]n spite of the many disadvantages and discriminations . . . we are better off than many minority groups," the letter agued, "imperfect as our present situation is, we still have the *right* and *opportunity* to use every legitimate means to improve our condition. This most certainly would not be possible under an Axis dominated country."[88] Charles H. Thompson, professor at Howard University and founder of the *Journal of Negro Education*, agreed, arguing that "despite the unenviable status of the Negro at the present time his position could be worse under fascism or Nazism."[89]

The most direct way that (White) U.S. educators addressed the race issue during the war was through the Intercultural Education movement. New Jersey teacher Rachel Davis DuBois had established the cultural gifts movement in the 1920s to challenge ethnic stereotypes and to introduce students to positive images of non-Whites and minority White immigrant groups. Using assemblies, cultural fairs, and classroom activities, DuBois emphasized the cultural contributions of all ethnic and racial groups in America. Throughout the 1930s, DuBois had worked cooperatively with the American Jewish Committee on a number of projects to reduce anti-Semitism. The Nazi treatment of the Jews in Germany threatened to derail much of the work that intercultural educators had done to develop tolerance of German and Jewish-Americans and to assuage tensions between these minority groups. Intercultural educators worked primarily to hold the nation together under the stresses of war. However, with the persecution of Jews in Europe, the American Jewish Committee began to withdraw its support for the cultural gifts movement because DuBois continued to depict Judaism as a culture instead of a religion. Others critiqued that the focus on ethnic pride sounded too much like fascism. The movement abandoned the term "cultural gifts" and adopted "intercultural education," which focused more on similarities than differences. Starting in 1939, the U.S. Office of Education sponsored a radio broadcast called *Americans All, Immigrants All* to boost intercultural sentiment. DuBois lobbied for the inclusion of Blacks in the broadcast "because our democracy, after all, will rise or fall according to the way we treat that group."[90]

Ruth Benedict, a professor of anthropology at Columbia University, argued that all American students should learn about discrimination against Jews abroad and against Blacks at home. Benedict was a former student of the influential anthropologist Franz Boas, who along with Benedict and Margaret Mead combatted scientific racism in the 1920s and 1930s.[91] In 1940, Benedict published *Race: Science and Politics*, which drew on recent research to attack the scientific basis of racism. Both Benedict's book and Ashley Montagu's *Man's Most Dangerous Myth: The Fallacy of Race* were bestsellers. In the work, Benedict discussed the treatment of both Southern Blacks and Jews under the Nazis as examples of oppressive policies based on the dubious claims of scientific racism. She also explained that the latest research showed Jews were not actually a race, despite what the Nazis claimed. Benedict insisted that the war presented teachers an opportunity to confront domestic racism against Blacks, as the nation was fighting overseas for ideals that had not been fully realized at home.[92] In a 1942 volume on intercultural education published by the NEA, Benedict insisted that "[a]n intercultural program which does not face our Negro problem fairly would be about on par with a German program which omitted Nazi treatment of the Jews." Domestic prejudice, she implored, "must be faced squarely."[93]

In 1943, Benedict turned *Race: Science and Politics* into an educational pamphlet for teachers called *The Races of Mankind.* She co-authored the pamphlet as a "general refutation of Nazi race theories," and so she reiterated that Jews were not a race.[94] The text also challenged the validity of intelligence tests to determine the alleged inferiority of Blacks, a controversial position that angered many Southern White politicians when the pamphlet was sent to U.S. servicemen during the war. Similarly, in an article for *Social Frontier*, Mead reiterated that "scientific research has documented the absence of any proof of reliable differences in intelligence and emotional make-up; differences, that is, which are impervious to the forces of cultural change."[95] Mead dismissed both the multiple white race theory employed by the Nazis and the alleged inferiority of American Blacks proposed by American Southerners. Both Mead and Benedict linked American virtue with the values of tolerance and open-mindedness and made a case that a war against totalitarianism underscored the importance of improving race relations at home.

Overall, intercultural educators referenced the Nazi persecution of Jews as a rhetorical device to bring attention to how race prejudice was a pressing concern in the United States. They repeatedly pointed to the irony of criticizing the Nazi treatment of Jews while ignoring the blatant discrimination aimed at Blacks in the United States. The full extent of the Jewish persecution was not yet known, but the educators cited above knew enough to make passing references to how Jews were being treated, or had been treated, by the Nazis, and they assumed that their audience would know what they were taking about.

After the war, the concerns for intercultural understanding continued, but the racial hatred expressed by the Nazis in the Holocaust presented a paradox for American postwar liberals and educators during the Cold War. On the one hand, the continued mistreatment of African Americans in the South was a major public relations problem abroad; the Russians were quick to point out American hypocrisy on race, and the mistreatment of Blacks was an embarrassment to American diplomats trying to court non-White nations to choose democracy over communism. As one U.S. official insisted in 1954: "Racial discrimination furnishes grist for the Communist propaganda mills."[96] Yet, on the other hand, race was a divisive domestic issue, especially in the South, that could potentially disrupt the social solidary policymakers and educators had worked so hard to construct and were working so hard to maintain. Postwar liberals pointed to the steady progress Blacks had made and urged them to be patient. Too much emphasis on conflict could create the kind of social division upon which communists preyed and could damage the image of democracy abroad. The message from policymakers was that African Americans ought to be thankful for the steady progress they had made up to that point and patiently wait for things to get better. "A course which emphasizes racial discrimination and scarcely mentions the humanitarian movements of the last hundred years," a group of Harvard professors averred, "is likely to foster either cynicism or romantic zeal for quick remedy, which may turn into disillusion at the first contact with the difficulties and complexities inherent in the attainment of true reforms."[97]

Despite these pleas for patience, World War II had awakened the demand for civil rights by American Blacks, especially those who served in the war on behalf of preserving freedom only to return to racial segregation at home. In addition, many Blacks had gained employment during the war in areas from which they had previously been barred. This led to raised expectations and political activism. For example, the National Association for the Advancement of Colored People (NAACP) increased its membership from 50,000 to 400,000 during the conflict. In addition, films made during the war highlighted the multicultural and multiethnic make-up of the American troops, and how they worked together to defeat their totalitarian enemies.

The Office of War Information deliberately sought to boost American morale by contrasting pluralistic democratic life with the intolerance and rigidity of life under totalitarianism.[98]

Despite these wartime pleas for tolerance, overall the complacent mentality of wartime and postwar consensus liberalism dampened discussions of domestic racism because educators universalized discrimination into broader discussions of life under totalitarian regimes, and approached institutional racism as an open-ended issue in need of careful debate and consideration. While domestic racism and the anti-Semitism of the Nazis would have created ample opportunity to teach "how to think, not what to think," these topics were—with a few exceptions—mostly ignored until the 1960s because they proved to be problematic for the consensus-building approach of wartime and postwar liberalism. Thus, postwar consensus liberalism was an inadequate framework for addressing the race issue, and ultimately served to reinforce the existing racial inequalities of U.S. society. Scholars and grassroots organizers ultimately needed to reintroduce the ideas of conflict, moral conviction, and commitment to social reform before meaningful improvements in race relations could take place.

As the paradox of race demonstrates, despite its tepid embrace of open-mindedness, the teaching "how to think, not what to think" approach to education was, in essence, a way to circumvent certain controversial issues by focusing only on those issues that lent themselves to compromise and consensus. Dissent within very narrow bounds was encouraged, but discussion of major social reforms, collectivist ideologies, structural inequalities, and/or moral convictions—which the race problem demanded—were too easily dismissed by consensus liberals as mere fodder for totalitarianism.

CHAPTER 5

In the Shadow of Totalitarianism

Scholars and journalists first introduced the term *totalitarianism* during the 1930s to describe fascist Italy. By mid-decade, many began applying the term to Soviet Russia and Nazi Germany as well. Duke University economist Calvin B. Hoover gave the idea a sense of legitimacy when he outlined the convergence of the three totalitarian regimes in his book *Dictators and Democracies*. "The three totalitarian states have certain basic characteristics in common," Hoover explained. "They are alike in their contempt for democracy, liberalism, pacifism, and parliamentary methods, and their admiration of force, and in their reliance upon direct action."[1] Hoover's book marked a pivot away from the term *dictatorship* toward what would become the preferred term for the next 2 decades, *totalitarianism*—a term that seemed to convey the unprecedented nature of these new ideological threats. By the start of World War II, U.S. educators began using the term *totalitarianism* with greater frequency. In 1939, Sidney Hook and numerous other leading public intellectuals, including Dewey, formed the Committee for Cultural Freedom. As the Committee's manifesto proclaimed: "Under varying labels and colors but with an unvarying hatred for the free mind, the totalitarian idea is already enthroned in Germany, Italy, Russia, Japan, and Spain."[2]

By contrasting democracy with totalitarianism, postwar liberal educators followed leading social scientists and intellectuals in rejecting the progressives' ideological commitment to reform and embracing the values of ideological skepticism, open-mindedness, and scientific rigor.[3] As Harvard historian Arthur Schlesinger, Jr., explained in *The Vital Center*, published in 1949, the thrust of postwar liberalism was "away from fanaticism . . . toward compromise, persuasion, and consent in politics."[4] Postwar consensus liberal educators rejected elements of progressive education, especially those expressed by the radical collectivists, as excessively ideological and too similar to the epistemology of totalitarianism. Whereas progressives and totalitarians were allegedly ideological, postwar consensus liberals cast themselves as anti-ideological; whereas progressives and totalitarians emphasized conflict and reform, postwar consensus liberalism emphasized consensus and compromise.

Drawing upon this anti-ideological outlook, a new generation of social studies educators rejected the political commitments of their progressive forebears but embraced the progressives' focus on open-ended inquiry and scientific thinking. The new breed of postwar social studies educators shifted the focus of democratic education from reforming democratic life to merely sustaining it. However, they did not reject the work of Dewey outright, despite his affiliation with the radical collectivists in the 1930s. Rather, postwar educators refashioned Dewey's work to meet the needs of the new anti-ideological context by embracing his apolitical work *How We Think* in an effort to sustain democracy in the face of totalitarian threats. In other words, despite the backlash against naturalistic philosophy and progressive education that took place during the postwar years, the idea of teaching students how to think, not what to think continued to gain ground among theorists of democratic education.

SCIENCE AND DEMOCRACY

After World War II, science became an important metaphor for how democratic life ought to function. The link between ideology and science has been present since the origins of naturalism in the late 19th century. Reform-oriented scholars during the progressive era often used "science" as a lever to implement change and dismissed what came before as "tradition." Reform-oriented scholars such as James, Beard, Dewey, and Rugg often cited the ways in which recently discovered facts, attained scientifically, demanded that social reform take place by replacing the old, unscientific knowledge of the past with the new, scientific knowledge of the present. As a result, prior to the late 1930s, politics, ideology, and science worked conterminously. However, during and after World War II postwar consensus liberals recast science in apolitical and nonideological terms. Science in a democracy represented the open-ended approach to knowledge, independent of ideology and politics. With authoritarian science as the *other*, science in a democracy became a metaphor for democracy itself, as both a way of life and a form of government. In contrast to science under authoritarian dictatorships, science in a democracy was seen as unfettered and ideologically neutral. As a result, democracy and science worked symbiotically. As one professor of political and social psychology wrote in 1944: "The scientific way is also the democratic way. Science and democracy cannot flourish without the other."[5]

Postwar liberal educators concluded that science and scientific thinking represented the best antidotes to totalitarian and ideological thinking. Just as Dewey had done, Sidney Hook articulately linked the themes of open-ended inquiry to science and democracy and contrasted these values with the methods of totalitarianism. In the 1930s, Hook had been a leading Marxist scholar who reconciled the ideas of Marx to the naturalism of Dewey. However, by the end of the decade, he became disillusioned with the communist experiment, distanced himself from Marxist dialecticism, forged a more moderate position, and became a leading anticommunist crusader. In his 1940 book, *Reason, Social Myths, and Democracy*, Hook articulated his new vision that embraced ideological neutrality, which he aligned directly with the scientific method. He argued that "the ultimate commitment of a democracy" must be based on a faith in the "method of intelligence, of critical scientific inquiry" as the "test of all values."[6] By aligning scientific inquiry with the democratic way of life, Hook diverted attention away from the substance and content of American life and reoriented the focus onto the processes of democracy itself. That is, he abandoned the 1930s emphasis on ideological commitment to collectivism and embraced the post-1939 focus on ideological agnosticism because both science and democracy shared a naturalistic approach to knowledge as open-ended and contingent. Unlike those citizens living under totalitarian dictatorships, citizens in a democracy were free to engage in open-ended scientific inquiry unfettered from state interference. As Hook explained, if the scientist/citizen was "not to find himself merely a productive arm of a totalitarian state, his scientific theories must not be subject to the dictates of a party, race, or state philosophy." By providing a foil to democracy, totalitarianism had highlighted the enduring strength of democratic life. "The greatest tribute to democracy as an ideal of social life," Hook reasoned, "is unwittingly paid to it in the apologias of the dictators of the modern world—Hitler, Stalin, Mussolini."[7]

Along these lines, sociologist Robert Merton of Columbia University authored an influential essay during World War II that would help guide the self-conception of U.S. scientists for the next 2 decades. Merton's "Note on Science and Democracy" argued that there was an unspoken "cultural structure of science" that was "legitimized in terms of institutional values." These values—universalism, communism, disinterestedness, organized skepticism—were able to flourish in a democratic society but were restrained in totalitarian ones. Scientists espoused these values, not only because they were "procedurally efficient, but because they are believed to be right and good." Merton argued that, if science was practiced properly, then truths could be verified and accumulated through the processes of observation, transparency, replication, and communal verification. Scientific findings discovered in such a way, Merton insisted in a direct contrast to Nazi Germany, cannot be "invalidated by Nuremberg decree." Merton suggested that science could take place in all types of social orders, but democracy was clearly the best context for scientific inquiry because the practice of democracy shared certain values with the practice of science. Scientists in democracies represented an autonomous community that operated independent of ideological pressures, but in "modern totalitarian society, anti-rationalism and the centralization of institutional control both serve to limit the scope provided for scientific activity."[8]

The importance of science to developing independent and rational thinking was a central theme of the Harvard Commission's *General Education in a Free Society*, published in 1946. The Harvard professors who authored the work sought compromise and consensus around a set of educational values that would carry the nation through the postwar years. On the one hand, the report recommended a general education grounded in science, humanities, and social sciences, because "ours is at present a centrifugal culture in extreme need of unifying forces." On the other hand, the Harvard Committee insisted that citizens needed the "habit of forming objective, disinterested judgments based upon exact evidence" and the ability "to communicate thought, to make relevant judgments, to discriminate among values." The emphasis on the vague, descriptive elements of education in a democracy reflected the paradox of both subscribing to "unifying" democratic values, while at the same time being pluralistic and skeptical toward the dogmatic interpretation of these values. More importantly, the Harvard Committee emphasized the importance of proper thinking and belief over the significance of prescribed subject matter. Echoing Dewey, Hook, and Merton, the Committee argued that scientific thinking "was both the outcome and the source" of democracy and was "of particular value in the formation of citizens in a free society."[9]

The Harvard report captured the postwar anti-ideological spirit of compromise and consensus by both absorbing and rejecting elements of progressive education and naturalistic epistemology. The authors explicitly articulated "a position somewhere between" the "practical courses" of progressive education and the "great books" approach suggested by Hutchins and Adler. "Education therefore cannot be wholly devoted neither to tradition nor to experiment," the authors explained. "It must uphold at the same time tradition and experiment." Regarding education for patriotism versus education for skepticism, they concluded: "Democracy is the attempt to combine liberty with loyalty, each limiting the other, and also each reinforcing the other." Regarding teaching how to think versus what to think, they concluded: "If toleration is not to become nihilism, if conviction is not to become dogmatism, if criticism is not to become cynicism, each [open-mindedness and patriotism] must have something of the other." Regarding absolute versus naturalistic epistemology, the Harvard professors concluded: "Freedom is submission to the best and fullest truth that can be known; yet it also recognition that truth is not fully known."[10]

The Harvard Committee reflected postwar anxieties over the psychological fragility of the American citizenry that would remain in place for the next 2 decades. With nearly 20 million Americans of voting age with less than a 6th-grade education, the Committee worried that "a large portion of the community" remained "ill equipped either as human beings or as citizens of a democracy." The Committee hoped to remedy this situation by putting more emphasis on critical, rational, and scientific thinking, open-mindedness, and citizenship. The Harvard report sold 40,000 copies over the next 5 years.[11] Although it is difficult to trace its impact on schools and classrooms, *General Education in a Free Society* captured the postwar mood of consensus liberalism and further endorsed the impulse to teach students how to think through an embrace of science, compromise, and moderation.

The Harvard Committee was presided over by Harvard University President James B. Conant, whose writings and actions helped forge postwar consensus liberalism with its emphasis on egalitarianism and meritocracy. To support this meritocratic vision, Conant supported the consolidation of smaller high schools into larger ones, so the different classes of students could mingle together, and the struggling and gifted students could both be accommodated with an appropriate curriculum. Conant considered the comprehensive high school to be one of the greatest American inventions, "an institution with no counterpart in any other country."[12] Furthermore, he helped proliferate the use of the Scholastic Aptitude Test to identify the most intellectually able students for college instead of merely rewarding the most financially well off. Like his liberal peers, he emphasized the importance of scientific thinking as an antidote to totalitarianism.[13]

THE END OF IDEOLOGY

During and after World War II, ideology became anathema to most scholars, as critics charged that communists, socialists, and fascists had employed ideology to distort the truth and implement unprecedented destruction upon the world.[14] Postwar consensus liberals compared totalitarians' ideological approach to knowledge with the collectivist proposals of the interwar progressives, as both totalitarians and progressives linked knowledge construction to reform in a way that liberals felt silenced dissent and bred social conflict and extremism. Leading social scientists agreed that the rise of totalitarianism and the resulting war had demonstrated clearly the need to reject all ideology and steer clear of grand narratives, overarching theories, and collectivist movements by rejecting extremism on the right and left. As one political scientist confirmed in 1941: "Liberalism invites open criticism. It welcomes a free examination of its fundamental precepts . . . It thus stresses the necessity of open-mindedness. It delights in the honest difference of opinion."[15] Scholars considered open-mindedness the best antidote to ideology because ideology interrupted and interfered with the process of open-ended inquiry that was so central to democratic life. As another social scientist affirmed in 1948: "Not only do the chief ideological banners of our age—capitalism and socialism—appear increasingly undifferentiated, but ideology itself seems to be dying."[16]

In *The End of Ideology*, published at the end of the 1950s, Harvard sociologist Daniel Bell critiqued progressives' tendency "to convert concrete issues into ideological problems" and concluded that democracy in the post-ideological world ought to be characterized by "bargaining between legitimate groups and the search for consensus." Bell argued in *The End of Ideology* that "the impulses of the past century and a half" toward "chiliastic hopes, to millenarianism, to apocalyptic thinking" have been "exhausted" and are now considered by most intellectuals to be a "dead end." Bell explained how the "calamities of the Moscow Trials, the Nazi-Soviet pact, the concentration camps, [and] the suppression of Hungarian workers" led to a decline "in simplistic, rationalistic beliefs."[17] Leading consensus liberals argued that political problems in the post-ideological world ought to be approached carefully and incrementally, not subsumed into some grand narrative, universal truth, or ideological system, as the progressives had done. This pluralistic approach to democracy should focus on commonalities, not differences, and allow competing groups to negotiate toward consensus.

This rejection of totalitarianism led scholars away from the reform agendas of the progressives toward an emphasis on incremental change, a mixed economy, and ideological skepticism, as such approaches were considered the best antidotes to the extremism of totalitarian thought and action. Democracy's "love of variety discourages dogmatism," Schlesinger explained in *The Vital Center*, "and its love of skepticism discourages hero-worship . . . the advocate of free society defines himself by telling what he is against; what he is for turns out to be certain means and he leaves other people to charge the means with content."[18] Schlesinger—along with a new breed of postwar consensus liberal historians such as Richard Hofstadter, Louis Hartz, and Daniel Boorstin—demonstrated how history could be written without the kind of economic, ideological, and social conflicts outlined by progressive historians such as Beard, Becker, and Robinson by focusing on shared American ideals, principles, and culture.[19] For example, in the introduction to his 1955 Pulitzer Prize–winning book *The Age of Reform*, Columbia University historian Richard Hofstadter critiqued the progressives for their moral absolutism and close-mindedness. He suggested that—as the Russians and Nazis had demonstrated—moral absolutism and moral relativity often look the same "because an excessively consistent practice of either leads to the same practical result—ruthlessness in political life." Instead of ideological certainty, Hofstadter espoused allegiance to "a certain set of values: freedom of individual intellectual inquiry, scientific attitude of mind, respect for facts."[20]

According to postwar consensus liberals like Hofstadter, the main problem with ideologues was their dangerous failure to face the hard facts of reality when the facts did not affirm their ideological preconceptions and rigid beliefs. Progressives, communists, and fascists, to different degrees, shared an excessively ideological approach that quashed dissent and failed to come to terms with reality of changing conditions on the ground. For example, in *The Vital Center*, Schlesinger specifically targeted "doughfaced progressivism" for its "distortion of facts for desire."[21] Similarly, as historian Richard Burkes explained in 1949: "The vitality of ideological belief has been movingly demonstrated in our own time by the refusal of western intellectuals, when confronted with the realization of the ideological character of such configurations as democracy and communism, to undertake a critical revamping of these patterns or to abandon them altogether."[22] In contrast to totalitarianism and progressivism, postwar consensus liberals determined and interpreted facts scientifically with an open-mind by avoiding rigid ideologies that distorted the truth and prevented adjustment and compromise. The scientific and objective reckoning with the facts is what differentiated postwar consensus liberalism from the alleged naivety of progressives because postwar scholars deliberately sought to examine rigorously the complexity of reality without preconceived ideological notions.

In *The Children of Light and the Children of Darkness*, Reinhold Niebuhr admonished both conservatives and radicals for their naive views on the perfectibility of human nature during the 19th and 20th centuries. Again critiquing the misguided ideals of progressive education, which made social reform a central purpose of the schools, Niebuhr dismissed those who think that "evil is no more than ignorance, and therefore waits for a more perfect educational process to redeem man from his partial and particular loyalties."[23] Niebuhr argued that ideologues were dangerous because they dismissed dissent as mere ignorance, and they looked to education to impose their particular views upon the masses, a tendency he observed in both totalitarian regimes and progressive education. Niebuhr was no absolutist; like the naturalists, he too was liberal, experimentalist, and pluralistic in his outlook. Despite his Biblical pessimism about the perfectibility of man, Niebuhr did not espouse a return to the absolutism of premodern Christian theology. Instead he praised the modern liberal values of individual rights, deliberation, and consensus-building as compatible with a Christian notion of man as inherently fallible. As the atheist historian Perry Miller commented in 1949, Niebuhr's "theology proves acceptable, even gratifying, to many who make no claims to possessing anything resembling 'faith.'" Miller related how he had encountered "scores" who "comprehend [Niebuhr] on wholly naturalistic grounds."[24]

The idea that Americans adhered to an unspoken set of democratic principles and values contained in the Bill of Rights and Constitution received articulate and convincing support in Gunnar Myrdal's magnum opus on race relations in the United States, *An American Dilemma*, which was published the same year as Niebuhr's text. Based on years of collaborative research in the American South, Myrdal concluded that racial discrimination against Blacks was in direct conflict with the values of equality and equal opportunity that Americans consistently professed. Although Myrdal prescribed social engineering as the best way to solve the race issue, thus linking him to progressive ideas of the interwar years, his idea of an American Creed based on a core set of democratic ideals resonated with educators and political theorists of the 1940s seeking to redefine themselves in contrast to totalitarianism. In fact, this was Myrdal's intent.[25]

Drawing on this anti-ideological outlook, numerous critics attacked progressive educators in the postwar years, not only for their excessively student-centered pedagogy, but more significantly for their use and abuse of ideology and their misguided desire to use the schools as levers of social reform. For example, in his widely read critique of progressive education, *Educational Wastelands*, Arthur Bestor, professor of history at the University of Illinois, asserted that progressive education was not merely a reform movement, but rather an "ideology" that "was widely held in professional educational circles throughout the country."[26] By 'ideology,' Bestor meant a self-fulfilling and mutually reinforcing set of rigid ideals that ignored or distorted the facts, demanded strict adherence, and dismissed dissent and compromise. Frederic Lilge, a professor of education at the University of California, rejected the progressive educators' tendency to "politicize" educational philosophy by transforming educational approaches into ideologies that "defend or oppose the social order." Lilge denounced the progressives' desire to turn "crucial problems of education" into "political problems."[27]

Similarly, Everett Kircher, professor of education at Ohio State University, argued that, despite their invocation of freedom, progressive educators inappropriately demanded that "philosophy abandon its liberal status for a doctrinal status" by making education "self-consciously the ideological center of reference for the culture." That is, like totalitarians, progressives had collapsed ideas, action, and politics to the degree that their philosophy had become all-encompassing and ideologically intolerant. As Kircher explained: "The Russian error was in the selection of a wrong philosophy . . . put into practice without fundamental modification."[28] Kircher suggested that, like the Russians, progressive educators' reform-oriented curriculum inherently conveyed a specific ideological vision for the future and was, therefore, a form of indoctrination. Isaac Kandel, professor of education at Teachers College and longstanding critic of progressive education, agreed, claiming that progressive education had devolved into a "dogmatism which arrogantly refuses to recognize any virtue in the past or any validity in opposing arguments."[29] Change for the sake of change and progress for the sake of progress had become the mantra of progressive educators without any set of apolitical criteria against which they could gauge their successes and failures.

Some critics aligned the social studies with progressive education and proposed a return to "straight" history. In 1942, historian Allan Nevins attacked the interwar social studies curriculum in an article that appeared in the *New York Times Magazine*. Nevins suggested that social studies had displaced traditional, patriotic history, but this history was vital for the war effort. "We cannot feel that we are all Americans together unless we know how the United States came to be and grow," Nevins insisted. "We cannot understand what we are fighting for unless we know how our principles developed." Nevins cited dismal results of national assessments of high school students' historical knowledge as evidence of curriculum degeneration, which he attributed to the rise of social studies. Nevins's critique capitalized on a growing backlash against progressive education.[30]

Bestor, Lilge, Everett, Kandel, and Nevins argued on behalf of recovering the rigorous liberal arts curriculum that had allegedly been displaced by progressive education because a liberal arts curriculum was inherently anti-ideological in its pursuit of transcendent truths independent of politics, ideology, and reform. By focusing on transmission of the national heritage and universal truths, the liberal arts curriculum was allegedly apolitical. "The liberal arts are the arts of freedom," Robert Hutchins reminded readers in his wartime book *Education for Freedom*. "To be free a man must understand the tradition in which he lives."[31] The critics of progressive ideology were quick to remind readers that progressive educators such as Dewey, Kilpatrick, Counts, and Childs had praised the collectivist schools of Soviet Russia in the 1930s, demonstrating how they had considered some of the dangerous totalitarian ideas such as indoctrination and imposition. Critics argued that education and scholarship in a democracy ought to steer clear of collectivism, dogmatism, indoctrination, and propaganda, approaches that some progressives had openly embraced.

The issue of indoctrination was front and center during a nationally publicized controversy in Pasadena, California, in the late 1940s. Under the leadership of superintendent Willard Goslin, Pasadena schools had implemented a number of progressive education reforms, such as discontinuing report cards and promoting a curriculum that focused explicitly on fostering citizenship and international relations. Angered by these new ideas, patriotic and pro-Christian groups launched a successful campaign to purge the Pasadena schools of progressive influence, leading to Goslin's dismissal. Critics charged Goslin with indoctrination and "trying to make guinea pigs and future socialists of our children."[32] This sentiment echoed a number of books published in 1949, such as John Flynn's *The Road Ahead*, which likewise proclaimed that "a number of progressive educators have for twenty years been trying to use the public schools to shape the minds of children in support of socialist theories," and Mortimer Smith's *And Madly Teach*, which accused progressive educators of an "un-American" ideology that pushed students "along the road to totalitarianism." Smith cast progressive educators as ideologues who represented a "cohesive body of believers with a clearly formulated set of dogmas and doctrines," who only certified teachers "who have been trained in the correct dogma." Similarly, one Pasadena resident, Mary Louise Allen, concluded in her partisan account of the controversy, *Education or Indoctrination*, that progressive educators espoused a "distaste for the American way of life and approval of the socialization of Soviet Russia"—a charge that may have been an accurate description of the radical collectivists in the early 1930s, but by World War II was no longer the case.[33] Historian Andrew Hartman described the successful purge of Goslin in Pasadena as part of a broader "change from education for world-mindedness to education for Cold-mindedness" that took place during the 1940s, as the conservative forces of patriotism, religious fundamentalism, and localism gradually overtook the peace-oriented internationalism of the immediate postwar years.[34]

The postwar critiques of progressive education overlapped with the critiques of progressive ideology in three ways. First, critics argued, progressives overlooked cultural consensus by exaggerating the need for conflict, progress, and reform. After World War II, the focus on conflict was considered dangerous in a world where totalitarians overemphasized conflict and preyed on class and social divisions. Second, postwar consensus liberals argued that progressives employed a reform ideology that was rigid, shallow, and naive. In their effort to reform society through education, progressives uncritically rejected all elements of the past as inherently outdated, ineffective, and wrong. However, postwar liberals argued, the rigor and neutrality of the pre-progressive curriculum needed to be restored, at least in part, for democracy to flourish. Third, progressives, especially the radical collectivists, had conflated politics and knowledge in the pursuit of reform, which was the most dangerous development because the conflation of politics, research, and education was precisely how the Nazis and communists had turned their distorted version of the world into reality. Postwar consensus liberals insisted that, to avoid totalitarianism, scholarly communities in democracies needed to remain autonomous by pursuing rigorous inquiries free from politics and ideology.[35]

TEACHING HOW TO THINK

During the war, professional organizations pledged their support for democratic government and individual human rights. In 1940, the NEA explicitly denounced totalitarianism with its "mockery of democratic principles of equality among men," "its denial of the dignity of the individual human being," and "its inculcation of sentiments of national and racial bigotry." The same year, the American Political Science Association passed a resolution pledging to "rededicate ourselves to the continuing task of promoting an understanding of democracy and generating confidence in its institutions."[36] Following the lead of social scientists, theorists of democratic education were faced with the difficult task of reaffirming the strengths of democracy without resorting to propaganda, indoctrination, or the ideological imposition characteristic of totalitarian regimes.

During and after the war, dozens of scholars and professional organizations published works calling for the strengthening of democratic education. These works explored the knowledge, skills, and dispositions that would be needed in a chaotic new world in which democracy was under constant attack.[37] As part of this literature, former collectivists Beard, Counts, Newlon, and Kilpatrick reiterated their newfound political moderation and proclaimed their rejection of ideology and totalitarianism.[38] All groups and authors reiterated the need for patriotism and the ability to think critically, and they rejected the rote memorization of facts. "To identify democratic education . . . with memorized words and phrases about American history," the Educational Policies Commission insisted, "probably does more harm than good," because democratic citizens needed the skills to think critically.[39] The Harvard Committee likewise identified the "mechanical repetition of uncomprehended words and phrases" as the "bane" of the social studies.[40] Balancing the allegiance to democracy with the need for critical thinking was a paradox that scholars would spend the 1940s and 1950s trying to resolve.

Even those educators who meekly carried the torch of democratic collectivism into the postwar years downplayed the role of economic and social conflict, explicitly denounced the use of indoctrination, and embraced teaching students the art of deliberation and problem solving. For example, William O. Stanley, professor of education at the University of Illinois, replaced the ambitious educational goals of collectivist social reconstruction with the more modest goals "of mutual thought, interpersuasion [*sic*], and personal reconstruction."[41] Similarly, R. Bruce Raup of Teachers College and his colleagues outlined a postwar agenda for social reform based not on indoctrination and ideological commitment, but on "a sense of community in which the self becomes identified as a functional part of the organic process" by developing the skills of "community persuasion as the basis of action."[42] In their book *The Improvement of Practical Intelligence*, Raup and his co-authors were sure to denounce the evils of ideological rigidity in a democracy because such rigidities—whether socialist, Marxist, or capitalist—"have in common the effect of shutting out great areas of human interest and human good from consideration and possible acceptance."[43] While retaining the interwar commitment to social planning, Raup and his colleagues carefully expressed their postwar vision in a curriculum aimed at developing judgment, persuasion, and critical thinking skills as part of a program of establishing communal goals.

Under the mentorship of Raup, Kenneth D. Benne addressed the issue of authority in the post-ideological world in his 1944 book, *A Concept of Authority: An Introductory Study*. Benne depicted both totalitarianism and classic liberalism as rigid ideologies that threatened the future of democracy. The former ideology led men to impose their authority upon others, while the latter "prompts men under its influence to fear and resent the development and exercise of any common, authoritative plan and direction." Yet, Benne averred, direction and authority were unavoidable, necessary, and desired in the modern world because technology and modern institutions had replaced the traditional authority of the church and family, but this new authority had to be derived through democratic means. In the place of rigid ideologies, Benne endorsed a version of community life in which authority was continuously renegotiated through processes of "criticism, discussion and deliberation." Benne awkwardly dubbed this "non-authoritarian authority," and implored teachers to take an active role in constructing this consciousness among students, even if it upset local administrators, parents, and community members.[44] In their heavily referenced books, Stanley, Raup, and Benne drew on the naturalistic philosophy of Dewey, as well as numerous other social scientists and political theorists, to hash out an ambitious program of educational reform that rejected dogmatism and indoctrination, but still tried to envision a program of social and economic equity in American society through social planning.

During and after the war, teaching how to think, instead of what to think, emerged again as a common reaction to totalitarianism. Scholars agreed that teaching must convey democratic values, such as open-mindedness and scientific disinterestedness, while avoiding indoctrination. "Any dictator uses men *for his own purpose*," one educator related. "The only effective weapon against dictatorship is an active, thinking citizenry."[45] Another educator stated clearly that to avoid indoctrination, teachers must "help students how to think, not what to think."[46] Robert Thouless's *How to Think Straight: The Technique of Applying Logic Instead of Emotion*, published in 1939, underscored the importance of proper thinking as the best antidote to propaganda, indoctrination, and totalitarianism.[47] However, even within the anti-ideological consensus, educators still debated how to find the right balance between teaching skepticism and a love of democracy. "Ability to think, to evaluate, to judge are essential characteristics of a developed personality," John Childs maintained. "To attempt to cultivate particular outlooks and values in the minds and affections of the young is indoctrination, not education."[48] In an essay entitled "Indoctrination versus Education," one author defined indoctrination as delivering "one version of a proposal . . . without supporting reasons." Education, on the other hand, the author explained, involved presenting students "not only with the widest possible horizontal spread of proposals in a controversial situation but also with the greatest possible depth of supporting reasons." Indoctrination, he continued, was "dogmatic and doctrinaire," while education was "tentative and liberal"; indoctrination was "at home in an autocracy," while education was "consistent with and conducive to democracy."[49] With totalitarianism serving as democracy's *other*, scholars stated the goals of civic education with greater emphasis on thinking.

Of course, the idea of teaching how to think, not what to think, had been suggested in one form or another for nearly 30 years. However, prior to World War II, it had been somewhat of an empty phrase often employed in vague ways as an antidote to the uncritical transmission of facts. The problem of teaching how to think, Raup and his co-authors explained in 1943, "has been vaguely and generally felt by the profession but has not been crystalized for effective discussion."[50] However, in the postwar years, a new generation of scholars took the task seriously by fleshing out more robust rationales and methodologies for why and how students ought to engage in clear thinking, class deliberation, and discussion of social issues. While interwar progressives and collectivists had used social problems as a scheme to organize content and convey a particular set of ideals, the postwar social studies educators, under the influence of consensus liberalism, focused on presenting social problems to students as a set of open-ended questions in order to teach them how to think in a rational and open-minded way.

In 1910 Dewey had written a book called *How We Think*, which had initially received little notice in comparison to his more popular works of the period, *School and Society*, *The Child and the Curriculum*, *Schools of To-Morrow*, and *Democracy and Education*. For example, the authors of the 1916 Committee on Social Studies report directly cited *Schools of To-morrow*, published a year earlier, while completely ignoring *How We Think*, published 6 years prior.[51] Yet by 1950, one popular social studies methods textbook, *Teaching Social Studies in High Schools*, cited only *How We Think* as an influential text on the field and completely ignored Dewey's other texts.[52] Likewise, another textbook, *Social Studies Instruction*, also ignored Dewey's other works and instead cited *How We Think* as the rationale for what he called "the problem method." According to the textbook's author, the problem method suggested attacking "a specific situation in a scientific manner . . . and is therefore . . . directly applicable to the secondary school level of instruction."[53]

In *How We Think*, Dewey outlined the generic elements of reflective thinking as "five logically distinct steps: (i) a felt difficulty; (ii) its location and definition; (iii) suggestion of possible solution; (iv) development by reasoning of the bearings of the suggestion; (v) further observation and experiment leading to its acceptance or rejection; that is, the conclusion of belief or disbelief."[54] When Dewey revised the text in 1933, he backed off the assertion that the steps were linear and distinct, yet he reiterated the generic steps of thinking that cut across all disciplines and life activities. Although written over 3 decades earlier, Dewey's description of the thinking process accurately reflected the kind of anti-ideological, open-minded consideration of evidence valued by postwar educators. Accordingly, the textbook *Education for Social Competence* ignored Dewey's *Democracy and Education* and instead cited *How We Think*. Under the section discussing the popularity of the problem-based curriculum approach in many schools, the authors explained how "the use of the problems approach in selecting and organizing curriculum materials and learning experiences is in reality the application of Dewey's definition of reflective thinking to group problems and situations."[55] Even those who did not directly cite Dewey adopted his language. "A social problem involves a felt difficulty," one social studies educator explained, borrowing the phrase "felt difficulty" from *How We Think*.[56]

How We Think became the handbook for postwar consensus liberal educators looking to teach correct, scientific thinking as a way to avoid indoctrination. In other words, postwar educators did not reject Dewey's work in the 1940s and 1950s, despite its affiliation with progressive ideology and ideological imposition. Instead, postwar educators refashioned Dewey's work to meet the needs of the new anti-totalitarian environment that valued open-mindedness and scientific disinterestedness. "In its tentative, experimental spirit, pragmatism best expresses the ideals of democracy," one educational philosopher explained in 1954. "But pragmatism must be constantly redefined; otherwise it becomes a dogma rather than a *living vision*."[57] During the postwar years, leading social studies educators drew on Dewey's *How We Think* to construct a new approach to social and political issues in the classroom appropriate for the postwar world. Education professors Alan Griffin, Maurice Hunt, Lawrence Metcalf, and Donald Oliver forged their anti-ideological approach to democratic education not only in response to totalitarianism and indoctrination abroad, but also to what they considered to be authoritarianism at home.

In 1942, Alan Griffin authored an influential dissertation under the supervision of Boyd Bode at Ohio State University. Griffin agreed with Dewey and Bode that the absolutism of patriotic traditionalists was as dangerous as embracing collectivism and indoctrination. Griffin insisted that there was no way to teach history "simply 'for its own sake' or 'to give the child the facts,'" because these approaches merely reflected the values of the status quo and were, therefore, also a form of indoctrination. Griffin likewise rejected inculcation to "any competing system of economic organization," as Beard, Counts, and Rugg had recommended in the early 1930s. What was needed in postwar democracy, Griffin argued, was a new, skeptical, scientific approach to social studies with deliberation at its core, "a reliance upon reflection, not as a method, but as *the* method for defining truth of any proposition about a subject." Griffin contrasted democracy with the relativity of "authoritarianism," which "can never stand off and examine or appraise the content of an accepted hierarchy of values" because "Nazis and Fascists . . . accept [values] on authority without doubt or testing." If "democracy as a way of life is to have a fighting chance for survival," Griffin insisted in the heightened rhetoric of the war, "the task of the democratic school is to make the student intelligent about his culture, rather than to win his adherence to a predetermined course of action."[58] Thus, Griffin rejected the ideological approach of both the radical collectivists and patriotic-liberal arts professors, embraced the postwar anti-ideological orientation of postwar consensus liberalism, and cited Dewey's *How We Think* as the document that best reflected his outlook.

Maurice Hunt and Lawrence Metcalf further developed Griffin's approach to democratic education in their 1955 textbook, *Teaching High School Social Studies: Problems in Reflective Thinking and Social Understanding*. Hunt and Metcalf specifically named Dewey, Bode, and Griffin as influences on their focus on applying reflective inquiry on what they called "closed areas" of society, defined as "islands of totalitarian thought and practice in the midst of a culture which is straining in democratic directions." By 1955, the totalitarian villains had shifted from the Nazis to the Russians. The authors related how education in the Soviet Union was once progressive, but now employed "official dogmas, . . . indoctrination and prescription, drill and rote memorization" to discourage any questioning of the official state ideology. Democracy, in contrast, did not have an official ideology, but rather consisted of pluralistic deliberation around "core values such as dignity and worth of individuals, the methods of intelligence and political freedom." Drawing on an extensive discussion of Dewey's *How We Think*, Hunt and Metcalf concluded that the social studies curriculum ought to have students "experience problematic situations of the general nature described by Dewey, situations which are puzzling, uncertain, doubtful." By focusing on closed areas of societal conflict and having students try to reach consensus with their peers, the authors postulated that students would experience firsthand the kind of scientific thinking necessary for sustaining a democracy. Addressing controversial topics in the classroom would stand in direct contrast to totalitarian schooling. Echoing the language of Merton's "scientific ethos," Hunt and Metcalf identified the "rules of the reflective method" as logical consistency, exhaustion of evidence, methodological transparency, and acceptance of the provisional nature of conclusions.[59] This was an ambitious program for high school teachers, many of whom were not even college graduates.[60] Nevertheless, Hunt and Metcalf articulated a clear rationale and vision for democratic education supported by developments in political theory, the hard sciences, and educational psychology. More significantly, they fleshed out what had up to that point been an empty phrase: teaching students "how to think, not what to think."

Two years later, Donald Oliver, professor of education at Harvard University, published in the *Harvard Educational Review* what would become a classic essay in the field of social studies education, "The Selection of Content in the Social Studies." Oliver aimed his critique directly at the progressive worldview espoused by Beard in his conclusion to the American Historical Association Commission on the Social Studies, the content guidelines issued by the National Council for the Social Studies, as well as the patriotic perspective of Nevins. Echoing Niebuhr, Oliver dismissed the approaches of all three as naive because they stressed "the ultimate goodness of society and the perfectibility of human societies" and downplayed the value conflicts at the center of a healthy democracy. Rather than teach students that value conflicts are unnatural or a result of ignorance, Oliver insisted, students ought to be taught how to engage with value conflicts in a rational way. He argued, "man [*sic*] is intellectually inadequate to define the ultimate truth, the ultimate criteria for 'the good life'" and so he must learn to live with the simultaneous existence of "a variety of value positions." To do so, students "should be taught to make thoughtful predictions about the consequences of various alternative methods of regulating human affairs."[61] Oliver argued that, in a democracy, a root focus on human dignity would have to be accepted on faith. The curriculum ought to consist of discussions on how to implement and interpret the protection of human dignity.

The work of Griffin, Hunt, Metcalf, and Oliver followed the contours of Schlesinger's "vital center," Merton's "scientific ethos," and Bell's "end of ideology" in their focus on open-mindedness, pluralism, transparency, use of evidence, and communal verification. Their work both drew on and repudiated the work of interwar progressive educators by embracing Dewey's apolitical *How We Think*. Most significantly, they shifted the emphasis on social issues from topics and facts to be discussed by the teacher to open-ended problems to be considered by individual students, thus fleshing out the idea of teaching students how to think, not what to think. This reorientation was driven by the rise of totalitarianism. "Attention to citizenship education had been stimulated by the rise of totalitarian governments," Teachers College professor Erling Hunt explained in 1952. "Yet the thinking and efforts that have resulted do not constitute merely an emergency program . . . [they] should be of major and lasting value."[62] Similarly, Oliver and his co-author, James Shaver, noted how "the success of Fascist regimes . . . as well as the Russian Revolution marked the beginning of a serious new challenge to modern democratic government."[63] This new challenge to democracy fueled a repudiation of radical collectivism and interwar progressive education, but it also redirected democratic education in a more student-centered direction focused on the cognitive processes of reflective thinking.

Like their predecessors, postwar consensus liberal educators desired to make an impact on improving citizenship education in local schools, but they met only limited success. Several social studies educators implemented grant-funded projects focused on teaching problem solving and critical thinking. These professors created instructional pamphlets and ran teacher workshops to equip teachers with the skills to teach good citizenship, including the ability to think critically about social issues. They also collected data on the effectiveness of their materials. They discovered that getting local teachers to embrace the new focus on thinking was difficult, and it was equally challenging to change the minds of students. For example, a study in Detroit found that teachers were hesitant to move beyond rote learning and felt unprepared to teach problem solving. The study concluded: "Courses of study, lack of varied instructional materials, and the earlier conditioning of pupils retarded attempts to teach by problem solving procedures."[64] Even more disappointing, a study from Syracuse University study found that students learned more about citizenship from home, church, sports, and other local community groups than they did from school. The study concluded: "Classroom instruction fails to achieve the citizenship goal; indeed it appears to be less effective than the extracurricular program." Furthermore, students from the Syracuse study often adopted a cynical attitude regarding politics and political action. "Students tend to leave our secondary schools with the concept that politics is a 'messy business,'" the study discovered. "In general they reject the idea of future responsible participation as individuals."[65] A study from Kansas also discovered a resistance among students to developing critical thinking. "So far as the evidence goes, the progress that high school students are making toward acquiring skills in the various aspects of critical thinking is not very great."[66] Much like the disappointing findings of the efforts to teach propaganda analysis between 1937 and 1940, the efforts at teaching active and critical citizenship had limited success. Further, the definition of citizenship with which students felt most comfortable was one of compliance, politeness, and respect, not political engagement and critical thinking.

Although their impact on school practice was limited, the classic works of Griffin, Hunt, Metcalf, Oliver, and Shaver influenced the field of social studies education for decades. Their work represented a golden age of theory and research on issue-based social studies education, and provided the field with a sense of coherence and identity that drew upon, but was distinct from, the social sciences.[67] The shift in pedagogical influence away from Dewey's more ideological books, such as *Schools of To-morrow* or *Democracy and Education*, toward his apolitical *How We Think* further rationalized the movement away from prescribed subject matter toward the process of thinking itself. The postwar emphasis on *How We Think* kept Dewey relevant throughout the 1940s, 1950s, and beyond, but it also deemphasized the social criticism and reform agenda of his earlier work.

DEWEY ON THE DEFENSIVE

Despite the enduring influence of *How We Think* on postwar consensus liberal educators, Dewey continued to be haunted by his affiliation with progressive education, the radical collectivists, and their embrace of relativity and indoctrination. After all, Counts had directly cited Dewey in his 1932 call-to-arms *Dare the Schools Build a New Social Order?*[68] Dewey continued to assert that naturalism was the most compatible philosophy with democracy, and that the growth of the social sciences proved this. In his 1950 article in the *American Historical Review*, Connecticut College historian Chester McArthur Destler argued that American relativists like Dewey "have neglected to indicate to prospective converts the intimate relation that the new Continental historiography has borne to the origins of fascism." As Destler explained, "the adoption of subjectivist-presentist-relativism as the basis of historical theory contributed to the rise of Fascism and Nazism and their conquest of the universities." As a result of Dewey's approach to history, Destler charged, the discipline had been turned into an instrument of propaganda. Destler traced this presentist approach to history not only to Dewey, but also to progressive historians such as Beard and Becker. For Destler, these theorists had turned history into something that exists only in the heads of historians; they had turned history from something about which historians think into something that was nothing more than thought itself. Destler insisted that if history were to remain less than a tool for the state, it needed to be based on the scientific method and accept objectivity as it major goal.[69]

A decade after Destler, another historian argued in the *American Historical Review* that "Dewey had closed the door to any effective distinctions between the finding of the historian and the reasons that lie behind his interest in any historical problem."[70] The historian considered the epistemological dualism that Dewey rejected as a necessary precondition for effective historical inquiry. Likewise, another historian remarked: "Because Dewey thought of knowledge in terms of power rather than truth, he could not understand that historians frequently undertake inquiries without trying to prove anything." [71] He criticized Dewey's contention that trained historians could not transcend the social views and narrow interests of their time. Further, in a critique of science under Marxism, another critic linked Dewey's naturalism to totalitarian research, suggesting that "the crudities of Soviet pragmatism are analogous to those of John Dewey's philosophy at the turn of the century" because both Marxism and pragmatism asserted that "only statements which are useful are really true."[72] For all of these critics, Dewey's naturalism was inherently relativistic because it denied that scholars could fully separate their understanding of the past from their own social milieus.

Beyond attacks on Dewey's epistemology, critics continued to blame the philosopher for what they considered to be the poor state of American education. Dewey was allegedly responsible for pushing secularism, relativism, child-centeredness, and communistic collectivism into the nation's schools. In 1949, in *Crisis in Education*, Episcopal minister Bernard Iddings Bell traced the removal of religious and absolute values from American classrooms to Dewey, quipping that progressive education "works so badly it must be wrong." Another critic accused Dewey of "unwittingly, undertaken to soften us up for the Red push" because Dewey and his followers could not adequately "give one good, radically theoretical reason, one that goes beyond experience, why he prefers democracy to totalitarianism." In *A Program for Conservatives*, published in 1954, Russell Kirk dismissed the "stifling empire of the doctrinaire Deweyites," and attacked Dewey's naturalism as "an intellectual corpse" that continued to haunt the education system with relativism and anti-intellectualism.[73]

Other critics of Dewey were more subtle and suggested that Dewey's detrimental influence on the schools was inadvertent. For example, Mortimer Smith suggested in *The Diminished Mind*, published in 1954, that "[o]ne of the primary flaws in the Deweyan philosophy, its failure to set up ends, its insistence 'that the educational process has no end beyond itself' . . . had undoubtedly had unfortunate classroom repercussions."[74] In *Anti-intellectualism in American Life*, Richard Hofstadter likewise chided Dewey for his vagueness and inability to clarify the limits of his metaphors. "[Dewey's] idea that education is growth is at first blush all but irresistible. Certainly education is not a form of shrinkage," Hofstadter joked. "[But] I believe that in the hands of some of Dewey's followers this idea became one of the most mischievous metaphors in the history of modern education."[75] Suggesting that Dewey's philosophy was sound, but misinterpreted, was a convenient way to avoid having to engage with his work in a serious and rigorous way.

Dewey's naturalism experienced a backlash during the anti-ideological days of the 1950s due, in large part, to its affiliation with progressive education and collectivist ideology; his reputation had never been (and would never again be) held in such low regard. Even those who cited him, such as the issue-centered social studies educators discussed earlier, stayed clear of any of Dewey's more ambitious educational aims related to social reform or reconstruction, and instead focused on his apolitical *How We Think*. Yet, Dewey's ideas such as scientific thinking, pluralistic interaction, the comprehensive high school, a relevant curriculum, and issue-centered instruction continued to gain traction in the postwar years, even if Dewey often was not given credit for it. Ultimately, for every scholar who attacked Dewey in the name of saving democracy from totalitarian ideas in the postwar years, there were several drawing on Dewey's ideas—directly or indirectly—to assert that Dewey's naturalism was the only path to take in the new anti-ideological mindset that valued democratic pluralism and scientific thinking.

CHAPTER 6

In the Shadow of Mind Control

In July 1953, at the conclusion of the Korean War, the United States and Korea exchanged their prisoners of war (POWs). To the astonishment of many, 23 American soldiers refused to return home, having allegedly been "brainwashed" to stay and live in the communist nation. "The defection of just one . . . would have been enough to sadden the heart," a magazine editorial lamented at the time, but the defection of twenty-three was "almost a blow in the face to us."[1] Background research on the 23 defectors revealed that only 10 of them had attended high school, and only three of them had graduated. This fact led some to link secondary education with intellectual fortitude, resiliency, and the love of country. Conversely, others blamed the schools for their inability to prepare the soldiers more to resist the brainwashing techniques of the Chinese and North Koreans.

A 1956 study by army psychologists reported that a third of all prisoners in Korea had succumbed to some form of communist brainwashing. As one psychologist explained: "From these things it is tragically clear that the American educational system, fine as it is, is failing miserably in getting across absolute fundamentals of survival in a tense and troubled international society."[2] Another psychologist blamed the POWs' defection on authoritarian parenting, writing: "Any POW who accepted communist propaganda as a result of Soviet mind washing techniques were men who, as children, gave up the struggle to be themselves and abandoned themselves to the dictates of father and mother." Although psychologists disagreed over the roots of mental vulnerability in the prisoners, they agreed that students who were well-adjusted, assertive, content, and loved democracy would not be persuaded by communist propaganda and would, therefore, have the psychic strength to resist brainwashing. However, students who were psychologically fragile, aberrant, and unassimilated were potentially vulnerable to brainwashing, propaganda, and conversion to communism. As the *New York Times* concluded, the defection of American prisoners to Korea proved that "brainwashing does work on some persons."[3]

Just as the term *totalitarianism* raised the stakes from the previously preferred term, *dictatorship*, the term *brainwashing* went far beyond previous concerns for mere indoctrination, imposition, and propaganda, to encompass, in the words of one journalist and brainwashing expert, a "mechanism of flesh and blood, with new beliefs and new thought processes inserted into a captive body."[4] Books published during and after the war on the role of education in brainwashing communists and fascists had captured the imagination of American readers, and feature films produced after the war, such as *My Son John* (1952), *Invasion of the Body Snatchers* (1956), and *The Manchurian Candidate* (1962), heightened fears about the risks of communist brainwashing and the potential threat it posed to American life. Moreover, dystopian novels such as George Orwell's *1984*, published in 1949, fueled the flames of paranoia about the success of brainwashing techniques. Not only were totalitarians willing to brainwash their citizens, prisoners, and victims, they were skilled at it.

Educators did not react immediately to the brainwashing scare because they had been responding to authoritarian threats for decades by emphasizing how to think, not what to think. However, during and immediately after World War II, psychologists and social scientists issued numerous warnings about the susceptibility of U.S. citizens to authoritarian thinking, and mental hygienists worried about the detrimental effects of undiagnosed mental disorders among students. In response to these concerns, policymakers launched the postwar program of life adjustment education—the most derided program in the history of American education. All agreed that the best defense against totalitarian thinking (and brainwashing) was to foster a well-adjusted, mentally fit, patriotic community of citizens. They also agreed that the schools represented the best avenue to accomplish this goal. However, by the end of the 1950s, most were convinced that life adjustment education—which marginalized academic content and focused on positive social attitudes and therapeutic interventions—was not the best way to meet the communist threat.

THE CULTURE OF THE COLD WAR

After World War I, the Committee on Public Information had quietly and quickly disbanded, the nation demilitarized, and most American intellectuals sank into postwar disillusionment, convinced they had been duped into supporting the war. In contrast, during the years following the Allied victory in World War II, the exact opposite occurred. The nation, including intellectuals and educators, seamlessly entered into what one historian called "state of near-permanent war."[5] The unconditional surrender of the Japanese left few ambiguities about who had won the conflict, and there was an overwhelming consensus that the war had been worth it. Despite over a million U.S. casualties (403,399 died; 670,846 were wounded), it had been a good war because democracy had been restored and fascism had been thoroughly defeated. The gruesome and incomprehensible discovery of piles of corpses in the Nazi concentration camps near the end of the conflict confirmed that the Nazi threat to humanity had perhaps been underestimated, not overestimated, and that the Allies were clearly on the moral high ground. Yet tensions with the United States' former ally, the Soviet Union, quickly escalated into a Cold War that would last for the next half-century. As a result, fears of totalitarianism did not abate; they escalated.

Domestically, to meet the perceived threat of Soviet aggression, the United States greatly expanded its state apparatus with an enlarged national security bureaucracy and surveillance infrastructure, including the Federal Bureau of Investigation and Central Intelligence Agency. A second Red Scare emerged, as the House Un-American Activities Committee and Senator Joseph McCarthy sought to purge the U.S. government, Hollywood, schools, and society of secret communists working to undermine democracy. In 1950, Alger Hiss, head of the Carnegie Endowment for International Peace, and Klaus Fuchs, an atomic scientist who had worked on the atomic bomb, were both convicted of spying and sharing state secrets with the Soviet Union. In 1953, Julius and Ethel Rosenberg were executed on charges of communist espionage. These convictions provided proof for accusers such as McCarthy that real communist conspiracies were being hatched on America soil, and that communists had infiltrated all aspects of American life. In 1955, Arthur Bestor was convinced that "American democracy is under attack by the agents of Soviet Communism."[6] As a result of McCarthyism and the Red Scare, thousands of U.S. citizens lost their jobs, and hundreds were jailed and/or deported. In 1940, 21 states required teachers to take loyalty oaths explicitly denouncing communism, and in 1948 the American Federation of Teachers voted against allowing communists to teach in public schools. New York State's Feinberg Law ordered principals to file reports on the loyalty of their teachers.[7]

Against this anxious and paranoid backdrop, postwar Americans experienced unprecedented prosperity. Immediately after the war, Americans consumed 50% more calories than their European counterparts, whose infrastructure had been decimated by the conflict. The Servicemen's Readjustment Act of 1944, also known as the GI Bill, aided U.S. veterans in buying new homes, starting businesses, and going to college. By 1956, half of all veterans had taken advantage of the opportunities. An innovation in mortgage loans, requiring only a 10% down payment and allowing 30 years to pay off the loan, led to a booming housing demand. To meet this need, builders constructed suburbs outside of major urban areas, which were linked to cities through the new Interstate highway system used by commuters in their newly bought automobiles to travel to and from work. Between 1948 and 1958, 85% of nonfarm housing was built in the suburbs. Further, a postwar baby boom began immediately after the war and extended into the early 1950s, which further fueled the demand for suburban housing and consumer goods. Between 1939 and 1948, clothing sales increased threefold, furniture sales increased fourfold, sales of household appliances such as television sets and washing machines increased fivefold, and millions of American-made cars were sold.[8] As *Life* magazine reported in 1955, a "revolution in consumer purchasing" created a new demand for immediate satisfaction, where "instead of saving for years to afford major purchases, customers buy on credit and enjoy the goods while they pay for them."[9]

Growth in high school enrollments accompanied this growth in consumer spending and suburbanization; the school's central role in the new suburban communities changed the social fabric of American society, as mostly White middle-class parents moved to the suburbs, in part so their children could attend the new, safer schools away from urban centers. Enrollment in U.S. high schools had been increasing steadily for decades. High school enrollment increased from 17% of 17-year-olds in 1920 to nearly 70% in 1960. The biggest jump in enrollment occurred in the 1930s, as the adolescent job market dried up, and parents and communities encouraged students to stay in school and off the streets. This change in school demographics fueled the effort to reduce the amount of academic content in the curriculum, and inspired educators to reimagine the high school as an institution that most Americans would attend, whereas most would not go on to college.

This period saw a steady increase in enrollment in social studies courses, from about 13% of the average student's course load in 1915 to about 16% in 1960, reflecting greater emphasis on civic education during and after the war. This increase in social studies enrollment, while modest, was telling because it took place against a backdrop of overall declining enrollments in academic classes and a relative increase in enrollment in vocational and commercial classes. In fact, by 1960, 100% of U.S. high school students took at least one social studies class, second in overall enrollment to classes in English and Health.[10] This slight increase in the importance of the social studies came at the expense of math and science classes. The Problems of Democracy course, which had been introduced by the progressive Committee on Social Studies, continued to be offered in about a third of U.S. high schools.[11]

Most educators viewed the explosion in high school enrollment and the variety of course offerings designed to cater to this intellectually diverse student population as a sign of democracy triumphant. Educators took seriously Dewey's proposal that U.S. schools served as embryonic democratic communities, although often these communities reflected the consensus values of White, suburban America. Educational films produced by Coronet Films during the 1940s and 1950s projected (literally) images of White, suburban, well-dressed, polite adolescents dealing with nonacademic issues such as how to make friends or ask a girl on a date.[12] Learning to live together in a polite, respectful, tolerant community was a desired outcome of leading educators, policymakers, and politicians, who actively fostered the "American way of life" through feature films, urban planning, and cultural events. In 1954, the Pledge of Allegiance added the words "one nation under God," reflecting a resurgence in church attendance, which rose from 43% during the interwar years to nearly 70% by the end of the 1950s.[13] In addition, publishers rewrote their textbooks during this period to place more emphasis on the strengths of democracy and the role of Communist subversives. They issued warnings about "false news" and "dangerous propaganda," and encouraged students to "report directly to its offices any suspicions they may have about Communist activity on the part of their fellow Americans."[14] Many of these textbooks followed the lead of U.S. Attorney General Tom C. Clark, who argued in 1947 that "indoctrination in democracy is the essential catalytic agent needed to blend our varying groups into one American family."[15] Collectively, these trends created, endorsed, and sustained a sense of American community, albeit one that was White and middle class.

However, beneath the veneer of postwar community, consensus, and prosperity, U.S. educators worried about the psychological health of the nation. Books like David Riesman's *The Lonely Crowd* (1950) and William Whyte's *The Organization Man* (1956) uncovered a new set of postwar middle-class values—inner-directedness and materialistic ambition—that suburban, white-collar life seemed to foster. "These are the days when men of all social disciplines and all political faiths seek the comfortable and the accepted," economist John Kenneth Galbraith complained in his 1958 book *The Affluent Society*. "When the man of controversy is looked upon as a disturbing influence; when originality is taken to be a mark of instability." Intellectuals and policymakers wondered whether this new sense of conformity was good or bad for American youth and society, and they debated whether conformity made you more vulnerable or less vulnerable to communism. For example, public intellectual Mary McCarthy worried that too much emphasis on patriotism and conformity was pushing students to adopt a stance of apathy and willful ignorance. "The student today is far from being in danger of [indoctrination] by Communism," she wrote in 1952; instead the student "is in danger of being stupified [*sic*] by the complacent propaganda of democracy."[16] Similarly, MIT professor Jerrold Zacharias observed that "our schools have been set up in such a way as to produce a sea of uniform mice; if you don't believe it, look at the lamps people buy, or the automobiles."[17] In contrast, others argued that the schools needed to do more to instill a love of democracy, not less. An official from the American Legion insisted that educators must "not only get Communism out of schools" but they must also "get Americanism into schools."[18] Overall, the 1950s was a time of economic prosperity and cultural consensus, undergirded by feelings of anxiety and apprehension about the psychological health of American youth and their potential susceptibility to communism, propaganda, and brainwashing.

MENTAL HYGIENE

Before the brainwashing scare following the defection of Korean POWs, educators had linked totalitarian education with mind control and indoctrination. Published in 1941, Gregor Ziemer's *Education for Death: The*

Making of a Nazi surveyed the educational techniques of the Nazis in the years leading up to the war. Ziemer's book reached an audience far beyond educators when the book was abridged for the *Readers Digest* and formed the basis of the 1943 movie *Hitler's Children*. Ziemer's book was part detective story, part thriller, part horror story, as the author, president of an American school in Berlin, related how he used deception, wit, and bribery to gain access to Nazi-run German schools that were officially closed to foreigners. As Ziemer explained, "The Nazi school, I discovered, was an auxiliary of the army, and its methods were as guarded as if they were military secrets." After gaining access to the schools, Ziemer uncovered a segregated, totalitarian system in which boys were raised from preschool to worship the *Fuehrer* and prepare for military service, while girls were taught to have children and raise strong Nazi men. "In Nazi Germany the ideal of self-sacrifice, of dying for Hitler, has taken on proportions that to an outsider would seem sadistic perversion," Ziemer related. "And for those who oppose Hitler deep hatred is aroused in the hearts of German youth." Ziemer concluded that to meet the formidable threat of Nazi education, the American schools would need to become more vigilant and rigorous in its patriotic fervor. "We hear it said that Hitler's methods and Hitler's techniques have no place in American Schools. Of course not!" he concluded. "But surely one cannot be accused of extolling Nazi methods if one points out that Hitler's system has worked with remarkable efficiency for Nazism." Ziemer did not offer specific prescriptions for how U.S. schools ought to be reformed, but he was clearly worried that educators were not taking the Nazi threat seriously enough.[19]

Although far less sensationalistic than Ziemer's study, George S. Counts and Nucia Lodge likewise highlighted the effects of brainwashing in the Soviet Union in 1949 with *The Country of the Blind: The Soviet System of Mind Control*. Counts's and Nucia's study collected official documents issued by the Soviet Union that, according to Counts, "tells the story in authentic detail of the operation of the Soviet system of mind control." As Counts related, the Communist Party "is engaged with great energy in systemically building, in the minds of young and old alike, two great myths—one about themselves and their country and the other about the rest of the world and the so-called camp of capitalism." In a chapter entitled "Education as Weapon," Counts related how all the forces of government, entertainment, arts, youth groups, and journalism worked together to run "the most gigantic and comprehensive marshaling of forces to shape the human mind in the whole history of mankind." Counts conveyed his love for the Russian people by casting them as helpless victims of Stalin, but he could not explain why the Communist Party met so little resistance. He pondered—based on the high-profile suicide of a Russian woman, Osaka Kasenkina, who leapt to her death from the Soviet consulate in 1948—that, perhaps, potential resistance to communism was waiting just below the surface. He asked: "[H]ow many Soviet schoolteachers envy the fate of Kasenkina and long for the opportunity to jump to freedom?"[20] Counts admitted that he did not know the answer, but he hoped there were many.

Counts's 1957 follow-up study, *The Challenge of Soviet Education*, was a more comprehensive and scholarly account of the Soviet apparatus of mind control, including the role of terror techniques of the Stalinist purges in maintaining a sense of paranoia, loyalty, and control. As Counts explained: "The process of indoctrination [begins] . . . in the nursery . . .and is continued systemically and comprehensively from grade to grade to grade to the final year of study in the University." Communist indoctrination was carried on through "all the agencies of communication" and "throughout the entire cultural apparatus." As a result, Russian children and adults did not have "the opportunity of encountering a vigorous presentation of opposing and contrary doctrines and outlooks."[21] Counts concluded that Soviet education "needs to be answered in terms of an education appropriate to a free society as the Soviet program is suited to the values and purposes of a totalitarian state," but he did not elaborate on what this was.[22] In a 1956 essay, English professor Robert Gleckner cited Counts's work as confirmation that the Russians employed brainwashing on its own citizens. Gleckner endorsed assigning Orwell's *1984* as the best way to convey to students exactly what the Americans were up against. "The psyche of the Russian individual can be allowed no independence or autonomy," Gleckner explained. "The human mind is prohibited from any chance for self-determination, organic integrity, or resistance to outside pressures." Gleckner concluded that the Russian pedagogical approach was "brain-washing... done on a national scale in the name of science, like the laboratory and torture chamber activity in *1984*."[23]

Ziemer and Counts were both disgusted by what they had observed in education under totalitarian rule. Ziemer, who observed the German schools firsthand, was convinced that the Germans had readily and freely absorbed the Nazi worldview, while Counts, who after the 1930s was banned from Russia and was merely working with official Soviet documents, was less certain that the Russian masses really believed what they were being fed. Both considered the totalitarian approaches inappropriate for U.S. schools, yet both worried that U.S. educators were underestimating the power of the mind-control techniques of its enemies. Neither Ziemer nor Counts endorsed teaching through indoctrination nor teaching what to think in place of how to think, but as the Cold War continued, others were willing to take this step. For example, using the Korean prisoners' defection as a call-to-arms, E. Merrill Root's *Brainwashing in the Schools* declared that Americans were losing the Cold War because the schools were failing to instill a love of democracy in its students. "The Communists, in carrying out their systemic brainwashing, knew what they could count on," Root explained in his 1958 study. In contrast, the American defectors in Korea had "yielded because they have never been taught to understand, as their Communist masters did understand, American politics, American economics,

American history and American ideals." Reviewing a dozen popular social studies textbooks, Root argued that the fear of nationalism in the years after the war had diluted the essential message about the absolute superiority of American constitutional democracy, but an unquestioned love of democracy needed to be reinstated in the schools to inspire the kind of patriotism that could withstand outside influence. Root demanded that students develop "a love of the United States of America that cannot be shaken by the brainwashers."[24] Root was, in essence, endorsing brainwashing U.S. students by inculcating them with a love of democracy.

Beyond these works by Ziemer, Counts, and Root, Jewish refugee scholars offered up more nuanced psychological insights into how totalitarians managed to gain and maintain control through various mind-control techniques that went beyond schooling. Drawing on their Freudian backgrounds in Europe, these refugees employed psychoanalytic constructs to explain the rise and acceptance of Nazism in provocative and influential ways.[25] Psychologist Bruno Bettelheim had spent nearly a year in German concentration camps before he was released and immigrated to the United States. While Bettelheim labored under horrific conditions in the camps, he studied its psychological effects on the captives as a survival technique to pass the time. After several rejections by journals due to Bettelheim's inability to record field notes during his ordeal, he eventually published his findings in a groundbreaking 1943 article, "Individual and Mass Behavior in Extreme Situations" for the *Journal of Abnormal and Social Psychology.* Bettelheim's article depicted the imprisonment as a psychological microcosm of the entire Nazi regime because the camps served as laboratories where the Nazis experimented with torture, indoctrination, and brainwashing. He explained how the longer the prisoners spent in the camps, the more they became "serfs who in many respects accept their masters' values" and concluded "that what happened in an extreme fashion to the prisoners who spend several years in the concentration camps happens in less exaggerated form to the inhabitants of the big concentration camp called Germany."[26] In *Childhood and Society*, published in 1950, psychologist Erik Erikson discussed the ways that Hitler's childhood and life experiences may have contributed to his irrational anti-Semitism and fanatical behavior. Arguing that Hitler shared many life experiences with his entire generation of Germans, Erikson concluded: "[I]t is our task to recognize that the black miracle of Nazism was only the German version—superbly planned and superbly bungled—of a universal contemporary potential."[27]

Drawing on Bettelheim's study, Hannah Arendt's *The Origins of Totalitarianism*, published in 1951, likewise depicted totalitarianism as a form of willful surrender by the citizenry and victims. "Through the creation of conditions under which conscience ceases to be adequate and to do good becomes utterly impossible," Arendt explained, "the consciously organized complicity of all men in the crimes of totalitarian regimes is extended to the victims and thus made really total."[28] Bettelheim, Arendt, and Erikson depicted totalitarianism as more than a form of government; it was a psychological potential in the subconscious that could afflict any person at any time under the right conditions. Totalitarianism originated as an existential crisis and the feeling of being alienated and unconnected from the modern world, and ended in the willful surrender of an individual's identity and rights to the broader goals of the regime. Since the potential for totalitarianism resided in the very nature of man, the totalitarian outlook could be present in the United States and other democracies. As Arthur Schlesinger, Jr., recognized in *The Vital Center*, totalitarianism represented "more than an internal crisis for democratic society. It signif[ied] an internal crisis for democratic man" because there was potentially "a Hitler, a Stalin in every breast."[29]

The willingness of citizens to surrender to the dictates of totalitarian leaders was the subject of one of the most influential and important psychological studies of the postwar years, *The Authoritarian Personality*. In their massive statistical study, psychologists Theodore Adorno, Else Frenkel-Brunswik, Daniel Levinson, and R. Nevitt Sanford constructed a battery of tests designed to detect dispositions and attitudes that made one more likely to adopt authoritarianism. The authors insisted that predicting potential authoritarian attitudes was no mere academic exercise; it was a pressing issue for a democratic society under constant totalitarian threat. "It seems apparent that any attempt to appraise the chances of a fascist triumph in America must reckon with the potential existing in the character of the people," the authors explained. "Here lies not only the susceptibility to antidemocratic propaganda but most dependable sources of resistance to it."[30] Predictably, their study found that many Americans did, in fact, demonstrate a preference for authoritarianism, and that this posed a problem for national culture. As Adorno and his colleagues warned: "If there should be a marked increase in antidemocratic propaganda, we should expect some people to accept and repeat it at once, others when it seemed that 'everybody believed it,' and still others not at all." Their study aimed to assess "this 'readiness level' in order to gauge the potential for fascism in this country."[31] The F-scale, developed during the study, became a widely used psychological instrument for the next 2 decades to assess noneconomic conservatism among subjects. A high score on the F-scale revealed a disposition considered potentially susceptible to fascism and incompatible with democratic life.[32]

Discrimination against both Jews and Blacks was analyzed throughout the *Authoritarian Personality* as well, because "a man who is hostile toward one minority group is very likely to be hostile against a wide variety of others." The authors found that individuals who were sympathetic to totalitarianism shared certain characteristics with racists because they were "superstitious, proud to be an individualist and in constant fear of not being liked by the others . . . and inclined to submit blindly to power and authority." Regarding prejudice against Jews and Blacks, the study found: "Increasing degrees of anti-Semitism were shown to be closely related to increasing opposition to . . . racial equality." *The Authoritarian Personality* was criticized for its assertion that prejudice could be reduced solely to issues of personality, instead of learned behavior, culture, and social structures. Yet the study pointed to the irrationality of persistent racism in the face of the lack of scientific evidence supporting racist views, making those with an authoritarian personality "potentially fascistic" and "particularly susceptible to anti-democratic propaganda."[33]

Even before the rise of totalitarianism and the emerging fears of brainwashing, educational psychologists had been concerned with the mental hygiene of American students. The rise of mental hygiene accompanied a growing therapeutic ethos among educators that sought to treat pathological mental conditions at the individual and group level.[34] The mental hygiene movement reached a peak during the postwar years because mental hygienists considered World War II and the Cold War as posing unprecedented psychological threats to students. This anxiety was underscored by the fact that nearly 30% of American draftees for World War II had to be dismissed as being mentally unfit for service, a number considered dangerously high for American society.[35] In 1946, Congress passed the National Mental Health Act, which reinforced the role of the federal government in the fostering of good mental health. The goal of mental hygienists was to identify and treat children before they became antisocial adolescents, thereby placing the school at the center of the movement. Some mental hygienists worried that an excessively academic curriculum demoralized many students and led to anxiety, feelings of inferiority, and antisocial behavior.

Even before the groundbreaking study by Adorno and his colleagues, mental hygienists correlated good mental health with democratic dispositions and poor mental health and authoritarian dispositions. As George Stevenson explained: "In this contest [between democracy and authoritarianism] mental hygiene as now conceived is identified more closely with democratic aims." Improving the mental health of the nation was not only humane and efficient, it was necessary for the maintenance of democracy in the face of authoritarianism. He continued: "The ultimate test of the principle of democracy lies not in its vulnerability to outside attack, but in the strength of the individual to withstand aggressions from within himself and his own society."[36]

Schools became the central location not only for teaching democratic dispositions but also for identifying and treating those students who lacked them. As one psychologist explained: "The public and private schools are admirable channels through which to foster a true, prophylactic mental hygiene program."[37] Citing the successful and efficient screening of millions of draftees during the war, Theodore Meltzer recommended that a trained psychiatrist examine every new high school and college student so that mental disorders could be identified and treated. A simple 10-minute evaluation, he explained, was all that was needed. Another mental hygienist suggested that group therapy could serve as a more practical way to reach large numbers of high school students than individual assessments. While not solving the overwhelming problem of the deteriorating mental health of the nation, he suggested, group therapy could at least arrest some of the feelings that may lead one to mental instability.[38]

The research on brainwashing, the authoritarian personality, race prejudice, and mental hygiene did not converge or overlap in any formal sense, but collectively these topics reflected an escalating anxiety over the mental health of the American citizenry in the 1950s. Researchers agreed that the mentally maladjusted individual was more likely to be persuaded by totalitarian influence. "Totalitarianism has shocked us into a reemphasis on the individual, the individual self-consciousness, and value of life, as of basic significance to all social services," mental hygienists John D. Griffin and William Line explained: "Hence the general search for satisfactory understanding of the psychodynamics of personal development."[39] Scholars' immediate and enduring concerns over healthy adjustment to postwar life help explain, in part, the implementation of the most ridiculed pedagogical program in U.S. history: life adjustment education.

LIFE ADJUSTMENT EDUCATION

Life adjustment education focused on curriculum flexibility, student guidance, and attention to previously neglected areas of social living such as mental hygiene, family living, drivers' education, and social relations with peers. Emphasis was on increasing the holding power of U.S. high schools by presenting students with a more meaningful and relevant curriculum and preparing them for a citizenship in the postwar world. In many ways, life adjustment education was the product of a longstanding antagonism to stand-alone academic subjects that originated with progressive education. However, life adjustment education was also a product of the same postwar anti-ideological context that inspired critics of progressive education because both were responses to broader fears of indoctrination, propaganda, and totalitarian thinking. After all, the term *adjustment* implied subtle, incremental change that adapted slowly and responsively to the actual conditions on the ground, as opposed to the term *reform*, which implied the wholesale rejection of existing conditions in light of some imagined utopian future. Reform was ideological; in contrast, adjustment was pragmatic, incremental, and slow. While academic critics sought a return to the traditional subjects as a way to bolster intellectual rigor, postwar educators sought well-adjusted citizens who would easily and readily resist communism through willful socialization to democratic norms. Leading social scientists believed that the authoritarian personality, aberrant behavior, and mental weakness had left adolescents vulnerable to communist propaganda and potential brainwashing, so proper adjustment served as an antidote to the feelings of alienation on which communists preyed. Adjusting students to middle-class life was the best antidote to these threats.

Life adjustment education also capitalized on the emphasis on teaching students how to think, not what to think, by focusing on the potential social problems that surrounded adolescents in their day-to-day life. Ultimately, with its focus on mere socialization, life adjustment education was a betrayal of both the traditional academic curriculum and the progressive curriculum because it circumvented the alleged irrelevancy of traditional academic subjects, while simultaneously undermining the consensus liberals' focus on teaching social issues. As one astute educator observed in 1954: "Many of the things going on in the schools today seem to appall some progressives as much as they do traditionalists."[40] Although contemporaries and historians have depicted life adjustment education as the culmination of progressive education, they have mostly ignored the broader context of anxiety surrounding mental hygiene, mind control, and brainwashing that provides much-needed context for understanding how and why schools implemented life adjustment education.

The movement formally began with the Prosser Resolution of 1948. Its author, Charles Prosser, was the director of Dunwoody Institute of Minneapolis and at the end of a long career in vocational education. Prosser designed his resolution to address the portion of the student population—believed to be about 60%—that did not benefit from either college preparation or vocational training. Concerns about general education had already been expressed by the reports of the American Youth Commission and the Harvard Committee in *Education in a Free Society*. In fact, the Harvard Committee had specifically drawn attention to the issue of social adjustment, writing: "The school will be concerned with the health of its pupils, both physical and mental." The Harvard Committee suggested that "the human body must be healthy, fit for work, able to carry out the purposes of the mind," and that schools focus on "personal adjustment, the individual's understanding of himself, his poise and adequacy in coping with real situations."[41]

However, unlike these reports, which merely issued recommendations, life adjustment education involved a mobilization of resources toward the rapid implementation of its goals that dwarfed previous efforts at systemic curriculum reform. A national conference on life adjustment was held in Washington, DC, in October 1951 and attended by more than 200 representatives from 38 states. The conference focused on two fundamental issues: (1) that many youth of secondary school age were not in school, and (2) that those who were in school "were not in programs well-adjusted to their interests, efforts, and probable future activity." The following year, over 200 representatives from 36 states attended another conference on life adjustment. The Second Commission of Life Adjustment estimated that more than 200,000 local teachers and administrators participated in workshops and conferences sponsored by state committees between 1951 and

1953, and 29 states had either appointed committees or designed programs on life adjustment. Between the issuing of the Prosser Resolution in 1948 and the 1951 conference, 25 different educational periodicals published a total of 116 articles on life adjustment education, and 40 bulletins were written in support of the movement. Supported by the U.S. Department of Health, Education and Welfare, life adjustment reformers were driven by an unprecedented sense of mission.[42]

Although certain social studies educators supported the goals of life adjustment education, the reform movement was primarily an external, top-down curricular initiative engineered by the second generation of curriculum specialists—that is, professionals with doctoral degrees in nonacademic curriculum design. In their doctoral programs, these specialists were trained specifically in the kind of scientific curriculum making first employed by Rugg in the late 1920s, and they applied this expertise to the curricula of state and local districts across the United States. "If the first thirty five years [of curriculum reform] were the day of the liberal arts professors," Rugg explained in 1947, "the last twenty have been that of the professors of education and the public school curriculum-makers."[43]

However, even though Rugg was a self-professed scientific curriculum designer, he was not entirely antagonistic to academic content, just its traditional arrangement. His issue-centered textbooks contained substantial academic content arranged thematically. As Rugg explained in the introduction to his 1940 textbook *Citizenship and Civic Affairs*, his interdisciplinary approach ". . . has not caused a reduction in the amount of history or of geography in the course. Rather it has produced a sharp increase in the amount of these subjects in the curriculum and, in addition, has added to the curriculum a wealth of new material."[44] On the other hand, the next generation of curriculum specialists was less deferential to the academic expertise of college professors. No one would be more influential on the design of curriculum in the postwar years than University of Chicago professor of education Ralph Tyler.

After the publication of his classic text, *Basic Principles of Curriculum and Instruction*, Tyler would become the most influential curriculum specialist in the country; his enduring influence would even exceed that of Rugg.[45] As Tyler explained, curriculum design involved four steps: selecting objectives, determining learning experiences, organizing activities, and planning for evaluation. Regarding the determination of objectives, Tyler explained: "[R]ecognize the fact that, fundamentally, education means changing the way human beings behave: the way students think, feel and act and that the ultimate success of any education enterprise must be judged in terms of individual growth in good living." Tyler also suggested that teachers select "learning experiences in response to real needs . . . when [the student] comprehends his personal relationship to the problem, the more probable it is that he will show changes in his behavior." When organizing activities, Tyler explained, it is crucial to connect the material to the lives and occupations of students. He insisted that teachers should ask: "How can the school connect democratic practices and real living so that citizenship can be practiced in students' actual behavior?"[46] Tyler adopted the postwar obsession with citizenship education and linked it with the concerns about scientific thinking, mental hygiene, authoritarian thinking, and mind control.

According to Tyler and the curriculum specialists, course objectives were not listed in terms of intellectual growth, but rather in terms of acquired or modified personal behaviors and attitudes that could be applied directly toward present social problems. On this point, I. James Quillen of Stanford University was explicit: "Social studies objectives should: (a) be stated as descriptions of behaviors; (b) be related to each other so as to focus on the development of the total personality of youth."[47] The dozens of social studies curriculum guides and programs published during the years of life adjustment education were virtually all organized in the manner described by Tyler and Quillen. They listed objectives in terms of observable behaviors and attitudes, listed possible learning activities, and suggested ways to evaluate the acquisition of the desired attitudes and behaviors. Although academic content was still included, the curriculum specialists emphasized the importance of organizing content around present and interdisciplinary problems instead of around academic subjects.[48]

As a result of the new curriculum specialists, an explosion in the production of curriculum guides occurred in the years following World War II, especially in the fields of language arts and social studies. In an exhaustive review of these new curricular materials published between 1951 and 1953, researchers reported that, instead of taking a chronological approach, 88% of the newly designed history/social studies courses were organized around learning units, "over half of which were based on combinations of aspects of social living, themes, and concepts." The reviewers also noted "a tendency to fuse history, geography, civics, and economics . . . in the study of state, city, or community."[49] The immediate effects of life adjustment education on the rhetoric of the social studies curriculum were present in Edwin Carr's 1956 assessment of current trends in the curriculum. In his review of the field, he identified increases in "matters of personal adjustment," "emphasis on better family living," "emphasis on improving intergroup relations," "emphasis on community study," and "pupil-teacher planning." Regarding the encroachment of such issues and approaches into the curriculum, Carr offered the following defense: "The legitimacy of dealing with personal-social topics in social studies is evident. . . . The question is not as to their propriety—the question is the provision of a greater amount of time for the social studies so that the teacher can do justice to individual and social needs."[50] Carr not only failed to express reservations about the abandonment of the traditional, academic arrangement of content, he wholly endorsed the revisions that sought to replace it. He was not alone in his enthusiasm about these reforms. His ideas were present in the numerous state, city, and local curriculum guides and programs, many of which were authored by or with curriculum specialists and consultants.[51]

In some schools, the senior Problems of Democracy course, originally designed by the 1916 Committee on Social Studies to combine history and the social sciences in light of present-day problems facing the U.S. democracy, morphed into problems facing the social life and adjustment needs of individual students. In other words, in many schools the concept of "problem" was reinterpreted from a collective, social science–based issue facing the nation—as recommended by the 1916 Committee on Social Studies—to a potential emotional challenge facing a student in her or his daily routine. Accordingly, the 7th-grade social studies objectives for the Course of Study (guide) for the State of Alabama listed the following: "To develop through guidance in suitable work, observation, reading, conference, and participation in home, school, and community life social attitudes and understandings." Activities listed under citizenship development included "[m]aking school lunch period a sociable one; and planning for recreation during the lunch period."[52]

Overall, life adjustment education had three major effects on the social studies curriculum as expressed in the local and state curriculum guides (although not necessarily in practice). First, these curricula employed the language of student "adjustment" and "needs" and often directly attacked in stand-alone academic subjects. Objectives were listed in terms of observable behaviors, not intellectual engagement or growth. Second, these curricula emphasized that teachers should include students in planning the substance of study and that teachers should make direct connections to the local community. The social studies curriculum, life adjustment educators argued, should be responsive and flexible. Third, these curricula demonstrate that in many states the definition of democratic education was expanded both internally and externally. Internally, the subject matter was broadened to include life adjustment topics that went well beyond the narrow limits of the academic disciplines, including social and marriage counseling, drivers' education, family living, and interpersonal relations. Externally, the entire school and curriculum often pursued the objective of "citizenship education" by linking community projects and student involvement to this broader goal. Through this process, the discourse of the social studies at the state and local level diverged from the recommendations of the 1916 Committee on Social Studies, the interwar collectivists, and the postwar deliberation-centered liberals, and instead followed the dictates of the scientific curriculum makers and mental hygienists. During the life adjustment education movement, the social studies curriculum in many schools became more of a process than a body of knowledge, and more of a list of narrowly conceived, observable behaviors than a path toward intellectual development. Despite its obvious and well-documented shortcomings, life adjustment education makes sense when understood in the context of broad concerns about the psychological health of adolescents, brainwashing, mental hygiene, and suburbanization.

EDUCATIONAL BRAINWASHING

When postwar critics attacked the foundations of progressive education, they focused mainly on two targets: its alleged anti-intellectualism and its ideological radicalism. When looking for evidence of anti-intellectualism, life adjustment education provided ample and current examples. However, when looking for evidence of radicalism, they often focused on the work of Theodore Brameld, because other former radicals such as Counts, Hook, and Childs had not only corrected their views but were currently leading the charge against communism and the ideas of Soviet Russia. The wealth of published teaching materials created for life adjustment education provided effective evidence for critics of progressive education. The exact impact of progressive education during the interwar years was notoriously local, opaque, and hard to document. In contrast, life adjustment education was centrally directed, transparent, and supported by reams of published rationales and curricula. As a result, critics not only found a plethora of evidence to support their assertions about the absurdity of life adjustment education, they clearly reveled in the act of mocking the anti-intellectualism they discovered in these documents.

For example, Arthur Bestor dismissed life adjustment as "a parody of education" that enthroned "the ancient doctrine that a clear majority of the people are destined from birth to be hewers of wood and drawers of water."[53] Mortimer Smith attacked life adjustment education as a "hotchpotch of unexceptional vague clichés."[54] *Time* magazine described life adjustment education as "the latest gimmick among U.S. educators," reflecting the belief that "the teacher's job was not so much to teach history or algebra, as to prepare students to live happily ever after."[55] Richard Hofstadter won the ridicule Olympics with his quip: "Life adjustment educators would do anything in the name of science except encourage children to study it."[56] Life adjustment education made the critiques of progressive ideology by Bestor, Smith, and Hofstadter seem trenchant, pressing, and persuasive. In fact, for the next 50 years, few, if any, educators (or historians, for that matter) defended the goals, materials, and rhetoric of life adjustment education. The movement was generally regarded as the worst idea in the history of U.S. education.[57]

In addition to life adjustment education, the other postwar target was Brameld, a professor of education at the University of Minnesota and New York University. Brameld had been one of the most radical collectivists in the mid-1930s, incorporating the ideas of Marx, focusing on class conflict as a central component of educational reform, and even suggesting that violence was sometimes necessary to effect change. Brameld's first book, *A Philosophical Approach to Communism*, employed Marxist rhetoric to call for a mobilization of the *proletariat* in the overthrow of *bourgeois* values, and he invited teachers to identify with the former and participate in the revolution. Dewey and Raup objected to Brameld's divisive focus on class and challenged his views in the *Social Frontier*. Brameld countered that Marx provided some analytic tools that naturalism could not and was therefore needed to bring about the kind of social change they all desired.[58] By combining Marxist analysis and naturalistic epistemology in the 1930s, Brameld was no different from Reinhold Niebuhr, Max Eastman, and Sidney Hook, but unlike these scholars, Brameld did not abandon his class-based analysis during and after the war. In *Design for America*, published in 1945, Brameld capitalized on the postwar spirit of internationalism and peace by doubling down on his international collectivism and call for radical reform.

Design for America reported on a study Brameld had conducted at Fleetwood High School in Minnesota in which he had students generate a list of social goals for the future and then designed a curriculum around the discussion of these goals. Brameld assessed how the program contributed to the increased "liberality" of students' thought regarding issues of social and economic justice. Based on this study, he forged a postwar vision for democracy grounded in goal setting, peaceful class conflict, mass persuasion, and democratic reconstruction through the discussion of controversial social and economic issues.[59] Published alongside a flood of books addressing the promise and challenges of international peace and postwar democracy, *Design for America* received little attention. However, Brameld's next major work, published 5 years later, met a hostile audience eager to pounce on any remnants of ideology, radical collectivism, and alleged attempts at brainwashing students.

Brameld's *Patterns of Educational Philosophy: A Democratic Interpretation* was intended as an introductory textbook on the philosophy of education. As such, he surveyed the philosophical landscape and identified four intellectual approaches to education: progressivism, essentialism, perennialism, and reconstructionism. He aligned the first with the student-centered pedagogy of Dewey and Kilpatrick, the second with the content- and test-centered focus of William Bagley and Edward Thorndike, the third with the epistemological absolutism of Hutchins, and the fourth with the radical collectivism of 1930s-era Counts, Beard, and himself. The final section of the book made a robust and reasoned case for the necessity of reconstructionism in education. Brameld controversially embraced "the twin principles, ideology and utopia" and denounced objectivity and scientific thinking as educational goals, thereby challenging the reigning anti-ideological approach of the period. "Reconstructionist education takes sides," Brameld clarified. "It encourages students, teachers, and all members of the community not merely to study knowledge and problems . . . but also to make up their minds about the most promising solutions and then to act concertedly." In place of detachment and ideological skepticism, Brameld endorsed a "commitment to agreed-upon future-looking goals." He considered indoctrination and propaganda to be unavoidable in teaching, and in certain instances they were "indispensable" in creating a more democratic utopian order. He employed Marxist rhetoric by inviting teachers to unite with "the growing militarism of other wage-earning citizens" so that "the education profession, and therefore public education as a whole" could "become truly great instruments in the remaking of civilization." But to do so, teachers needed to "become courageous, purposeful, united, and aggressive." *Patterns of Educational Philosophy* was published at the absolute peak of Cold War anxiety over communist infiltration. As such, references to class conflict, mobilization, aggressive action, conflict, propaganda, indoctrination, and ideology could not have been more out of step with postwar liberalism.[60]

Predictably, postwar critics reveled in the atavistic collectivist rhetoric Brameld employed and considered it extremely dangerous in a domestic front under communist threat. They equated his commitment to collectivism with brainwashing. In a chapter in *The Diminished Mind* entitled "Educational Brain-Washing, Democratic Style," Mortimer Smith specifically attacked the ideas expressed by Brameld in *Patterns of Educational Philosophy* and the less combative but similar ideas espoused by B. Orthanel Smith, William O. Stanley, and J. Harlan Shores in *Fundamentals of Curriculum Development*. These books "are written by men who call themselves scholars and are put forward as scientific discussions of educational matters," Smith argued, "but actually the authors are zealots and reformers who are writing propaganda." Former radicals "Counts and Sidney Hook," Smith reminded readers, "have long since learned the bitter lesson that communism is not just a more radical liberalism, but is actually a conspiracy against the whole non-Soviet world." Brameld, according to Smith, had not learned this lesson by continuing to espouse collectivism as a solution to the problems of democratic life. Specifically, Smith considered Brameld's attempt to increase the "liberality" of students described in *American By Design* to be a form of brainwashing—an approach preferred by totalitarians.[61]

Brameld countered that the greatest weakness of liberal democracy was "its very pride in open-mindedness and tolerance" that justified the status quo. He pondered: "Surely it is possible to advocate a planned democracy—for the precise purpose of meeting the challenge of totalitarianism" without being accused of supporting totalitarianism, but few were convinced.[62] Frederick Lilge further attacked Brameld's *Patterns of Educational Philosophy* in an extended review and critique for the *Harvard Educational Review*. According to Lilge, Brameld refused to accept the "waning of the earlier radical spirit" by seeking "to rescue what fragments of the bolder ideas of the thirties he can" while espousing ideas that can be traced "back to Marx rather than Dewey." Lilge objected to Brameld's dismissal of the non-reconstructionist philosophies as "ideologies of unstable defunct and reactionary societies" and saw his whole project as leading to "the dead end of anti-rationalism."[63]

Both Smith and Lilge admitted that the majority of educational theorists had long abandoned the radical collectivism espoused by Brameld, and that few teachers were likely to adopt his ideas. Yet they considered Brameld's ideas to be an extreme example of the broader threat of progressive education and naturalistic epistemology. The twin evils of radicalism and anti-intellectualism revealed that professors of education could not be trusted any more to run the schools and prepare the next generation of teachers. Academic professors, they convinced themselves, would need to step in to save education from the educationists. While retaining an allegiance to teaching how to think, not what to think, postwar consensus liberals looked to the academic disciplines as a way to rescue the curriculum from the ideological ideas of progressive educators. In place of alleged brainwashing, college professors claimed to offer disciplined inquiry and scientific rigor.

CHAPTER 7

In the Shadow of *Sputnik*

In October 1957—only a few years after the defection of the American POWs to Korea—the Soviet Union successfully launched a beach ball–sized satellite called *Sputnik* into orbit, propelling the Soviet Union ahead of the United States in the international space race. The satellite and its follow-up, *Sputnik II*, launched a month later, represented a huge blow to American self-esteem, and yet another sign that the Americans were losing the Cold War. "The Soviet Union's conquests of space, its capability of producing not only powerful weapons but also an effective industrial society," Harvard psychologist Jerome Bruner reflected, "have shaken American complacency to a degree that, looking back, would have seemed inconceivable a decade ago."[1] *Life* magazine insisted, "Let us not pretend that *Sputnik* is anything but a defeat for the United States," and Senator John F. Kennedy stated that the satellite proved that "the Soviet Union is on the march . . . and we were standing still."[2] The critics of life adjustment education and numerous reporters blamed U.S. schools for their inability to generate the manpower needed to compete with the Soviet Union. A multipart series in *Life* magazine and the *Los Angeles Times* insisted that *Sputnik* had revealed a "crisis" in education. While Russian children were studying math and science, American children were studying how to be popular and how to go on a date. George Counts pointed out that Russian scientists who designed *Sputnik* would have attended school during the 1920s and 1930s, so the current state of Russian education was irrelevant.[3] Nevertheless, calls for massive and fundamental reform of the U.S. curriculum met a receptive audience eager to purge the remnants of progressive education from the schools and restore the rigor needed to win the Cold War.

Moreover, the launching of *Sputnik* challenged the narrative that U.S. schools taught students how to think, while the authoritarian Russian schools merely taught their students what to think. *Sputnik* also complicated the alleged superiority of scientific inquiry in a democracy, as outlined by Robert Merton. After all, did the launching of *Sputnik* not require both critical thinking and cutting-edge science? Just as they had done in 1920s, several U.S. educators visited the Soviet Union to examine its schools. They discovered that previous reports of rote learning and indoctrination in Russian schools had been exaggerated. Based on his firsthand account of the Russian schools, U.S. Commissioner of Education Lawrence Derthick reported in 1958: "[W]e are simply not prepared for the degree to which the U.S.S.R. as a nation is committed to education as a means of national advancement. . . . The privileged class in Russia is the children." Senator Hubert Humphrey echoed this concern in 1960, declaring, "the real threat to America's world leadership comes not from Soviet rockets, but from Soviet schools."[4]

By 1957, the student-centered wing of progressive education had already been winding down (the Progressive Education Association had disbanded in 1955), and several curriculum projects were already underway to increase the rigor of American schoolwork in math and science. However, the architects of these projects did not hope to turn back the clock to the pre-progressive days of teacher-and-textbook centered instruction. Instead they forged ahead with an even sharper focus on teaching students how to think, not what to think. Only this time, instead of turning to professors of education and their discredited theories about relevance and student interests, policymakers looked to college professors in academic disciplines, who were seen to know better than anyone else how to teach critical thinking and disciplined inquiry in a rigorous way. Riding a wave of unprecedented prestige and awash in federal funding, college professors employed the inherent power of the academic disciplines in an effort to restore rigor to the U.S. curriculum and win the Cold War. Still using totalitarianism as their *other*, they hoped to employ the academic disciplines to inspire open-mindedness and creativity.

THE RHETORIC AND REALITY OF SCHOOL PRACTICE

After *Sputnik*, most critics agreed that the pervasive influence of progressive education was the reason U.S. schools were in such poor shape. However, throughout its history, both critics and proponents of progressive education tended to exaggerate the extent that reforms permeated the classroom at the local level. Attempts at changing teacher-centered instruction between 1916 and 1958 had been only partially successful. Even grant-funded programs such as core curriculum, propaganda analysis, and issue-based instruction left researchers frustrated, because teachers and students often resisted attempts at meaningful reform. Yet the language of life adjustment education had made a substantial impact on, at least, the rhetoric of local curriculum guides. This raises questions: What exactly was the overall impact of the 40 years of rhetoric about the importance of teaching students how to think, not what to think? Were critics correct about the social studies replacing traditional history? Were critics correct about the student-centered, functional curriculum replacing the academic one?

It is notoriously difficult to assess what was, or is, going on in U.S. classrooms at any given time. Without descriptions of classroom practice on a massive scale, the historian can make only informed inferences based on course offerings, course enrollments, and case studies of local districts about what was going on at the classroom level. Further, only the most ambitious teachers published in professional journals, schools retained a great deal of local control, and teachers and principals had the authority to simply ignore the recommendations of state bureaucrats and educational experts. Most teachers were underqualified and inexperienced, and counterprogressive forces such as the conservative recommendations of the College Board—which administered college entrance exams prior to World War II—blunted many of the proposed changes.[5] Some historians have argued that the U.S. curriculum remained more or less static throughout the 20th century as teachers, parents, and administrators successfully deflected any meaningful reform.[6] Others historians have argued that the ideas of progressive education fundamentally transformed American classrooms by the 1950s.[7] The truth lies somewhere in the middle, although the overall reality of classroom practices was probably characterized more by constancy than change.

Reflecting on why the problem-based instructional pamphlets he coauthored in the 1960s were at such a high intellectual level, one researcher explained that "we imagined three groups [of teachers]: those who would never agree to or would not understand this approach . . . those who be sympathetic and interested but would need significant staff development to succeed, . . . [and] those highly committed to the approach and able to implement if they only had adequate instructional materials."[8] The researchers aimed their issue-based instructional pamphlets at the most motivated group, knowing the majority of teachers would ignore, distort, or water down their approach beyond recognition. School survey data and local curriculum guides from the first half of the 20th century corroborates this assessment of teachers, schools, and pedagogy. Roughly a third of U.S. teachers, administrators, and schools were committed to a substantial degree of meaningful reform related to incorporating a relevant, student-centered curriculum, social issues, critical thinking, and/or life adjustment; roughly another third of teachers and schools incorporated the language of reform at a superficial level without fundamentally altering their teacher-and-subject-centered curriculum and pedagogy in any major way; and another third of teachers and schools completely ignored these reforms altogether. Overall, the number of students who experienced the discussion of social issues in the classroom increased substantially between 1916 and 1958, yet, overall, the *majority*—likely two-thirds of students—never experienced anything beyond teacher-and-textbook-centered, chronological history with no reference to deliberation, inquiry, or critical thinking whatsoever. In other words, prior to *Sputnik*, only a third of students were really being taught how to think, not what to think, despite what progressive critics and advocates proclaimed.[9]

When critics of progressive and life adjustment education made claims about the pervasive displacement of traditional history by social studies, or academic classes by progressive ones, and teacher-centered methods by student-centered ones, they were greatly exaggerating. Survey data on course enrollments by the U.S. Bureau of Education was easily available, but these critics—inadvertently or advertently—had not done their homework. Writing in 1957, the same year as the launch of *Sputnik*, two educators from Maryland provided a more accurate and sobering assessment. They recognized an overall increase in "provisions made for common citizenship education," but otherwise observed only superficial change in the curriculum since World War II. Despite "an increase in the number and variety of courses offered, greater emphasis on guidance, more attention to extra-curricular activities," they concluded, "there has been relatively little *basic* change to the curriculum. . . . Academic courses continue to hold their time-honored position."[10]

The reality of the impact of progressive education on classroom practice was irrelevant since the media and critics echoed the perception that U.S. schools had lost their way and that progressive educators were to blame. The 1959 book by Admiral H. G. Rickover, *Education and Freedom*, marked an important pivot point away from earlier concern about the epistemological vulnerability to communism that progressive education was said to create, toward the more pressing concern that U.S. schools were not generating enough manpower to compete with the Russians in scientific expertise. "The future belongs to the best-educated nation," Rickover insisted. "[I]ntellectual discipline is essential to our national purpose."[11] This sentiment echoed an earlier 1955 report by Nicholas DeWitt, *Soviet Professional Manpower*, which demonstrated that ideological indoctrination in Marxism-Leninism did not necessarily impede Russian scholars' ability to conduct research in the hard sciences. DeWitt confirmed: "[T]he Soviet educational system offers much more than our own in the teaching of science at the secondary-level."[12] Congressmen, Senators, and eventually President Eisenhower agreed. In response to *Sputnik*, they passed the National Defense Education Act in 1958, which provided modest support for improvements in math, science, and foreign language instruction and ended a longstanding antagonism to federal funding in education.[13]

THE TWO CULTURES OF SOCIAL SCIENCE

To fix the schools, policymakers turned to college professors in the academic disciplines and deliberately away from professors of education. The most recognized figure in educational reform during the postwar years was Jerome Bruner, professor of psychology at Harvard University. Bruner was a leader in cognitive psychology, a subfield he had helped found after World War II. Focused on the nonobservable aspects of thinking, cognitive psychology required methodological creativity and interdisciplinary study of the mind. Bruner's dissertation, completed in 1941, analyzed Nazi propaganda techniques. He discovered that Nazi propaganda exploited the Germans' irrational, emotional, and erroneous misconceptions about the world by telling them compelling, but false, stories that confirmed their personal experiences and fears. Bruner concluded that democratic education ought to do the exact opposite by teaching accurate information that challenged people's preconceived notions through critical thinking about how the world actually worked. The academic disciplines were the best tools to do this. Throughout his work, Bruner also emphasized that the rational side of the brain must work in tandem with the creative side of the brain.[14] Both were necessary for true critical thinking to occur.

In the 1950s, social scientists had worked hard to separate the rational and creative approaches, so Bruner entered a field initially antagonistic to his cognitive approach. Historian Andrew Jewett argues that there was "two cultures" of social science research during the postwar years: one culture that approached social science in an objective, positivistic, narrowly defined way, and another culture that accepted a more holistic, cultural, and qualitative explanations of phenomena. In other words, one culture of social science defined itself in opposition to the humanities, while the other looked to the humanities as a source of creativity and innovation. Both research cultures embraced the postwar scientific ethos of political independence and rejected the progressives' embrace of ideology, but they differed over what counted as scientific.[15]

In psychology, the first culture was represented by behaviorist B. F. Skinner, whose 1954 article "The Science of Learning and the Art of Teaching" dismissed the study of all nonobservable psychological objectives—such as "develop[ing] the mind" and "understanding"—as vague, unscientific approaches that were impossible to study with precision.[16] In his famous (or notorious) article, Skinner reduced teaching to mere conditioning through positive reinforcement, introduced his Skinner box as a teaching "machine" that could guide students toward the correct response through rewards, and suggested that teachers focus their energy on the nonscientific aspects of teaching, such as tending to students' personal and emotional needs. Thus, Skinner controversially sought to establish a sharp distinction between the *science* and the *art* of teaching; the former was the masculine domain of behavioral psychology, the latter the feminine domain of humanism.

The second culture was represented by Bruner, who dismissed the narrow rigidity of behavioral psychology, embraced a developmental/Freudian approach to mind, and employed the interdisciplinary, humanistic, and creative study of thinking. Bruner crafted his cognitive approach to psychology in direct opposition to Skinner's behaviorism, which had dominated the field since World War I. As historian Jamie Cohen-Cole explains, after World War II, cognitive psychologists viewed behaviorists "as both fascistic and unscientific" because behaviorists "narrow-mindedly" conducted "research from the perspective of a single discipline." One psychologist even insisted that the methodological and epistemological rigidity of behaviorism was the equivalent of an "ideology" because it both limited the questions that could be asked about the mind and prevented creativity in proposing solutions and new methodologies.[17] Bruner believed that cognitive psychology was not only a more accurate way to study and understand the working of the mind, but was also a better fit for the post-ideological world that valued open-ended inquiry and creativity as civic virtues. Bruner's cognitive approach aligned with the growing trend toward cultural and humanistic explanations of social phenomena.

Bruner's cognitive psychology shared a holistic, interdisciplinary, psychoanalytic, and holistic approach to knowledge with the new subfields of intellectual history, American studies, and cultural anthropology. All of these fields explored American exceptionalism through the lens of culture. The academic disciplines under totalitarian regimes had been perverted and distorted, so Bruner and like-minded social scientists sought to explore the ways in which disciplined inquiry in a democracy—and specifically American democracy—differed from inquiry under fascism and Marxism-Leninism. Behavioral approaches to knowledge did not allow researchers to address the issue of American exceptionality convincingly, so they turned to more creative, interdisciplinary, and cultural methodologies. As Bruner wrote in 1966: "Knowing is a process, not a product."[18]

The key to Bruner's new interdisciplinary approach was that inquiry went through multiple disciplines, but it did not circumvent the disciplines altogether. One of the major postwar critiques of progressive education was that it did not afford proper respect for disciplined inquiry. Because progressives viewed disciplines as detached from real-world problems, they either dismissed academic disciplines as outdated and irrelevant, or, in the case of Dewey, denied the inherent superiority of disciplined inquiry over other forms of inquiry.[19] In contrast, postwar theorists of disciplined inquiry, such as Bruner, argued that disciplines offered the best, most accurate way to examine the world. To make their case, they tried to free the academic disciplines from their alleged rigidity and irrelevance by casting the disciplines in broader civic and cultural terms. The phrase "structure of the disciplines" reflected this effort by placing academic disciplines at the center of the school curriculum, and by conveying the disciplines' conceptual, intuitive, and flexible nature. Bruner and like-minded professors argued that understanding the structures of the discipline allowed students to apply the rigor and creativity of the disciplines to their civic life.

THE STRUCTURE OF THE DISCIPLINES

Despite their exaggeration of the impact of progressive education on the curriculum, the accusations made by postwar critics such as Arthur Bestor, Mortimer Smith, Robert Hutchins, and Admiral Rickover found a receptive audience.[20] Bestor, author of *Educational Wastelands* and *The Restoration of Learning*, was the most effective, convincing, and prophetic critic of recent educational reforms. Bestor's critique resonated so well with many of his colleagues in higher education because he insisted that education must *necessarily* pass through the "scholarly and scientific disciplines." His focus on thinking, and specifically *disciplined* thinking, diverged from the discussion/deliberation approach of social studies educators like Griffin, Hunt and Metcalf, the premodern Socratic seminars of Hutchins and Adler, and the generic problem-solving techniques of Dewey, but converged with postwar liberals' focus on ideological skepticism and scientific thinking. It also emphasized teaching how to think, not what to think, by aligning disciplined thinking with democratic life. "[I]f the schools neglect their vital function of intellectual training, the loss to society is an irreparable one," Bestor explained. "Intellectual training may seem a formidable phrase. But it means nothing more than the deliberate cultivation of the ability to think."[21] During the late 1950s and early 1960s, the focus on how to think, not what to think, continued to gain ground, but instead of focusing on predisciplinary or extra-disciplinary thinking, as the progressives had done, the academic professors who sought to rescue the curriculum focused specifically on inquiry *in* and *through* the academic disciplines.

Joseph Schwab, a profession of education at the University of Chicago, was a key figure in the postwar transition from an emphasis on the generic five steps of reflective thinking outlined by Dewey in *How We Think*, to the new focus on the nonlinear messiness of discipline-specific thinking. Schwab was a prodigy who graduated high school at age 15. He obtained an undergraduate degree in English and graduate degrees in zoology and genetics, all from the University of Chicago. His training and background made him uniquely qualified to write on the relationship among the humanities, sciences, and pedagogy. Under the tutelage of President Hutchins, Schwab was encouraged to make these connections and implement them in the University's general curriculum for undergraduates. Schwab drew on the work of Dewey to make his case for a discipline-centered, rigorous curriculum that aligned with the goals of liberal, civic, and general education. Throughout his work, Schwab depicted the discipline of science, including its methods, as dynamic, pluralistic, open-ended, and creative, instead of rigid or formulaic.[22]

In an article published in 1949, "The Nature of Scientific Knowledge as Related to Liberal Education," Schwab recommended that college students first be introduced to the methods, procedures, and dispositions of science before they learned the facts and theories that these methods produced. This was a reversal of the order in which these things were usually taught. Instead of focusing on "coverage," Schwab argued that an introductory science course should be focused on "the complexities of science, philosophy, and history" but also on ". . . learning the exercise of analytic and critical thinking."[23] That is, as Dewey had pointed out decades earlier, the methods of science were themselves historical and philosophical events that reflected cultural assumptions about the period in which they were employed. Approaching science as historical and contextual not only linked science to the humanities but also conveyed the dynamic, fluid, and creative nature of the discipline. Further, Schwab argued, by focusing on the inquiry methods of the discipline instead of its facts, the student "sees that authority consists not in possession of information but in possession of competence in inquiry."[24] "Competence in inquiry" was just another way of saying that teaching how to think was as important as teaching what to think in the postwar world.

In an essay on "the structures of the discipline," Schwab asserted: "[T]o know what structures underlie a given body of knowledge is to know what problems we shall face in imparting this knowledge." Schwab's suggestion that the problems of teaching were to be found exclusively in the discipline, instead of in the student, classroom, community, or society, demonstrated how far scholars had come from the assumptions of progressive pedagogy. According to Schwab, the structure of the discipline consisted of four aspects: first, the subject matter; second, the competencies and habits of the disciplinary practitioners; third, the "the modes of enquiry by which the enquirer brings himself to bear on the subject matter;" and fourth, the ends to which the practitioner puts his or her work. These four aspects were dynamic and evolved in relation to one another. Schwab asserted that learning the structures of the discipline would better equip students for democratic life than a "the purely dogmatic, inculcative" curriculum because "indoctrination" would "create division and failure of communication among our citizens."[25] Understanding the structures of the discipline would also allow students to consider future advancements and revisions within each field, thus preparing them for the rest of their lives. Schwab's approach to the disciplined inquiry represents yet another example of how postwar liberals adopted some aspects of progressive education, such as the focus on thinking and the dynamic, contextualized nature of knowledge, while rejecting others, such as ideology, student interests, and using the school as an instrument of social reform.

Schwab's prose was dense, difficult, and expressed in academic jargon. However, Jerome Bruner introduced the structure of the disciplines in an accessible and inviting way in his 1960 book, *The Process of Education*, which would go on to sell several hundred thousand copies and be translated into 21 languages.[26] "Professor Bruner's little book *The Process of Education* may eventually prove to be the most influential volume ever written about curriculum," one professor commented in 1966. "Bruner has become a latter-day John Dewey."[27] The book was the product of a September 1959 conference in Woods Hole, Massachusetts, attended by 35 scientists, scholars, and educators who sought to "examine the fundamental processes involved in imparting to young students a sense of the substance and method of science." As Bruner related at the conference: "[T]eaching machines were demonstrated by professor B. F. Skinner of Harvard, and the demonstration led to a lively, at times stormy discussion," but the findings Bruner presented in the book reflected a complete rejection of Skinner's behavioral psychology, which he affiliated with mere fact recall and formulaic thinking skills. Instead Bruner proposed that the curriculum should not be focused on the transmission of information or the conditioning of behaviors; rather, it should focus on developing an appreciation for and application of the structures of the disciplines. "Mastery of the fundamental ideas of a field involves not only grasping of general principles," Bruner reasoned, "but also the development of an attitude toward learning and inquiry, toward guessing and hunches, toward the possibility of solving problems on one's own."[28] Understanding the structures of the disciplines would not only make learning more active, it would generate deeper understanding of the content and allow for the transfer of knowledge to novel situations. The structure of the disciplines could also serve as an antidote to indoctrination and the kind of rigid conformity that totalitarianism demanded.

Beyond Bruner, the most influential figure in introducing the "structure of the disciplines" approach to the schools was Massachusetts Institute of Technology (MIT) professor Jerrold Zacharias, who was one of the attendees at the Woods Hole conference. As Bruner later reflected, "I think it was Zach, more than anybody else, who converted the Sputnik shock into the curriculum reform movement." Zacharias had received funding from the National Science Foundation in the early 1950s to create the Physical Science Study Committee. The Committee would ultimately produce 56 films, a textbook, and numerous materials for laboratory experiments in physics, all based on narrowing "the gap between knowledge locked up in university library or the scholar's mind and the fare being taught in schools." Like Schwab and Bruner, Zacharias hoped to bridge the breach "between intellectuals and non-intellectuals" and "between humanitarians and scientists" with the physics materials he helped create.[29]

Schwab, Bruner, and Zacharias framed their "structure of the disciplines" approach to pedagogy in civic terms, and they viewed disciplined thinking as a defense against authoritarian thinking at home and abroad. To teach anything less than disciplined inquiry, Schwab reasoned in opaque language referencing the totalitarianism of Nazi Germany and the Soviet Union, was "to capitulate to the notion of Mass and Class—the latter managerial and manipulative; the former, managed servants, unaware."[30] In *The Process of Education*, Bruner asserted: "One thing seems clear: if all students are helped to full utilization of their power, we will have a better chance of surviving as a democracy in an age of enormous technological and social complexity."[31] Behavioral and progressive approaches to social science and learning overlooked the open-mindedness of disciplined reasoning, and thus these approaches left the individual vulnerable to totalitarianism. Yet, understanding disciplined inquiry and the use of evidence to support assertions enabled students to approach their world critically. "Having lived through World War II, Hitler, Stalin, Joe McCarthy," Zacharias explained, "it was perfectly clear that you had to get used to the notion that you have to understand why you believe what you believe . . . where's the evidence? Show me . . ."[32] These scholars likely packaged their curriculum vision in Cold War fears of totalitarianism, in part, to help gain funding, influence, and acceptance. Nevertheless, their belief in the power of the academic discipline to save the American curriculum and American culture from authoritarian and closed-minded thinking was sincere. This faith—one could call it arrogance—reflected a period in which the university professor was held in the highest esteem.

ACADEMIC PROFESSORS TO THE RESCUE

Policymakers turned to the academic disciplines as potential saviors of the U.S. curriculum for three reasons. First, there was a dialectical aspect to their emphasis on disciplined thinking. The traditional, pre-progressive curriculum was characterized by rote learning and teacher-and-textbook centered instruction in academic subjects, which was justified, in part, by the mental faculties approach to learning, positing that memorization and recitation strengthened the mental muscles of the mind. The research of Edward Thorndike on transfer discredited this mental faculties theory. Progressive educators used Thorndike's research to target the academic curriculum and replace it with a more relevant, functional and student-centered curriculum focused on critical thinking.[33] The structure of the disciplines approach espoused by Schwab, Bruner, and Zacharias steered a middle course between traditional and progressive pedagogy by rejecting the rote memorization of the traditional approach and the student-centeredness of the progressive approach, yet retaining the traditional focus on academic content and the progressive focus on critical thinking. Thus, the structure of the disciplines approach aimed to transcend the teacher-centered/student-centered divide by combining the rigor of the traditional curriculum with the critical thinking of the progressive curriculum.

Second, the structure of the disciplines approach aimed to foster an open mind that could make connections, understand evidence, and defend conclusions. Critics had accused both traditional and progressive education of being forms of indoctrination, propaganda, and/or brainwashing. In theory, no one would accuse the disciplined inquiry approach of being indoctrination, as for nearly 2 decades scholars had been making a case that the academic disciplines represented an anti-ideological model for pluralistic democratic deliberation and life that avoided totalitarian thinking. Inquiry in the disciplines reflected the same pluralistic, tentative, intersubjective methods as democratic life because both academic disciplines and democratic government rejected ideology, sought consensus, invited self-criticism, and approached their views with skepticism and humility. Since democracy shared so many overlapping attributes with scientific and academic inquiry, it made sense to base the curriculum on these same values.

Finally, the influence on academic disciplines reflected the growing prestige of college professors in American society during the postwar years. Scientists in particular were held in high esteem after World War II, having designed the atomic bomb that won the war. "[W]e were at the time pretty much imbued with the idea that we could do anything if we started from scratch," Nobel Prize–winning physicist Edward Purcell recalled. "It was, of course, a time of almost euphoria in that respect, because the wartime successes of high technology and physics applied to new problems were still fresh in our minds."[34] Beyond scientists, all college professors benefitted from what would later be known as the Golden Age of college education due to exploding postwar enrollments. By 1956, more than 2 million servicemen had entered colleges and universities as a result of the GI Bill; between 1940 and 1960, enrollment more than doubled from 1.5 to 3.6 million students. Despite initial reservations about their academic potential, these veterans turned out to be disciplined, focused, and driven scholars who would ultimately transform the culture of higher education through their maturity and work ethic. When the baby boom generation came of age, college enrollment continued to increase. In 1948, only 10 universities had over 20,000 students, but by 1967 there were 55 schools of that size. Between 1945 and 1975, college enrollment had increased nearly 500% and graduate enrollment had increased nearly 900%. More students led to the hiring of more professors; more professors led to more graduate programs and greater research specialization; greater research specialization led to more professional organizations, research centers, and the launching of new academic journals. Congress founded the National Science Foundation in 1950 to serve as a buffer between basic research, the security state, and the military-industrial complex. The National Science Foundation would provide tens of millions of dollars to professors and universities for research without any ideological interference.[35]

The National Science Foundation funded the initial wave of school curriculum reform projects in disciplined inquiry, such as the Physical Science Committee, the University of Illinois Committee on School Mathematics, the Biological Sciences Curriculum at University of Colorado in Boulder, and the School Mathematics Study Group. All of these projects implemented some form of the structure of disciplines approach by recasting their respective subject areas as rigorous, open-ended, and inquiry-based. By 1965, one educator referred to the structure of the disciplines approach as "nothing less than a revolution in American education."[36] Accordingly, the new math curriculum aimed to overcome the view of the discipline as rigid and formulaic by approaching the subject as conceptual, dynamic, and creative. Historian Christopher Phillips explained: "The point of the new reforms was to cultivate habits of thought more consistent with the image of 'open' creative American minds than with that of 'closed' inflexible Soviet minds." The new math was immensely popular in terms of school adoption; one survey estimated that the materials had been adopted by 85% of schools by the mid-1970s.[37]

Eventually, federal funding was extended to the social studies and humanities as well, which made sense given the centrality of the stated civic purpose of these reforms. The social studies projects began with a meeting of 47 scholars at Endicott House in Cambridge, Massachusetts, in June 1962. As arguments broke out among historians and social scientists, the two cultures of postwar social sciences research revealed itself in ways that surprised the conference host, Jerrold Zacharias. Participants eventually agreed on some vague concepts that aligned with the structure of the disciplines approach: that the factual coverage approach to the social studies was ineffective; that there should be some interdisciplinary integration, especially in the elementary and middle school grades; and that focus should be on deeper investigations of fewer topics—an approach that came to be known as "post-holing." Three of the most successful projects that emerged from the social studies conference were the primary-source inquiry materials of historian Edwin Fenton of Carnegie Institute for Technology, the social studies pamphlets by Donald Oliver at Harvard University, and Bruner's own, *Man: A Course of Study* (*MACOS*).[38]

Fenton's inquiry textbooks were the first of the projects to be published. The books were aimed at helping "each student develop to the limit of his ability into an independent thinker and responsible citizen of a democratic society." In place of the fact-driven narratives of traditional textbooks, Fenton's innovative materials focused on open-ended questions in history and the social sciences by presenting students with primary source documents, graphs, data sets, and excerpts from interpretive secondary accounts. "This skill—the ability to find an argument and to determine whether or not evidence supports it—is an important technique as well as vital preparation for citizenship," Fenton claimed. "It will put the student on guard against accepting everything he reads. . . . Thus he will become an effective member of a democracy."[39] Fenton's curriculum recommended replacing the senior capstone class, Problems of Democracy, with a semester-long course on Introduction to the Behavioral Sciences and another one on Humanities in Three Cities (Athens, Florence, and New York City). His 9th-grade course on Comparative Economic Systems had students examine "the values of Kwakiutl Indians, contemporary Americans, and leaders of the Soviet Union."[40] The primary sources and data sets presented in the old textbooks were often disjointed, void of context, and followed by long lists of questions focused mainly on reading comprehension. As a result, students were not really getting a sense of history and social science as interpretive and creative disciplines. Instead, Fenton's inquiries were set up mostly as searches for right answers—only students were looking for the right answers in primary sources instead of in traditional textbooks. Fenton was also unclear on whether his textbooks were supposed to supplement or replace the traditional textbook. Nevertheless, his texts were highly innovative in their incorporation of social scientific concepts and primary sources. They anticipated an explosion in research and interest on historical thinking that would take place in the 1990s and 2000s.[41]

The social issue pamphlets authored by Donald Oliver and Fred Newmann were less concerned with the structures of the disciplines; they focused on inquiry methods, classroom discussion, and how they related to the desired dispositions of citizenship. Having already articulated a clear rationale in 1957 for designing a curriculum around a jurisprudential approach to social issues, Oliver had a head start on rethinking the curriculum for the postwar world. He and his collaborators ultimately designed over two dozen pamphlets between 1967 and 1971 on topics such as the American Revolution, Jacksonian America, the Civil War, religious freedom, immigration, and "Negro Views of America," designed to make students "more than a spectator; as more of a thinking, acting participant in history and modern life."[42]

Finally, the *MACOS* materials were formally published in 1970—a full decade after the Woods Hole conference, and 8 years after the Endicott House meeting. While Fenton had designed an entire middle and high school curriculum by the late 1960s, Bruner and his associates had spent nearly 5 million dollars and close to a decade in designing a curriculum for only the 5th grade. Nevertheless, when finally complete, the *MACOS* curriculum was widely praised; Bruner and his associates won awards from the American Education Research Association and the American Educational Publishers Institute, and teachers across the nation expressed their excitement about the materials. Since culture had always been so central to Bruner's cognitive psychology, it made sense that anthropology would be the focus of his innovative curriculum. *MACOS* explored culture as a central component of life through the question: What does it mean to be human? The curriculum compared baboons to modern man and the Netsilik Eskimos, including extensive film footage of hunter-gatherer cultures, graphic images of Netsiliks skinning a seal, and a discussion on how to handle an elderly Netsilik grandmother who could no longer care for herself. Along with games and role-playing activities, the curriculum reflected the cultural relativism of Boasian anthropology, the latest advancements in audiovisual materials, and the inductive inquiry methods Bruner valued. Before formally publishing the curriculum, Bruner had piloted the materials in several classrooms, made substantial adjustments—including throwing out an entire unit on African Bushmen because of the potentially racist implications of depicting people of color as a premodern culture—and established an extensive professional development program for teachers.[43]

The new curriculum materials in science, math, and social studies were based on three assumptions. First, they were aimed at engaging the brightest students. Since *Sputnik*, policymakers were not only concerned that the U.S. curriculum had lost its rigor, but specifically that gifted students were not being intellectually challenged. They hoped that open-ended and discipline-based new materials would excite all students, and especially those most likely to go on to study these topics in college and graduate school. Second, by producing videos, teacher manuals, and prepackaged experiments, the college professors were doing their best to create teacher-proof materials that could not be watered or dumbed down. They deliberately included some flexibility, such as choice of topics, but they viewed the teacher mainly as a conduit for their own disciplinary ideas, not as a collaborator. Finally, the authors of the materials emphasized the civic function of disciplined inquiry by emphasizing the centrality of thinking to democratic life. As historian John Rudolph explained, the structure of the disciplines approach to physics and biology "emerged from the scientists' desire to showcase the intellectual power of science to combat all forms of dogmatism—religious, ideological, and even curricular (as found in life adjustment programs)."[44] Yet, like the proposed reforms of progressive education, these new materials represented a movement away from the textbook-and-teacher centered curriculum that many teachers and community members still valued. Ironically, the same Cold War context that helped launch the reform movement created an environment that made its universal acceptance unlikely. As Zacharias later reflected: "It's easier to put a man on the moon than to reform the public schools."[45]

OUT WITH THE NEW

As demonstrated earlier, the ambitious reforms of progressive education likely influenced only about a third of U.S. classrooms. With the exception of the new math, the new curriculum materials based on disciplined inquiry, especially those in the social studies, were even less successful. At its highest point, inquiry textbooks—including Fenton's—made up only about 15% of the textbook market, and *MACOS* was sold to only about 1,700 of a potential 58,000 schools.[46] The problems with the disciplined inquiry approach to curriculum were threefold. First was timing. By the time the new curriculum materials were rolled out, the anti-ideological milieu of consensus liberalism that valued objective, open-ended inquiry had partially evaporated. Had the curriculum redesign started immediately after the war and been ready to implement in the mid-1950s, teachers and the public likely would have greeted them more enthusiastically. However, by the 1960s and 1970s, the prestige of academic professors was on the wane, and domestic turmoil (see Chapter 8) made the disciplinary objectivity that postwar scholars valued seem somewhat irrelevant and out of touch.

Second, the professors' plan of teacher-proofing their materials and aiming them at the brightest students backfired. Since teachers were the ones who would ultimately choose to implement or ignore the materials, their participation needed to be solicited more directly and enthusiastically. Most teachers spend the bulk of their time and effort trying to engage their struggling and disengaged students, not the high-performing students, who were usually well behaved, engaged, and motivated. As a result, the vast majority of teachers mostly ignored the inquiry materials because they did little to address the needs of their struggling students.[47]

Third, basing the curriculum exclusively on the structure of the disciplines was inherently flawed. As historian Louis Menand pointed out, the academic disciplines were designed at the end of the 19th century specifically to be "transmissible but not transferable." That is, the professional expertise of disciplines is transmitted solely and exclusively by experts in each respective discipline, so that only experts in each discipline had oversight over what was considered appropriate knowledge in each area. "The non-transferability," Menand explains, ". . . ensures that competence in one profession can never be exercised in another profession." Thus, academic disciplines had nontransferability built right into them because they were designed to address discipline-specific problems, some of which were applicable to the real world, but many (if not most) of which were, by design, only relevant to other disciplinary experts. As Menand explains: "The inaccessibility of physics is built into the rationale of physics departments; that is, we need physics departments precisely because special training is necessary to teach and do research in physics."[48] This circular logic protected disciplinary experts from political and market pressures throughout the 20th century, but it also hindered the success of the structures of the discipline approach because it failed to acknowledge the broader goals of public schools, which went far beyond inquiry and knowledge construction for its own sake.

Despite Bruner's efforts at forging a theory of disciplinary transfer, the proponents of disciplined inquiry never made a convincing case why their approach was inherently better than traditional or progressive methods at preparing citizens for a rapidly changing world. For example, when asked by a publisher why he chose to focus *MACOS* on Netsilik Eskimos, Bruner responded: "Why not?"[49] Bruner's flippant response implied that because the topic was important to the discipline of anthropology, then *that* was all the justification needed. Teachers, publishers, principals, and school board members required more justification. However, the architects of the new materials were hesitant to fall into the same trap into which progressives had fallen by trying to make the materials too functional and/or relevant. Beyond broad statements about the development of critical thinking for civic life—a justification that became less and less frequent and convincing over the course of the late 1960s and early 1970s—the architects of the structure of the disciplines were not interested in answering questions about relevance or utility. As a result, most teachers ignored the inquiry methods, despite the extensive efforts Bruner, Zacharias, and others had made to engage teachers in the excitement of their fields.

The postwar liberal social studies educators in the tradition of Griffin, Hunt, and Metcalf were skeptical of the structure of the disciplines approach as well, although they were happy to acquire and employ the available grant money that emerged in the shadow of *Sputnik*. For example, in a classic 1960 article, Shirley Engle, an Associate Dean at Indiana University, distinguished the social sciences from the social studies because the "impelling purpose of the two is quite different." The social sciences were focused on research because the "absorbing interest is to push back the frontier of dependable knowledge," while the social studies were focused on the "quality of decisions" on "public and private matters of social concern."[50] Proponents of the structure of the disciplines approach made the mistake of thinking that the goals of social science aligned with the goals of citizenship; Engle argued that they did not. Although the social studies had to draw on the social sciences to analyze public issues with rigor, the goals of the social studies were far broader than the limited research goals of the social sciences. Looking back with frustration at the failed reforms of the new inquiry-based social studies, James Shaver expressed his dismay. "For many years . . . social studies personnel were too busy with teaching 'academic' content to pay much attention to values and valuing as part of citizenship education," Shaver complained in 1976. "In fact, the structure of the discipline approach that dominated most of the curriculum . . . was a fad that exemplified our long standing and unthinking subservience to professors in the academic disciplines."[51] He implored his colleagues to regain their confidence and get back to the Dewey-inspired rationales that characterized the field during the immediate postwar years.

However, mere resistance of teachers and social studies educators was not enough to stop the momentum of disciplined inquiry. It was ultimately Cold War politics that led to the purge of structure of the disciplines materials from the schools. The first sign of trouble emerged in 1971, when the Georgia Basic Education Council accused Fenton's textbooks of including "un-American teachings" and lobbied successfully to have them removed from a list of state-approved books. Echoing the Rugg textbook controversy of the 1940s, Fenton countered that the removal of his texts represented a "national conspiracy" that "eroded the strength of our democratic political institutions" by robbing "the children we teach of the right to learn from the social studies we know are best for them."[52] Criticism spread to the new math as well. In 1973, mathematician Morris Kline published an article in the *New York Times* accusing the new math of "irresponsible innovation" in its deliberate de-emphasis on mathematical computation, a critique he fleshed out in his book published the same year, *Why Johnny Can't Add*. By 1976, parents complained: "They have gone overboard on teaching . . . what they call the new math. I don't think any kid through third grade can multiply 3 times 3 and get 9."[53] By the mid-1970s, the new social studies inquiry texts and textbooks employing the approaches of the new math began to be phased out of U.S. schools, as many teachers, administrators, and parents wanted to move back to basics.

However, *MACOS* inspired the biggest backlash because of its disciplinary embrace of cultural relativity, its use of graphic imagery, and its posing of questions about the nature of man that bordered on the theological. The inclusion of these ideas would have been controversial enough, but because *MACOS* had used millions of federal dollars not only for the design of the program, but also for its dissemination, critics accused the organization of supporting biased materials aimed at delivering a particular social agenda. "The tax supported school system," one critic of *MACOS* charged, "has become the leading vehicle for transporting Marxist revolution to the streets." A nationally syndicated columnist accused the National Science Foundation's backing of *MACOS* as "an ominous echo of the Soviet Union's promulgation of official scientific theory," and Congressman John B. Conlon of Arizona concurred, considering the curriculum part of a "propaganda campaign . . . aimed at changing children's social values and behavior and questioning their religious upbringing."[54] George Weber of the Council for Basic Education recognized "an air of indoctrination about the course" because the *MACOS* curriculum had "definitive ideas about what conclusions the children should come to . . . [and] an underlying assumption that young children must be made to understand that cultural relativism and environmental determinism are the only 'scientific' answers to the place of man in society."[55] Many Americans were not ready to accept the basic epistemological assumptions of college professors, such as the relativity of Boasian cultural anthropology and the open-ended nature of knowledge.

Ultimately, no educational movement took the mantra of teaching students "how to think, not what to think" more seriously than the proponents of the structure of the disciplines. Under the right circumstances, the approach could have been successful, but just as the materials were finding their way into schools, the United States experienced the most volatile years of domestic turmoil since the 1930s, shifting attention away from Cold War fears of generating manpower toward equipping students to deal with ethical and moral conflicts about civil rights and the Vietnam War. Further, when the United States successfully landed a man on the moon in 1969, concerns about losing the space race to the Russians evaporated. For example, as late as 1966, a textbook entitled *Inquiry in the Social Studies* by Byron G. Massialas of the University of Michigan and C. Benjamin Cox of the University of Illinois maintained the postwar liberal anti-ideological stance of objective, reasoned deliberation. The authors cited the influence of Lawrence Metcalf, discussed the importance of Dewey's *How We Think*, denounced the perils of the "authoritarian personality," and argued that "reflective thinking can be patterned after a model of thought" by approaching a problem through "formulating, testing, and revising hypotheses."[56] Yet only a few years later, virtually the entire textbook needed to be rewritten in response to what would be called "the affective revolution" in the social studies. The revised version added the subtitle "Coping in an Age of Crisis," a reference to the domestic and political turmoil engendered by the Civil Rights Movement and Vietnam War that upended the curriculum and the nation.[57] Learning how to think, not what to think, continued to gain ground in the late 1960s and 1970s, but the emphasis shifted from concerns about public life to concerns of students' personal and emotional life.

CHAPTER 8

In the Shadow of Moral Relativity

In 1945, an 18-year-old Jewish American from Bronxville, New York, named Larry Kohlberg joined the U.S. Merchant Marines to do his part in the world war against Nazism. He served for 2 years in Europe, during which he met many Holocaust survivors. After the war, Kohlberg continued the fight on behalf of these Jewish victims as a civilian. But to do so, he needed to engage in a form of civil disobedience. With the aid of the Jewish group *Hagenah*, Kohlberg helped smuggle Jewish refugees out of Europe to Palestine, an act that was illegal because the route involved circumventing a British blockade. As a result, he was captured and confined, eventually escaping by using false papers provided by the *Hagenah*.[1] When Kohlberg returned home, he reflected on the moral dilemmas he and his peers had faced during the ordeal. He would go on to obtain a graduate degree in psychology so he could further study the process of working through moral dilemmas in a way that avoided both the moral relativity of the Nazis and the political indoctrination of the Russians. Drawing on psychology, philosophy, and ethics, Kohlberg developed a highly influential developmental framework to guide and assess the complex nature of moral growth in a democracy. He framed his approach as a counter to authoritarian thinking. Kohlberg explained that "the Russians know how to make the hidden curriculum explicit and how to make it work." However, he dismissed the communist approach to morality because "the definition of moral character as the promotion of collective national discipline . . . is neither rational ethics nor the American constitutional tradition."[2]

Although Kohlberg forged and refined his theory under the assumptions of postwar consensus liberalism, ironically, his theory did not rise to prominence until that consensus had collapsed under the weight of domestic turmoil brought on by the Civil Rights Movement and the Vietnam War. The rise and fall of Kohlberg's theory in the educational imagination mirrored the rise and fall of "the affective revolution" in U.S. schools between 1968 and 1983.

In educational circles, as well as within the culture at large, the turbulent 1960s marked a turning point. When the nation witnessed the war, assassinations, protests, civil unrest, and the formation of a counterculture, the structure of the disciplines approach no longer seemed appropriate to address these concerns. Social unrest seemed to peak in 1968, as students across the country demanded rapid curricular reform that would speak to their issues and worries. "Relevance" became the educational buzzword of the day, and many schools responded by offering elective classes and addressing moral and ethical issues in the classroom.[3] By the late 1960s, the curriculum materials that emphasized the structure of the discipline, which had been formulated during a time when scientific objectivity was highly valued, could not have been more out of step. Leading educational theorists were still committed to having their students learn how to think, not what to think, but thinking through and about the academic disciplines was not going to equip students for the social turmoil they witnessed and experienced on a daily basis. As a result, they attempted to redesign their curriculum and pedagogy to address more directly the affective elements of learning.

THE FALL OF CONSENSUS LIBERALISM

By 1960, the Civil Rights Movement that had begun in the 1950s continued to escalate into a more confrontational phase. Freedom Riders provoked Southern racists to violence by riding integrated buses through the South. The Student Non-Violent Coordinating Committee began registering Black voters in the Deep South, and the Southern Christian Leadership Conference compelled Black churchgoers to confront segregation through protests, marches, and boycotts. In 1963, an estimated 1 million activists participated in protests across the country, culminating in the March on Washington, DC, where Dr. Martin Luther King, Jr., delivered his famous "I Have A Dream" speech to a quarter-million protesters. Dozens of activists were killed during these protests, and hundreds were beaten. Despite victories like the Civil Rights Act of 1964 and the Voting Rights Act of 1965, African Americans grew more frustrated by the slow pace of reform, the impunity with which Southern racists could harass protestors and murder Black victims, and the continually poor socioeconomic standing of Blacks in America. Riots broke out in New York in 1964, Los Angeles in 1965, and Detroit, Newark, Washington, DC, and Chicago in 1968. In 1966, Stokely Carmichael was elected the chairman of the Student Non-Violent Coordinating Committee, expelled the White members of the group, and declared the importance of Black power. The same year, Black nationalists formed the Black Panthers to defend African American interests against White supremacy, through violence, if necessary.

The assumption of postwar consensus liberalism came crashing down with the rise of ethnic consciousness. African Americans, women, Hispanics, gay people, and Native Americans began to assert themselves through newly formed organizations that pursued their rights and their inclusion in the American society and the curriculum. By the 1960s, many intellectuals viewed the Cold War approach of apolitical, procedural neutrality as essentially endorsing the status quo of unjust domestic and foreign policies. However, rather than return to the functional and pragmatic approach of Dewey, with its quaint belief in social progress, scholars and activists of the 1960s and 1970s forged a more skeptical approach focused on the relationships among knowledge construction, perspective, and power. The "linguistic turn"—a reference to the ways that scholars use language to shape reality and impose power upon the oppressed—affected all the major disciplines. Scholars became particularly interested in the ways that claims of objectivity often obscured the hegemonic and oppressive structures of society. In science, Thomas Kuhn explored the impact of "paradigms" to limit what questions are asked and how scientific data are interpreted; in history, Hayden White examined the role of narrative tropes in shaping and distorting how the past is studied and presented; in anthropology, Clifford Geertz endorsed a local, symbolic, self-referential approach to culture that rejected claims of universality; in philosophy, Richard Rorty implored his peers to give up their fruitless search for an accurate representation of reality.[4] In education, A. S. Neill's *Summerhill* espoused an educational experience for children without any rules or set curriculum, and Brazilian philosopher Paulo Freire in *Pedagogy of the Oppressed* exposed the classist, oppressive assumptions in transmitting traditional knowledge to marginalized and oppressed groups. In addition, Rachel Carson's *Silent Spring* kicked off the environmentalist movement, and Michael Harrington's *The Other America* drew attention to the persistence of poverty in the United States.[5] Much of this work was aimed at what was considered the rigid, bureaucratic, racist, classist, and assimilationist ideas of postwar consensus liberalism. It was as if the dam of moderation had broken and waves of activism had burst forth. Every problem facing U.S. society that had been overlooked or suppressed in the 1950s demanded immediate remedy in the 1960s.

These new concerns and perspectives shattered the postwar liberal consensus, especially on college campuses. Many New Left professors replaced the epistemology of compromise, consensus, and complacency with one that embraced diversity, perspective, power, and conflict.[6] After the 1960s, intellectual historian Louis Menand explains: "The vocabulary of 'disinterestedness,' 'objectivity,' 'reason' and 'knowledge' and talk about things like 'the scientific method,' 'the canon,' and 'the fact/value distinction' began to be superseded . . . by attention to 'interpretations' (rather than facts), 'perspective' (rather than objectivity), and 'understanding (rather than 'reason' or 'analysis')."[7] The new emphasis on diversity in education was further endorsed by the 1978 Supreme Court decision *Regents of University of California v. Bakke* that struck down race-based quotas but endorsed racial and gender diversity as a laudable and legal objective in education. As Justice Harry Blackman explained in his dissenting opinion: "In order to get beyond racism, we must first take account of race. There is no other way. And in order to treat some persons equally, we must treat them differently."[8] Emphasis on equal access to education became replaced by an emphasis on equitable outcomes.[9] The

National Council of the Social Studies responded to these changes by including more material on racial issues in its curriculum and focusing its attention on student activism and identity. It devoted the entire April 1969 issue of *Social Education*, its flagship journal, to minority issues.[10]

The Vietnam War became another divisive issue during the 1960s. Based on the domino theory of communist aggression, U.S. leaders feared that the loss of South Vietnam to communism would allow all of Asia eventually to fall to the ideology. As the United States committed more and more troops to the effort, a vigilant anti-war movement emerged, as millions of protestors took to the streets to demand an immediate end to the war. In 1969, half a million protestors marched on Washington, DC, the largest protest ever to take place in the United States. The war protests were linked to the Civil Rights Movement, with participants often contributing to both movements. "[I]n the Vietnam war you are using all your might and all your modern technology to destroy a country, a poor backward country, where people are colored," Gunnar Myrdal explained in a 1968 interview for an education journal. "This is an association which incidentally makes both your war in Vietnam and the race riots at the present time a cause of revulsion in the whole world."[11]

Writing in 1971, Donald Oliver and Mary Jo Bane offered the following advice on how to elicit responses from reluctant students about a public issue during the time of domestic turmoil: "Questions, for example, could be phrased in personal rather than general terms: 'Should *you* participate in civil disobedience in protest against the Vietnam war?' Rather than 'Should peace groups use illegal means in pursuit of their aims?'" This recommendation not only reflected Oliver's 2 decades of experience in introducing social issues to students in the classroom, it also inadvertently reflected the fundamental change in the curriculum that took place between 1957, when Oliver authored his classic essay on the selection of content in the social studies, and 1971, when many schools were radically reforming their curriculum to meet the needs of student relevance and diversity. This shift—from the public to the personal—reflected U.S. educators' continued focus on teaching students how to think, not what to think, but emphasized the moral and ethical aspects of the social issues under consideration. The shadow of authoritarianism still hung over the discussion about how to teach morals in a democracy, but the communist threat was somehow more distant and abstract than divisive domestic issues. By the late 1960s, the threat of moral relativism that emerged from counterculture radicals was as much of a concern for teachers as the relativism of Soviet Russia.

THE AFFECTIVE REVOLUTION

In 1972, one educational researcher conducted a comparative study of moral education in the democratic regimes of the United States and England and the communist regimes of China and the Soviet Union. The study marked several differences between the approaches, but the author was particularly struck by the idea that in democratic countries one could be considered moral by adhering consistently to an individualized set of ethical rules, but under communism this was not possible: "Communist morality is achievable only by the political and collective man."[12] That is, communist morality was about socializing to the expectations and norms of the group, but in the United States, socialization to the norms of others was only sometimes valued, especially if the social norms of the majority were considered to be unjust. This made moral education in a democracy much more complicated. The author was agnostic about which approach was better, but others took a clear position. "In nondemocratic societies, education . . . is a weapon or an instrument for shaping the minds of the ruled in accord with the favored dogmatic myth of the rulers." As another researcher explained: "To choose the democratic ideal for society is wholly to reject the conception of education as an instrument of rule; it is to surrender the idea of shaping or molding the mind of the pupil."[13]

In light of these rapid social changes, educational psychologists were faced with an epistemological dilemma regarding the transmission of values. One the one hand, most social scientists embraced the cultural relativistic approach of Boasian cultural anthropology and the cultural pluralism of naturalistic philosophy, both of which approached cultural values as contextual, instrumental, and relativistic. On the other hand, they accepted that social justice needed to be defended on absolute, but secular, grounds and in contrast to the authoritarian approach of the Soviet Union. They wondered how they could prepare future citizens for a multicultural world in which students must be tolerant of different religious and philosophical values, while at the same time being intolerant toward rigid ideologies that denied human rights and social justice. They wondered how they could provide students with the tools to reach their own conclusions on issues of value conflicts without imposing a particular set of values on them or leading them to knee-jerk skepticism or nihilism. They wondered how to teach students how to think, not what to think, in a world that demanded allegiance to democratic justice and tolerance of different cultures. "[T]eaching certain values as desirable inclines students to believe that people in foreign lands who hold other value systems are necessarily wrong and ought for their own good to be corrected," Edwin Fenton explained in 1966. Yet if teachers "try to avoid teaching values, or at least teaching about values, we run the danger of leading students to believe that no values are worthwhile."[14]

By the mid-1960s, many high school students were facing real ethical dilemmas about whether to serve in Vietnam or to try to avoid what they considered to be an unjust war, while many others faced difficult decisions about whether to participate in, ignore, or oppose the Civil Rights Movement. Despite its focus on critical thinking, the structure of the disciplines approach seemed inadequate to address these moral and ethical issues. Educators responded with a focus on relevance and a slew of developmental schemes to assess the levels of complexity in forming values. By the 1970s, even Edwin Fenton had abandoned his earlier structure of the disciplines approach and become one of the leading advocates for the "affective revolution"—a term that social studies theorists applied retrospectively to educators' intense interest during the late 1960s and 1970s in students' identity, morality, emotions, and values. These reforms lost momentum at the end of the 1970s when they were replaced by the "back-to basics" and standards movement.[15]

Discussions of the affective elements to learning were actually introduced during the Woods Hole conference, only to be deliberately dismissed as irrelevant to the objective, scientific structure of the disciplines approach the professors were hoping to pursue. However, in the shadow of Vietnam and the Civil Rights Movement, the affective domain could no longer be ignored. In 1964, educational psychologists David R. Krathwohl, Benjamin S. Bloom, and Bertram B. Masia first outlined the elements of the affective domain in the *Taxonomy of Educational Objectives Handbook II: Affective Domain*. Working backward from existing published curricula, the authors asserted that the curriculum already contained unidentified affective elements, so they constructed a formal framework for assessing them. Krathwohl and his colleagues outlined the progression of affective development in students using five levels, "the continuum progress[ing] from a level at which the individual is merely aware of a phenomenon, being *able to perceive it*."[16] At the highest level, "values already have a place in the individual's value hierarchy, are organized into some kind of internally consistent system, have controlled the behavior of the individual for a sufficient time."[17] While Bloom's and Krathwohl's taxonomy of cognitive objectives, which drew on the work of Ralph Tyler and was published in 1956, become one of the most useful and cited educational resources of the 20th century, their taxonomy of affective objectives was less popular.[18] Nevertheless, their taxonomy pointed the way to the importance of affective elements of education in the next decade.

An even greater influence on the "affective revolution" was that of Lawrence Kohlberg, who addressed issues of morality from a cognitive point of view. Building on the work of Dewey and Swiss psychologist Jean Piaget, both of whom developed frameworks for analysis of moral development, Kohlberg designed his own framework involving six stages. His stages progressed gradually from an "obedience-punishment orientation," in which one simply followed the rules to avoid extrinsically imposed consequences, to a "conscience or principle orientation," in which one's actions arose from an intrinsically derived set of principles. Kohlberg's approach, which he termed "cognitive-developmental," boldly insisted that, while particular cultural values were relative, his developmental stages were not; they transcended cultural norms and contexts. Based on his research in the United

States, Israel, Turkey, Mexico, and Taiwan, he defended the universality of his theory until his death in 1987.

Although Kohlberg's developmental theory would come to prominence in the late 1960s and 1970s, his moral framework was formed in the intellectual milieu of postwar consensus liberalism. Kohlberg believed that by focusing on the process, instead of the content, of people's moral reasoning he could establish a hierarchy that could be prescriptive without imposing a specific set of values on others. He connected the imposition of specific values through normative socialization with Soviet Russia, an approach he considered to be a "horrifying innovation" based on "collective responsibility, collective punishment and reward." On other extreme, he also denounced the moral relativity of A. H. Neill's approach that "moral values should not be taught in school at all, since they are arbitrary and irrational."[19] Both approaches, he pointed out, were essentially relativistic and circumvented how real values and morals were developed and formed. The Russian approach simply socialized students to a predetermined Marxist ideology, regardless of its applicability to reality, and Neill's approach avoided morality altogether by leaving students with no guidance or direction whatsoever in the face of emerging dilemmas. Like many of his postwar liberal colleagues, Kohlberg sought to establish a moral framework that avoided both indoctrination and relativity but still championed the superiority of democratic life.

Kohlberg argued that the human mind was equipped with a standardized moral framework into which various cultural values could be processed. This framework, he explained, was composed of "basic moral concepts believed to be present in any society [that] . . . must be conceived of in terms of cognitive-structural changes . . . rather than in terms of the learning of cultural patterns."[20] In Kohlberg's case, the term "affective" was not appropriate, as it implied that values were inherently personal and relativistic. By tying moral development to the cognitive processes of the mind, Kohlberg argued that his stages were universal. Morality, he suggested, emerged from within through social interaction, as opposed to being something imposed from without through externally enforced discipline, as in the Soviet Union.

Kohlberg's six moral stages of development include (1) *obedience and punishment orientation*—egocentric deference to superior power or prestige, or a trouble-avoiding mindset; (2) *naively egoistic orientation*—right action is that which instrumentally satisfies the self's needs and occasionally those of others; (3) *good-boy orientation*—orientation to approval and to pleasing and helping others; (4) *authority and social-order-maintaining orientation*—orientation to "doing duty" and showing respect for authority and maintaining the given social order for its own sake; (5) *contractual logistic orientation*—recognition of an arbitrary element or starting point in rules or expectations for the sake of agreement; and (6) *conscience or principle orientation*—an orientation not only to ordained social rules but also to principles of choice involving appeal to logical universality and consistency.

His research revealed that the vast majority of adolescents and adults were at levels two or three, but level four was a prerequisite, he argued, "to have the capacities and motivation to enter positions of participation and public responsibility later."[21] He and his colleagues argued that the curriculum ought to be aimed at moving students as close to level four as possible. The sixth stage, critics later joked, could apparently only be attained by Jesus, Gandhi, Martin Luther King, Jr., and Kohlberg himself. He later redacted the sixth stage from his framework altogether after his own empirical studies failed to confirm its existence. He later joked: "Perhaps all the sixth stage persons of the sixties had been wiped out . . . perhaps they had regressed, or maybe it was all in my imagination."[22]

In the late 1960s and 1970s, in collaboration with Edwin Fenton, Kohlberg promoted the applicability of his theory to U.S. classrooms. Movement from one stage of moral development to the next, Kohlberg argued, was not inevitable or natural. Moral growth involved "the communication of definitions of situations which elicit socially appropriate affect."[23] In other words, growth required that students be confronted with hypothetical and real moral dilemmas and work them out through class discussion. Guided peer discussion, according to Kohlberg, would stimulate movement from one stage of moral reasoning to the next.[24] It was particularly important for individuals to consider the values of others and try to empathize with them. "Morality," he wrote, "is a natural product of a universal tendency toward empathy or role-taking . . . [and] a product of a universal concern for justice, for reciprocity or equality in the relation of one person to another."[25] Kohlberg's cognitive-developmentalism provided further evidence that teachers needed to introduce class discussion of contemporary issues into the curriculum. Such discussions would not only be relevant to student concerns but would also be grounded in the latest psychological research. Early research on the use of Kohlberg's approach in the classroom demonstrated that it did result in cognitive growth in most, but not all, students.[26]

"The Kohlberg Bandwagon," as one critic called it, peaked in the mid-1970s as his graduate students and colleagues continued to expand, tweak, and endorse his approach for use in U.S. schools. Scholars offered many critiques of his program: that it did not adequately account for God and religious belief; that he failed to define ideas such as morality and justice with precision; that his theory was too complicated for teachers to understand and implement; that the program was too time intensive and led to only minimal growth in students; that his approach focused solely on thinking and not on action; that his presented moral dilemmas were hypothetical and ignored real-world context; that his theory approached morality from the personal level instead of from the social or institutional level, and that—despite Kohlberg's claims to the contrary—his theory was morally relativistic. Kohlberg and his colleagues defended the framework from most of these criticisms through written responses and the further revision of his stages. However, over time it became apparent that Kohlberg's cognitive-developmentalism was a leftover from postwar consensus-building liberalism.

Since Kohlberg's theory was politically and epistemologically moderate, it made sense that attacks from both the New Left and the New Right ultimately led to its demise in U.S. schools. In "In a Different Voice," a 1977 article published in the *Harvard Educational Review*, psychologist Carol Gilligan argued that Kohlberg's framework reflected a male bias that caused women to score consistently lower. She suggested that men and women make moral decisions in fundamentally different ways. Men make decisions based on principled rationality, while woman were more concerned with personal relationships, compassion, caring, and love. These were stylistic differences that could and should not be ordered hierarchically. Using a feminist epistemology adopted from the New Left, Gilligan attacked the very idea of constructing stage theories that valued certain moral styles over others. She insisted that such efforts ought to be abandoned. Similar attacks by the New Left had been made against the "modernization theory" framework social scientists had constructed to assess the socioeconomic growth of developing nations. Overall, the popularity of stage theories—whether psychological or sociological—continued to wane after the 1970s as New Left critics tied them to excessive rationalization, hegemonic structures, cultural imperialism, and oppressive bureaucracies.[27]

From the New Right, William J. Bennett attacked Kohlberg's framework for its refusal to name the specific values it was hoping to transmit. Bennett would later serve as Secretary of Education under President Reagan. Calling his approach to values "character education," Bennett espoused the importance of knowing "the difference between right and wrong, good and evil," which he contrasted with Kolhberg's approach, which failed to prescribe any desired behaviors, values, or outcomes whatsoever.[28]

The affective revolution proved to be the last in a long line of approaches that emphasized how to think, not what to think. Ironically, the affective revolution paved the way for the resurgence in prescriptivism in the 1980s, not only by taking student relevance and curriculum fragmentation to its extreme, but also by abandoning the high schools' longstanding role in fostering democratic citizenship for the fight against authoritarianism. As much as the Vietnam War and Civil Rights Movement were Cold War events, and the New Left directly attacked the assumptions of Cold War consensus liberalism, many educators did not frame addressing the affective domain in ideological or existential terms, or as part of the fight against totalitarianism. That is, they did not argue that addressing students' values would help win the Cold War or combat authoritarian tendencies. In fact, unlike in previous wars, the education of communists in North Vietnam was completely left out of discussions of how to prepare democratic citizens in the 1960s and 1970s. It was primarily domestic issues, rather than foreign ones, that drove the need to teach students how to think about their own values. Nevertheless, Kohlberg and other theorists of moral education cast the Soviet Union as the ultimate *other* against which to design their own moral systems. Because the communists defined their moral system as a set of predetermined Marxist answers to be slavishly followed, their system was both a form of indoctrination and relative to the social norms and values of the proletariat; that is, Soviet morality was both indoctrinating and relativistic in a way that democratic regimes sought to avoid.

WHAT TO THINK

By the 1980s, the U.S. curriculum had never been more disjointed and disparate. The affective revolution spawned thousands of elective classes in the American high school. This context was great for the launching of innovative classes but detrimental to the idea of having schools transmit a common culture to future American citizens. In 1922, schools offered 175 different courses to students in U.S. high schools, but by 1973 this number had risen to 2,100. This explosion in course offerings occurred during a time when many of the smaller high schools had been consolidated into comprehensive high schools, specifically so they could meet the needs of their diverse student populations. The rise of electives had completely killed off the Problems of Democracy course, which dropped from being offered in 25% of schools in 1960 to only 4% in 1980; in 1982, less than 1% of students enrolled in the course.[29] One set of scholars argued that the multiple course offerings amounted to a "shopping mall" mentality where students chose their own path to graduation, and teachers had to compete for student attention through their relevant and disparate course offerings.[30] In 1983, the idea of a general curriculum that appealed to all students was essentially dead.

By the late 1970s, exhausted by waves of curriculum reform, social and political strife, and the top-down dictates of college professors, U.S. educators turned away from scholarly experts and toward the common-sense wisdom of local teachers and communities. This movement would be called "back-to-basics," which in essence meant a return to teaching students what to think. By "what to think," I mean the idea that the state should be in the business of prescribing what facts, ideas, texts, and specific skills every student ought to know—an idea leading educational theorists had rejected for nearly 70 years on the grounds that this is what authoritarian regimes did. Studies of the U.S. curriculum in the late 1970s concluded that schools had "simply given up on any attempt to exert any moral authority relative to students' education."[31] By the end of the decade, some states began to implement minimum competency examinations, not only to provide some degree of coherence and rigor to the curriculum but also to provide the appearance of equity among schools, which were becoming more segregated along racial lines as a result of White flight to the suburbs.[32]

In 1983, two publications marked the official return of the idea of teaching what to think in American schools. The first publication was *Nation at*

Risk: The Imperative for Educational Reform by the National Commission on Excellence in Education, which relayed the importance of a "shared education" and "common culture." The second publication was an article by E. D. Hirsch, an English professor at the University of Virginia, who proposed that schools ought to do a better job of transmitting a common set of facts to American students. He called this shared body of knowledge "cultural literacy" and would spend the next 40 years espousing the importance of shared background knowledge to reading comprehension and academic success.[33] These two publications articulated sentiments in circulation since the mid-1970s, but their positive reception was unprecedented and paved the way for the standards movement. Both publications conveyed an idea that had more or less been abandoned since World War I—that American schools needed to focus on transmitting a shared body of content knowledge to its students. That is, students needed, at least to some degree, to be taught what to think through a curriculum that transmitted specific facts. In 1987, Hirsch and his colleagues provided a list of facts, dates, figures, phrases, and allusions that every American ought to know—the first attempt at compiling such a list since Harold Rugg and others had done it in the 1920s. This pivot away from teaching how to think, not what to think, marked a major reorientation from viewing the school as a major tool in the ideological battle against authoritarianism toward a new view of the school as an engine of economic growth to better compete in the global marketplace.

In reaction to the "widespread public perception that something is seriously remiss in our educational system," President Reagan's Secretary of Education, Terrell H. Bell, commissioned the study that resulted in the *Nation at Risk* report in August 1981. In April of 1983, the Commission reported its findings. It concluded that despite advancements in school attendance and graduation, "the average graduate of our schools and colleges today is not as well-educated as the average graduate of 25 or 35 years ago." The report identified deficiencies in curriculum requirements, academic rigor, and teacher education. In an oft-cited passage specifically designed for maximum impact, the Commission provocatively concluded: "If an unfriendly foreign power had attempted to impose on America the mediocre educational performance that exists today, we might well have viewed it as an act of war."[34] Did that "unfriendly foreign power" imply the Soviet Union? Not necessarily.

Although the Cold War had thawed in the 1970s, in the 1980s President Reagan rekindled the hardline rhetoric of international competition between the competing ideologies of the free and communist nations by sharply increasing military spending and famously dubbing the Soviet Union "the evil empire." In this context, the most striking thing about *Nation at Risk* was its failure to frame educational reform in Cold War terms. Despite the centrality of international competition among nations, the Commission did not mention communism, totalitarianism, or the Soviet Union even once. Instead, according to the report, the primary threat to American dominance on the global stage was not ideological but economic. The report singled out other democratic nations (and U.S. allies) such as Germany, South Korea, and Japan as potential threats to the nation's economic future. The opening lines of the report were "Our Nation is at risk. Our once unchallenged preeminence in commerce, industry, science, and technological innovation is being overtaken by competitors throughout the world." Only after the economic threat to Americans was fully explained did the report add: "For our country to function, citizens must be able to reach some common understandings on complex issues, often on short notice and on the basis of conflicting or incomplete evidence."[35] Thus, the American school's civic function had been overtaken by its economic function.

A Nation at Risk made no reference to teaching how to think, not what to think, no references to conveying the strengths of democracy in the face of authoritarian threats, and no references to developing students' ability to analyze social issues or think like a disciplinary expert. The message was clear: The primary purpose of the American school was to prepare students for the workplace, and only secondarily to prepare the "intellectual, moral, and spiritual strengths of our people which knit together the very fabric of our society."[36] For policymakers, workforce preparation and international economic competition would be the driving purposes of American schooling for the next 30 years. The few references in the report to developing citizenship were vague and emphasized the importance of conveying a common culture regardless of race, ethnicity, or religion.

Hirsch published his influential article "Cultural Literacy" at virtually the same time as *A Nation at Risk*. However, as a liberal English professor, he had little concern for the nation's ability to compete in the global economic marketplace. His main concern was explaining why verbal SAT scores had been falling for over 2 decades—a fact cited and discussed in the *Nation at Risk* report as well. Hirsch hypothesized that the decline in SAT scores was directly linked to the decline in the transmission of a common culture in U.S. schools. He identified two culprits for the decline in common culture: formalism and pluralism, which in later works he traced back to Dewey and progressive education.

Formalism was the erroneous belief that "specific materials of reading and writing are interchangeable so long as they are 'appropriate' and 'high quality.'"[37] Pluralism was another word for multiculturalism, the belief that content should be diverse and culturally relevant to local students. Formalism and pluralism, Hirsch argued, worked in tandem to justify and ensure no common set of facts, texts, or ideas was being taught in U.S. schools. Since formalists/pluralists erroneously believed that learning could take place independent of content, any content would work to develop literacy so long as it was at the appropriate reading level. In other words, while one school district might assign J. D. Salinger's *Catcher in the Rye*, another district might assign Richard Wright's *Native Son*; the text did not matter because each was written at approximately the same reading level. As a result of the pervasive impact of formalism and pluralism, states, districts, schools, and even different teachers within a school had been employing a vast assortment of texts to meet the perceived needs and interests of their students. This flexibility, Hirsch argued, came at a high cost: Students, especially low-income students, were not learning the common culture that the best private and suburban schools were teaching. Hirsch concluded that the best way to remedy the situation was to restore the common curriculum for all students. "I am persuaded that if we want to achieve a more literate culture," he argued, "[w]e shall need to restore certain common contents to the humanistic side of the school curriculum" because "literacy implies specific contents as well as formal skills."[38]

The most iconoclastic idea Hirsch introduced was that to acquire the kind of cultural literacy he envisioned students need not develop a deep knowledge of any one topic. Instead, students required a knowledge a mile wide and an inch deep. He argued that to comprehend a sentence containing the word "beech" or "elm," students need not know the specific differences between a beech and an elm tree; they merely needed to know they were both trees. The same was true for the terms "First Amendment," "General Lee," and "DNA." Hirsch's "cultural literacy" approach proposal contradicted every major educational theorist for the past century, from Dewey to Kilpatrick to Hutchins to Bestor to Zacharias to Bruner to Kohlberg, all of whom proposed deeper learning of fewer topics. Nevertheless, Hirsch implored American educators to abandon their "culturally neutral skills approach" to teaching social studies and English and work to design a list of "proper names, important phrases and conventions" that all students should know.[39] When Hirsch turned his article into a best-selling book in 1987, he and two of his University of Virginia colleagues generated a list of words, dates, names, and phrases that constituted cultural literacy. They then used this list as the basis for the *Dictionary of Cultural Literacy* and a series of textbooks (*What Your First Grader Needs to Know*, etc.).[40]

The *Nation at Risk* report and Hirsch's "Cultural Literacy" article shared three commonalities. First, they both decried the fall of SAT scores, which they linked to fragmentation of the American curriculum since World War I. This link was correlational, not causal. Nevertheless, the link resonated with many Americans who likely remembered their own school as being more rigorous and rigid than the schools of the 1960s and 1970s. It seemed plausible that an easier and less rigid curriculum would lead to falling SAT scores, although critics later attacked these claims.[41] Second, both publications dismissed the idea that teaching students how to think was more important than teaching them what to think. These authors were not opposed to teaching students how to think, but they considered the transmission of common background knowledge to be a priority over merely learning to think. That is, they posited that content knowledge was a precondition for thinking. Finally, both publications proposed that reform required leadership at the national level, an idea that 20 years earlier would have led to accusations of authoritarianism, federal overreach, and indoctrination. The fact that both documents suggested, in essence, that a national curriculum be established through course requirements and a list of common terms demonstrated that, even before the Cold War had formally ended, the U.S. curriculum had emerged from the shadow of authoritarianism.

Of course, after 1983, the idea of teaching how to think, not what to think would remain vital in the years to come, but the purpose of doing so was more often framed, especially by those outside of social studies education, in vocational and economic terms.[42] That is, educators often demonstrated how learning how to think could equip students to be successful in the postindustrial domestic and global economy. Without an authoritarian enemy against which to define democratic education, educators marginalized the importance of schools in fostering democratic dispositions. As a result, U.S. citizens began to view the school more as a means toward personal economic advancement than as an indispensable ingredient in the national, civic project to create a nation of free-thinking individuals, as educators had originally envisioned.[43] Without the concrete examples of totalitarian regimes to serve as foils to democratic life, the civic function of education today has been diverted and subsumed in the current emphasis on college and career readiness. The threat of totalitarianism may have been detrimental to the political, psychological, financial, and cultural health of the nation, but it appears to have been beneficial to educators seeking to place thoughtful civic education at the center of the curriculum.

Notes

Introduction

1. Arthur M. Schlesinger, Jr., *The Vital Center: The Politics of Freedom* (New York: Riverside Press, 1949), 250.
2. Edwin Broome, Report of the Committee on Propaganda in the Schools: Presented at the Annual Meeting of the NEA, July 1929 (Washington, DC: NEA, 1929), 5.
3. Wayne Soper, "What Species Propaganda?" *The Elementary School Journal*, 30 (Nov. 1929): 224.
4. Editors, "Introductory Remarks on Indoctrination," *Teachers College Record*, 1 (1935): 8.
5 Carleton Washburne, "Indoctrination versus Education," *Teachers College Record*, 2 (1936): 213; R. Roderick Palmer, "Education and Indoctrination," *Peabody Journal of Education*, 34 (Jan. 1957): 228.
6. H. Gordon Hullfish and Phillip G. Smith, *Reflective Thinking: The Method of Education* (New York: Dodd, Mead, and Company, 1961), 59.
7. Israel Scheffler, "The Moral Content of Education" in *Moral Education . . . It Comes with the Territory*, ed. David Purpel and Kevin Ryan (Berkeley, CA: McCutchan Publishing Corp., 1976), 23.
8. Donald Oliver and James Shaver, *Teaching Public Issues in the High School* (Boston: Houghton Mifflin, 1966), 14. The quotation is from a chapter attributed to Shaver.
9. David Angus and Jeffrey E. Mirel, *The Failed Promise of the American High School, 1890–1995* (New York: Teachers College Press, 1999), 203.
10. Norman Foerster, "Education Leads the Way," *The American Review*, 1 (Sept. 1933): 403.

Chapter 1

1. Charles Beard, "Politics and Education," *Teachers College Record*, 17 (May 1916): 225.
2. Isaac Kandel, "Political Theory and Education," *Teachers College Record*, 17 (May 1916): 232.
3. John Dewey, "Organization of American Education," in *John Dewey, The Middle Works*, 410.
4. John Dewey, *Democracy and Education: An Introduction to the Philosophy of Education* (New York: New Press, 1997): 93, 87.
5. Andy Green, *Education and State Formation: Europe, East Asia and the U.S.A* (New York: Palgrave Macmillan, 2013); Jurgen Herbst, "Nineteenth Century

Schools between Community and the State: The Case of Prussia and United States," *History of Education Quarterly*, 42 (Autumn 2002): 317–341.

6. James McConaughy, "The Myth of German Educational Superiority," *Journal of Education*, 86 (July 1918): 31.
7. Calvin Ellis Stowe, *Common Schools and Teachers' Seminaries* (Boston: Marsh, Capen, Lyon, and Webb, 1839), 57; Horace Mann, "Mr. Mann's Seventh Annual Report: Education in Europe," *The Common School Journal* (March 1844): 119, 73.
8. Henry Barnard, "Public Instruction in Prussia," *American Journal of Education*, 8: 431.
9. Howard Gardner, *The Mind's New Science: A History of the Cognitive Revolution* (New York: Basic Books, 1987), 102.
10. Dorothy McMurry, *Herbartian Contributions to History Instruction in American Schools* (New York: Teachers College Press, 1946), 30–40.
11. Charles De Garmo, *The Essentials of Methods, A Discussion of the Essential Forms of Right Methods of Teaching Observation, Generalization, Application* (Boston: D.C. Heath and Co., 1889). See also Sir John Adams, *The Herbartian Psychology Applied to Education* (New York: D.C. Heath and Co., 1897) and Catherine Isabel Dodd, *Introduction to the Herbartian Principles of Teaching* (New York: Macmillan Co, 1898).
12. Quoted in Keith C. Barton, "Home Geography and the Development of Elementary Social Education, 1890–1930," *Theory and Research in Social Education*, 37 (Fall 2009): 494.
13. National Education Association, *Report of the Committee of Ten on Secondary School Studies with the Reports Arranged by the Committees* (New York: NEA, 1894); American Historical Association, *The Study of History in Schools: Report to the American Historical Association by the Committee of Seven* (New York: AHA, 1899).
14. Jurgen Herbst, *The German Historical School in American Scholarship: A Study in the Transfer of Culture* (Ithaca, NY: Cornell University Press, 1965); Daniel T. Rodgers, *Atlantic Crossings: Social Politics in a Progressive Age* (Cambridge, MA: Harvard University Press, 1998). Herbst writes that "Between the years 1820 and 1920 nearly nine thousand students set sail for Europe to enter the lecture halls, seminars and laboratories of German Universities," 1.
15. See Peter Novick, *That Noble Dream: The Objectivity Question and the American Historical Profession* (New York: Cambridge University Press, 1987), 88.
16. Herbert Baxter Adams, "The Germanic Origin of New England Towns," Johns Hopkins University Studies in Historical and Political Science, 1 (1883): 8.
17. Milton Bennion, Citizenship: An Introduction to Social Ethics (Yonkers-on Hudson, NY: World Book Company, 1917), xvi; Philip Van Ness Myers, *A Short History of Medieval and Modern Times* (New York: Ginn and Company, 1906), 3–5.
18. Lucy Salmon, "The Study of History in Elementary Schools," Educational Review (May 1891): 438. On Diesterweg see Robert Ulich, A *Sequence of Educational Influences: Traced through Unpublished Writings of Pestalozzi, Froebel, Diesterweg, Horace Mann, and Henry Barnard* (Cambridge, MA: Harvard University Press, 1935), 17–39.
19. G. Stanley Hall, "Introduction" in *Methods of History*, ed. G. Stanley Hall (Boston: D.C. Heath and Co., 1883), vii, ix, xi.

20. Adams quotation from McMurry, *Herbartian Contributions to History Instruction*, 13.
21. Randolph Bourne, *History of a Literary Radical and Other Essays* (New York: B.W. Huebsch, 1920), 32, 33.
22. Christopher Lasch, *The American Liberals and the Russian Revolution* (New York: McGraw-Hill, 1962), 26.
23. William Bagley, "Education and Utility," and "Education and Our Democracy," in *Forgotten Heroes of American Education: The Great Tradition of Teaching Teachers*, eds., J. Wesley Null and Diane Ravitch (Greenwich, CT: Information Age Publishing, 2006), 71, 117.
24. J. H. Phillips, "The Educational Ideal in Germany," *Journal of Education*, 80 (Nov 1914): 484; McConaughy, "The Myth of German Educational Superiority," 32; Paul Hanus, "Germany Indicted," *Journal of Education*, 83 (Nov 1918): 451.
25. V. H. Friedel, *The German School as War Nursery* (New York: Macmillan, 1918), 20–21.
26. M. E. Sadler, Preface to *The German School as War Nursery*, 9.
27. Thomas Alexander, *The Prussian Elementary Schools* (New York: Macmillan, 1919), v.
28. Gustavus Ohlinger, The German Conspiracy in American Education (New York: George H. Doran Company, 1919) 13, 93. These accounts of Prussian education during the war seem to be relatively accurate. See Andrew Donson, *Youth in the Fatherless Land: Pedagogy, Nationalism, and Authority in Germany, 1914–1918* (Cambridge, MA: Harvard University Press, 2010).
29. Helen Louis Cohen, "Americanization by Classroom Practice," *Teachers College Record*, 20 (May 1919): 245. Socialized recitation was a bit of a fad during the 1920s. See Edward Krug, *The American High School, Volume 2 1920–1941* (Madison: University of Wisconsin Press, 1972), 172–174.
30. Alexander, *Prussian Elementary Schools*, 539.
31. James Earl Russell, "Education for Citizenship," *Teachers College Record*, 17 (March 1916): 125.
32. Beard, "Politics and Education," 224.
33. Christopher Capozzola, *Uncle Sam Wants You: World War I and the Making of the Modern American Citizen* (New York: Oxford, 2008), 179, 183.
34. Friedel, The German School, 237, 269; Ohlinger, *The German Conspiracy in American Education*, vi, vii, 19, 92.
35. Cited in David M. Kennedy, *Over Here: The First World War and American Society* (New York: Oxford University Press, 1980), 54.
36. Cited in Capozzola, *Uncle Sam Wants You*, 181.
37. Capozzola, *Uncle Sam Wants You*, 183, 192.
38. Ohlinger, The German Conspiracy, 107.
39. Gary Gerstle, *American Crucible: Race and Nation in the Twentieth Century* (Princeton, NJ: Princeton University Press, 2001).
40. William Z. Ripley, *The Races of Europe: A Sociological Study* (New York: D. Appleton and Co, 1899), 437, 37, vi.
41. Ellwood P. Cubberley, *Changing Conceptions of Education* (New York: Houghton Mifflin, 1909), 13–15.
42. Quoted in Jeffery E. Mirel, *Patriotic Pluralism: Americanization Education and European Immigrants* (Cambridge, MA: Harvard University Press, 2010), 42.

43. Hamilton Cravens, *The Triumph of Evolution: American Scientists and the Heredity-Environment Controversy, 1900–1941* (Philadelphia: University of Pennsylvania Press, 1978), 53.
44. Gerstle, *American Crucible*, 94, 103.
45. Department of the Interior, Bureau of Education, Americanization as a War Measure: Report of a Conference Called by the Secretary of the Interior, and Held in Washington, April 3, 1918 (Washington, DC: Government Printing Office), 61.
46. Royal Dixon, *Americanization* (New York: Macmillan, 1916), 179, 181.
47. Quoted in Mirel, Patriotic Pluralism, 95–96.
48. Neil Coughlan, *Young John Dewey: An Essay in American Intellectual History* (Chicago: University of Chicago Press, 1975); George Dykhuizen, The Life and Mind of John Dewey (Carbondale, IL: University of Chicago Press, 1973).
49. John Dewey, "From Absolutism to Experimentalism" (1930) in The Later Works, vol. 5, 153.
50. John Dewey to William Torrey Harris, 4 December 1894 (record 00493) in *The Correspondence of John Dewey, Vol. 1: 1871–1918*, 3rd edition, CD-ROM version, ed. Larry Hickman (Carbondale, IL: Center for Dewey Studies, Southern Illinois University, 2005).
51. William Bagley, "Educational Survey," *School and Home Education*, 25 (1915): 3
52. On Kallen and Bourne see *Louis Menand, The Metaphysical Club: A Story of Ideas in America* (New York: Farrar, Strauss, and Giroux, 2001); David Hollinger, Post-ethnic America: Beyond Multiculturalism (New York: Basic Books, 1995).
53. Quoted in Menand, Metaphysical Club, 393.
54. Quoted in Thomas Fallace, *Race and the Origins of Progressive Education 1880–1929* (New York: Teachers College Press, 2015), 111.
55. Morton White, *Social Thought in America: The Revolt against Formalism* (New York: Oxford, 1947).
56. Thorstein Veblen, *Imperial Germany and the Industrial Revolution* (New York: Macmillan, 1915), 86.
57. John Dewey, *German Philosophy and Politics* (New York: Henry Holt, 1915), 37, 15, 73, 130, 132.
58. "John Dewey's Latest Book," *Journal of Education*, 83 (May): 518; A. Moore, "Review of John Dewey, Democracy and Education," International Journal of Ethics, 26 (Fall 1916): 547; John Dewey to Horace Kallen, July 1, 1916 (record 03236) in *The Correspondence of John Dewey, Vol. 1: 1871–1918*, 3rd ed., CD-ROM version, ed., Larry Hickman (Carbondale, IL: Center for Dewey Studies, Southern Illinois University, 2005).
59. Dewey, "Nationalizing Education (1916)," in *Middle Works*, vol. 10, 203, 204, 205, 206.
60. Dewey, "Nationalizing Education," 97, 99.
61. William L. Ettinger "The Schools and the War," *Journal of Education*, 88 (Dec. 1918): 453.

Chapter 2

1. Erwin Fellows, "Propaganda: History of a Word," *American Speech*, 34 (Oct 1959): 182–189. The definition in the quotation comes from Edwin Broome,

Report of the Committee on Propaganda in the Schools: Presented at the Annual Meeting of the NEA, July 1929 (Washington, DC: NEA, 1929), 3.

2. M. E. Sadler, Preface to *The German School as War Nursery*, 13.
3. Howard Parker, "A Plan for Sifting Propaganda in the Schools," *Elementary School Journal* (Dec. 1932): 279.
4. George Creel, *How We Advertised America: The First Telling of the Amazing Story of the Committee of Public Information that Carried the Gospel of Americanism to Every Corner of the Globe* (New York, Harper and Brothers, 1920), 4.
5. Creel, *How We Advertised*, 114, 111.
6. William R. Hood, compiler, *State Laws Relating to Education: Enacted in 1915, 1916, and 1917*, Department of the Interior, Bureau of Education, Bulletin 1918, No. 23 (Washington, DC, 1919), 164; "Americanization through Education," in *Report of the Commissioner of Education for The Year Ended June 30, 1918*, Department of the Interior, Bureau of Education (Washington, DC, 1918), 42–49.
7. Charles Judd, "Introduction," in *Lessons in Community Life: Series A, for the Upper Classes of the High School* (Washington, DC: Government Printing Office, 1918), 7.
8. George L. Mehaffy, "Social Studies in World War One: A Period of Transition," *Theory and Research in Social Education*, 15 (Winter 1987): 23–32; Lewis Paul Todd, *Wartime Relations of the Federal Government and Public Schools, 1917–1918* (New York: Bureau of Publications: Teachers College, Columbia University, 1945), 32–34.
9. See Celia Malone Kingsbury, *For Home and Country: World War I Propaganda on the Home Front* (Lincoln: University of Nebraska Press, 2010); Ross F. Collins, "This is Your Propaganda Kids: Building a War Myth for World War I Children," *Journalism History*, 38 (Spring 2012): 13–22.
10. Woodrow Wilson, Letter of the President, *Lessons in Community and National Life, Series A, for the Upper Classes of High School*, Department of the Interior, Bureau of Education in Cooperation with the United States Food Administration (Washington, DC, 1918), 5.
11. National Board for Historical Service, Department of the Interior Bureau of Education, *Opportunities for History Teachers: The Lessons of the Great War in the Classroom, Teachers Leaflet No. 1.* (Washington, DC: Government Printing Office, 1917), 18.
12. See J. R. Shannon "Exploitation of Our Schools," *American School Board Journal*, 72 (June 1926): 59, 158.
13. Shannon, "Exploitation of Our Schools," 7; National Board for Historical Service, *Opportunities for History Teachers: Lessons of the Great War in the Classroom, Teacher's Leaflet No. 1*, Department of the Interior, Bureau of Education (Washington, D.C: Government Printing Office, 1917); Charles A. Coulomb, Armand J. Gerson, and Albert E. McKinley, preparers, Under the Direction of the National Board For Historical Service, *Outline of an Course of Instruction on the War, Teacher's Leaflet No. 4*, Department of the Interior, Bureau of Education (Washington, DC, 1918), 5, 6, 13, 5.
14. Diane Ravitch, "Tot Sociology, or What Happened to History in Grade Schools," *American Scholar*, 56 (1987): 348.

15. See Thomas Fallace, "Did the Social Studies Really Replace History in American Secondary Schools?" *Teachers College Record*, 110 (2008): 2245–2270.
16. See Gary B. Nash, Charlotte Crabtree, and Ross E. Dunn, *History on Trial: Culture Wars and Teaching the Past* (New York: Vintage, 1997); Robert Orrill and Linn Shapiro, "From Bold Beginnings to an Uncertain Future: The Discipline of History and History Education," *The American Historical Review* 110 (2005): 727–751; Diane Ravitch and Chester Finn, *What Do Our 17–Year-Olds Know: A Report on the First National Assessment of History and Literature* (New York: Harper and Row, 1987); Paul Gagnon (Ed.) *Historical Literacy: The Case for History in American Education* (Boston: Houghton Mifflin, 1989); Diane Ravitch, "Who Prepares Our History Teachers? Who Should Prepare Our History Teachers?" *The History Teacher 31*(3) (1998): 495–503.
17. Wilson, "Letter of the President," 5.
18. Samuel Harding, "What the War Should Do for our History Methods" *Historical Outlook*, 10 (1919): 190.
19. Quoted in Stephen Vaughn, *Holding Fast the Inner Lines: Democracy, Nationalism, and the Committee on Public Information* (Chapel Hill, NC: University of North Carolina Press, 1980), 109.
20. NEA, *Report of the Commission of the Reorganization of Secondary Education. U.S. Bureau of Education Bulletin 35* (Washington, DC: Government Printing Office, 1918), 7–16.
21. National Industrial Conference Board, *A Case of Federal Propaganda in our Public Schools* (Boston: NCIB, 1919), 7, 3, 4, 13.
22. Charles Beard, "Propaganda in the Schools," *Dial* (June 14, 1919): 598.
23. See Edward K. Strong, Jr., "Control of Propaganda as a Psychological Problem," *The Scientific Monthly*, 14 (March 1922): 235.
24. National Board for Historical Service, *Opportunities for History Teachers*, 18; National Board for Historical Service, *Outline for Emergency Course*, 11.
25. Committee on Public Information, *The German-Bolshevik Conspiracy* (Washington, DC: Government Printing Office, 1918), 3. On the forgery of the Sisson documents, see Vaughn, *Holding Fast*, 77; Lasch, *The American Liberals*, 88.
26. Quoted in Novick, *That Noble Dream*, 163.
27. Lucy W. Wilson, *The New Schools of New Russia* (New York: Vanguard Press, 1928), viii, ix.
28. Guy Stanton Ford, "The Committee on Public Information," *The Historical Outlook*, 9 (2): 100.
29. "Reconstruction Editorial," *Dial* (Dec. 1918): 561.
30. Eastman, Becker, and Niebuhr quoted in Stuart I. Rochester, *American Liberal Disillusionment in the Wake of World War I* (University Park: Pennsylvania State University Press, 1977), 92, 91, 93.
31. C. E. Montague, *Disenchantment* (New York: Brentano's, 1922), 172.
32. Charles Beard and Mary Beard, *The Rise of American Civilization* (New York: Macmillan, 1927), 640.
33. Carter G. Woodson, "Negro Life and History in our Schools," *The Journal of Negro History* 4 (July 1919): 279.

34. Ross L. Finney, *Causes and Cures for Social Unrest: An Appeal to the Middle Class* (New York: Macmillan, 1922), 1.
35. See Edward A. Purcell, Jr. *The Crisis of Democratic Theory: Scientific Naturalism and the Problem of Value* (Lexington: University of Kentucky Press, 1973); Mark C. Smith, *Social Science in the Crucible: The American Debate over Objectivity and Purpose, 1918–1914* (Durham, NC: Duke University Press, 1994).
36. National Board for Historical Service, *Opportunities for History Teachers*, 7.
37. Donald Taft, "Historical Textbooks as Provocatives of War," *Advocate of Peace through Justice*, 87 (April 1925): 226, 227. See also Jonathan French Scott, *The Menace of Nationalism in Education* (London: G. Allen and Unwin, 1926), which focuses on textbooks in England, France, and Germany.
38. Quoted in Rochester, *American Liberal Disillusionment*, 91.
39. Upton Sinclair, *The Goose-Step: A Study of American Education* (New York: AMS Press, 1923), 18–19. See also Sinclair, *The Goslings: A Study of American Education* (New York: AMS Press, 1924).
40. Walter Lippman, *Public Opinion* (New York: Harcourt, Brace, and Co., 1922), 46, 42, 43, 14, 31, 408.
41. Randolph Bourne, "Twilight of Idols," in *John Dewey: Critical Assessments: Vol. II: Political and Social Practice*, edited by J. E. Tiles (New York: Routledge, 1992), 199. See also Carl Resek, ed., *War and the Intellectuals: Essays by Randolph Bourne, 1915–1919* (New York: Harper and Row, 1964).
42. Harold Lasswell, *Propaganda Technique in the World War* (New York: Peter Smith, 1927), 2.
43. Harold Lasswell, "The Theory of Political Propaganda," *The American Political Science Review*, 31 (Aug 1927): 3.
44. Harold Lasswell, *A Pre-View of Policy Sciences* (New York: American Elsevier, 1971), xiv.
45. Philip Marshall Brown, "Propaganda and Education," *The Review*, 2 (April 3, 1920): 343.
46. Frederick E. Lumley, *The Propaganda Menace* (New York: The Century Company, 1933).
47. James Sullivan, "History Teaching as Propaganda in Dealing with After-war Problems—Its Use and Abuse," *Proceedings of the Meeting Held* (Philadelphia: Association of History Teachers of the Middle States and Maryland, 1919), 24, 25, 27.
48. Wayne Soper, "What Species Propaganda?" *The Elementary School Journal*, 30 (Nov. 1929): 224.
49. Edward K. Strong Jr., "Control of Propaganda as a Psychological Problem," *The Scientific Monthly*, 14 (March 1922): 236.
50. *The New Republic*, "Federal Trade Commission's Investigation" (Nov. 1928), 28; "Fight for Propaganda in Nation's Schools," *New York Times* (Nov. 1928), sec 2, 1:1.
51. Lumley, *Propaganda Menace*, 316.
52. Marlen E. Pew, "Propaganda," *Teachers College Record*, 31 (Jan. 1929): 37–38.
53. Stephen Raushenbush, *High Power Propaganda* (New York: New Republic, Inc., 1928) and *The Power Fight* (New York: New Republic, Inc., 1932); Carl D. Thompson, *Confessions of the Power Trust* (New York: E. P. Dutton, 1932).

For detailed testimony on the power trust scandal, see Ernest Gruening, "Power and Propaganda," *American Economic Review*, 21 (1931): 202–241; George W. Norris, "The Power Trust in the Public Schools," *Nation*, 129 (Sept. 18, 1929): 296–297.

54. Dewey, "The New Paternalism (1918)," *Middle Works*, vol. 2, 118, 119.
55. Dewey, "Impressions of Soviet Russia," *Later Works*, vol. 3, 221.
56. Dewey, "Impressions of Soviet Russia," 221–222.
57. As Lumley wrote, "[a] number of year ago some writings of Professor John Dewey directed my attention to the phenomena of propaganda" (p. vii).
58. Broome, *Report of the Committee on Propaganda in the Schools*, 26.
59. Broome, *Report of the Committee on Propaganda*, 5.
60. William Carr, "The School Child and Propaganda: The Conundrum of the Educator," *Official Proceedings of the Annual Meeting of the National Conference on Social Welfare* (1931), 600–601, 603.
61. Historians have extensively explored the use and effect of propaganda on the U.S. during World War I, but they have failed to consider the lasting effect of propaganda on U.S. schools. In addition to previously cited sources, see Alan Axelrod, *Selling the War: The Making of American Propaganda* (New York: St. Martin's Press, 2009); Jonathan Auerbach, *Weapons of Democracy: Propaganda, Progressivism, and American Public Opinion* (Baltimore, MD: Johns Hopkins, 2015); George Blakey, *Historians on the Home Front: American Propagandists for the Great War* (Lexington: University of Kentucky Press, 2015); Brett Gary, *The Nervous Liberals: Propaganda Anxieties from World War I to The Cold War* (New York: Columbia University Press, 1999); Stewart Halsey Ross, *Propaganda for War: How the United States was Conditioned to Fight the Great War of 1914–1918* (San Diego: Progressive Press, 2009); Michael J. Sproule, *Propaganda and Democracy: The American Experience of Media and Mass Persuasion* (New York: Cambridge University Press, 1997).
62. See William James, *The Meaning of Truth, A Sequel to Pragmatism* (New York: Longman, Green, & Co, 1909), vi; James Harvey Robinson, *The New History: Essay Illustrating the Modern American Outlook* (New York: Macmillan, 1912), 130.
63. See Novick, *That Noble Dream*, 124–128.
64. Broome, *Report of the Committee on Propaganda*, 5; italics in original.

Chapter 3

1. Albert Pinkevitch, *The New Education in the Soviet Republic* (New York: John Day, 1929), vi.
2. Yordanka Valkanova, "The Passion for Educating the 'New Man': Debates about Pre-Schooling in Soviet Russia," *History of Education Quarterly*, 49 (May 2009): 211–221. See also Larry E. Holmes, *The Kremlin and the Schoolhouse: Reforming Education in Soviet Russia 1911–1931* (Bloomington: Indiana University Press, 1991).
3. Leo Pasvolsky, "Education under Communism: The Results of Soviet Education," *School and Society* (Nov. 21 1921): 331.
4. Abraham Epstein, "The Schools in Soviet Russia," *School and Society* 16 (Oct. 7, 1922): 399.

5. Lloyd Storr-Best, "Review of *Changing Man: The Soviet Education System* by Beatrice King," *The Slavonic and East European Review*, *15* (Jan 1937): 465.
6. Scott Nearing, *Education in Soviet Russia* (New York: International Publishers, 1924), 9, 13, 15.
7. See John Dewey, *Impressions of Soviet Russia and the Revolutionary World* (New York: New Republic, Inc., 1929).
8. Dewey, *Impressions of Soviet Russia*, 129.
9. Kilpatrick quoted in Lewis Feuer, "American Travelers to the Soviet Union, 1917–32: Formation of a Component of New Deal Ideology," *American Quarterly*, 14 (Summer 1962): 123. See also Peter Filene, *Americans and the Soviet Experiment, 1917–1933* (Cambridge, MA: Harvard University Press, 1967).
10. Kilpatrick quoted in Ravitch, *Left Back: A Century of Failed Schools of Reform,* (New York, Simon & Schuster, 2001), 209.
11. Wilson, *The New Schools of New Russia*, 2.
12. George S. Counts, *The Selective Character of American Secondary Education* (Chicago: University of Chicago Press, 1922); Counts, "The Selective Principle in American Secondary Education I," *The School Review*, 29 (Nov. 1921): 657–667; Counts, "The Selective Principle in American Secondary Education II," *The School Review*, 30 (Feb. 1922): 95–109; Counts, *The Social Composition of School Boards* (Chicago: University of Chicago Press, 1927).
13. George S. Counts, "Needed Research in Secondary Education," *The Phi Delta Kappan*, 5 (Feb. 1923): 27.
14. See Ellen Condliffe Lagemann, "Prophesy or Profession? George S. Counts and the Social Study of Education," *American Journal of Education*, 100 (Feb. 1992): 137–155; Gerald H. Gutek, *George S. Counts and American Civilization: The Educator as Social Theorist* (Macon, GA: Mercer University Press, 1984).
15. George S. Counts, *A Ford Crosses Soviet Russia* (Boston: The Stratford Co., 1930); Counts, *The Soviet Challenge to America* (New York: John Day, 1931). Counts also wrote a brief foreword to William Clark Trow, ed., *Character Education in Soviet Russia* (Ann Arbor: University of Michigan Press, 1934) and an introduction to Pinkevitch, *The New Education in the Soviet Republic.*
16. R. D. Charques, "Education in the Soviet Union," *International Affairs*, 11 (July 1923): 495.
17. Beatrice King, *Changing Man: The Education System of the U.S.S.R.* (New York: Viking Press, 1937), 50. The statistics on literacy come from King.
18. Gajanan S. Khair, "Glimpses of Secondary Education in Soviet Russia," *Junior-Senior High School Clearing House*, 9 (Nov. 1934): 143
19. Counts, *The Soviet Challenge*, 329.
20. Counts, "Education and the Five-year Plan of Soviet Russia," *The Journal of Educational Sociology*, 4 (Sept. 1930): 29.
21. Counts, "Introduction," to Pinkevitch, *The New Education in the Soviet Republic*, xii.
22. King, *Changing Man*, 22.
23. Quoted in Ravitch, *Left Back*, 234.
24. King, *Changing Man*, 24.
25. Samuel Northrup Harper, *Civic Training in Soviet Russia* (Chicago: University of Chicago Press, 1929), 377.

26. Philip Cox, "Russian and Danish Guideposts for American Education," *Journal of Educational Sociology*, 2 (March 1929): 416, 415.
27. Counts, *The Soviet Challenge*, 322, 328; italics in original.
28. Charques, "Education in Soviet Union," 503.
29. Lumley, *The Propaganda Menace*, 327.
30. Boyd Bode, "The Confusion in Present-Day Education," in *The Educational Frontier*, ed., William H. Kilpatrick (New York: D. Appleton-Century Company, 1933), 23, 24.
31. Counts, "Introduction," in Pinkevitch, *The New Education in the Soviet Republic*, xii.
32. Purcell, *The Crisis of Democratic Theory*, 122; see John T. McGreevy, *Catholicism and American Freedom: A History* (New York: Norton, 2003).
33. John Diggins, "Flirtation with Fascism: American Pragmatic Liberals and Mussolini's Italy," *American Historical Review*, 71 (Jan. 1966): 487–506.
34. Adolph E. Meyer, "Education in Modern Italy," *School and Society*, 22 (July 25, 1925): 99.
35. Fredericka Blankner, "Education in Italy," *School and Society*, 32 (July 5, 1930): 21; E. A. Miller, "Il Fascismo, Italian Education, and the Church," *The School Review*, 38 (Sept. 1930): 510.
36. Emma Menna, "The Gentile Reforms in Italian Education," *Educational Administration and Supervision*, 22 (1936): 555.
37. Quoted in Purcell, *The Crisis of Democratic Theory*, 122, 123.
38. John Dewey and John Childs, "The Socio-Economic Situation and Education," in *The Educational Frontier*, 72.
39. W. F. Russell, "Address," *Bulletin of the American Library Association*, 21 (Oct. 1927): 275.
40. Valmai Burwood Evans, "Education in the Philosophy of Giovanni Gentile," *International Journal of Ethics*, 43 (Jan. 1933): 210–217; Herbert W. Schneider and Shepard B. Clough, *Making Fascists* (Chicago: University of Chicago Press, 1929), 83–109.
41. Giovanni Gentile, "The Philosophical Basis of Fascism," *Foreign Affairs*, 6 (Jan. 1928): 303.
42. Blankner, "Education in Italy," 21.
43. Benito Mussolini, "The Schools of Italy," *The High School Journal*, 16 (Nov. 1933): 264, 263, 262.
44. W. Y. Elliot, "Mussolini, Prophet of the Pragmatic Era in Politics," *Political Science Quarterly*, 42 (June 1926): 164.
45. William Kilborne Stewart, "The Mentors of Mussolini," *The American Political Science Review*, 22 (Nov. 1928): 863.
46. Hook quoted in Horace Kallen, "Mussolini, William James, and the Rationalists," *Social Frontier*, 4 (May 1938): 253.
47. Quoted in John Diggins, *Mussolini and Fascism: The View from America* (Princeton, NJ: Princeton University Press, 1972): 253.
48. See Maurice Parmelee, "Liberal Democracy, Fascism, and Bolshevism," *The Annals of the American Academy of Political and Social Science*, 180 (July 1935): 47–54.
49. R. Bruce Raup, "The New Conception of the Professor of Education" in *The Educational Frontier*, 78.

50. Patricia Albjerg Graham, *Progressive Education from Arcady to Academe: A History of the Progressive Education Association, 1919–1955* (New York: Teachers College Press, 1967).
51. Quoted in Richard H. Pells, *Radical Visions and American Dreams: Culture and Social Thought in the Depression Years* (Urbana: University of Illinois Press, 1973), 50.
52. Counts, *Soviet Challenge*, ix.
53. Charles Judd, "Education, the Nation's Safeguard," *Superintendence Report* (1932): 37
54. George S. Counts, "Secondary Education and the Social Problem," *School Executives Magazine*, 51 (Aug. 1932): 500.
55. Charles Beard, *Conclusions and Recommendations of the Commission: Report of the Commission on Social Studies of the American Historical Association* (New York: Charles Scribner's and Sons, 1934), 46.
56. On Beard's life and career see the chapter on the historian in Mark C. Smith, *Social Science in the Crucible*, 159–211.
57. See John Franklin Bobbitt, *The Curriculum* (New York: Houghton Mifflin, 1918); Carleton Washburne, "Basic Facts Needed in History and Geography: A Statistical Investigation," in *The Twenty-second Yearbook of the National Society for the Study of Education*, edited by G. M. Whipple (Bloomington, IL: Public School Publishing Company, 1923); William C. Bagley and Harold O. Rugg, *The Content of American History as Taught in the Seventh and Eighth Grades: An Analysis of Typical School Textbooks* (Urbana, IL: University of Illinois, 1916); W. W. Charters, *Curriculum Construction* (New York: Macmillan, 1923); Ernest Horn, "The Application of Methods of Research to Making the Course of Study in History," in *The Twenty-Second Yearbook of the National Society for the Study of Education*, 234–259.
58. Ernest Horn, "The Application of Scientific Method to Making the Course of Study in Civics," *The Elementary School Journal*, 19 (1919), 762.
59. Harold O. Rugg, "How Shall We Reconstruct the Social Studies Curriculum?" *The Historical Outlook*, 12 (May 1921): 186; Harold O. Rugg, "A Century of Curriculum-Construction in American schools," in *Making Past and Present: The 26th Yearbook of the National Society for the Study of Education* (Bloomington, IL: Public School Publishing Company, 1933), 50.
60. Neal Billings, *A Determination of Generalizations Basic to the Social Studies Curriculum* (Baltimore, MD: Warwick and York, Inc., 1928).
61. John Childs, *Education and the Philosophy of Experimentalism* (New York: The Century Company, 1931), 7, 118.
62. George Counts, "Education and the Social Problem," *Southern Review*, I (Autumn 1935): 303.
63. Charles Beard, "The Education in the Quest for National Security," *Social Frontier*, I (April 1935): 14.
64. John L. Childs, "Dr. Bode on 'Authentic' Democracy," in *John Dewey: The Later Works*, Vol. 3 of *The Collected Works of John Dewey*, ed. Jo Ann Boydston (Carbondale: Southern Illinois University Press, 1983), 389.
65. Harold Rugg, "The American Scholar Faces a Social Crisis," in *The Social Frontier: A Critical Reader*, ed. Eugene F. Provenzo, Jr. (New York: Peter Lang, 2011), 97.
66. Jesse H. Newlon, "Teachers and Politics—1940," in *The Social Frontier: A Critical Reader*, ed. Eugene F. Provenzo, Jr. (New York: Peter Lang, 2011), 245.

67. R. Bruce Raup, *Education and Organized Interest in America* (New York: G. P. Putnam's Sons, 1936), 37, 39.
68. Beard, *Conclusions and Recommendations*, 16.
69. Editorial Board, "Orientation," in *The Social Frontier: A Critical Reader*, ed. Eugene F. Provenzo, Jr. (New York: Peter Lang, 2011), 21.
70. Harold Rugg, *Foundations for American Education* (New York: World Book Company, 1946), xi.
71. Charles Beard, *The Nature of the Social Sciences: Part VII Report of the Commission on the Social Studies, American Historical Association* (New York: Charles Scribner's Sons, 1934), 50.
72. George S. Counts, *Dare the Schools Build a New Social Order?* (New York: John Day, 1932), 7.
73. Thomas H. Briggs, "Propaganda in the Curriculum," *Teachers College Record*, 34 (1933): 476.
74. Boyd Bode, "Dr. Childs and Education for Democracy," in *John Dewey: The Later Works*, vol. 3 of *The Collected Works of John Dewey*, ed. Jo Ann Boydston (Carbondale: Southern Illinois University Press, 1983), 380, 381.
75. John L. Childs, "Dr. Bode on 'Authentic' Democracy," in *John Dewey: The Later Works*, vol. 3 of *The Collected Works of John Dewey*, ed. Jo Ann Boydston (Carbondale: Southern Illinois University Press, 1983), 390.
76. John Dewey to Horace Kallen, 1932, 02. 11 (rec. 08463) in *The Correspondence of John Dewey, 1871–1952.*
77. Horace Kallen to John Dewey, 1932, 02. 16 (rec. 08464) in *The Correspondence of John Dewey, 1871–1952.*
78. John Dewey, "Education and the Social Order," in *John Dewey: The Later Works*, vol. 9 of the *Collected Works of John Dewey*, ed. Jo Ann Boydston (Carbondale: Southern Illinois University Press, 1983), 182.
79. John Dewey, "The Economic Basis of the New Social Order," *Later Works*, vol. 13, 320. For a discussion of the influence of these reactionary forces on educational policy and textbooks in the 1920s and 1930s, see R. Bruce Raup, *Education and Organized Interests in America*. This text also documents the transition from propaganda anxiety to the educational radicalism of 1930s.
80. John Dewey, "Can Education Share in Social Reconstruction?" in *John Dewey: The Later Works*, vol. 9 of *The Collected Works of John Dewey*, ed., Jo Ann Boydston (Carbondale: Southern Illinois University Press, 1983), 207.
81. John Dewey, "What is Social Study?" in *John Dewey: The Later Works*, vol. 13 of *The Collected Works of John Dewey*, ed., Jo Ann Boydston (Carbondale: Southern Illinois University Press, 1983), 341.
82. John Dewey, "Education, Democracy, and Socialized Economy," in *John Dewey: Later Works*, vol. 13 of *The Collected Works of John Dewey*, ed., Jo Ann Boydston (Carbondale: Southern Illinois University Press, 1983), 307.
83. John Dewey, "The Economic Basis of the New Social Order," *Later Works*, vol. 13, 321; italics in original.
84. See Frederick S. Breed, "Indoctrination at Atlantic City," *The Phi Delta Kappan*, 16 (March 1935): 147–149. Some of the articles from the *Social Frontier* were republished online in *Teachers College Record*. See Harry D. Gidoense, "Non-Partisan Education for Political Intelligence," *Teachers College Record*, 1 (1935): 15–18; The Editorial Board, "Teaching Democracy in the Present Crisis," *Teachers College Record*, http://www.tcrecord.org, ID Number: 14168, date published: April 09, 2007; date accessed: August 18, 2016; William Stanley and Kenneth Benne,

"The Ohio School of Democracy and Education," *Teachers College Record*, http:// www.tcrecord.org, ID Number: 13930, date published: March 27, 2007; date accessed: August 18, 2016; Carleton Wolsey Washburne, "Indoctrination versus Education," *Teachers College Record*, 2 (1936): 212–215. For a more in-depth discussion of the contents of *Social Frontier* journal, see C. A. Bowers, "The Social Frontier Journal: A Historical Sketch," *History of Education Quarterly*, 4 (Sept. 1964): 167–180; Bowers, *The Progressive Educator and the Depression*, 92–198; Sonia Murrow, "Depicting Teachers' Roles in Social Reconstruction in the Social Frontier, 1934–1943," *Educational Theory*, 61 (2011): 311–333.

85. "Appendix C: Dr. Isaiah Bowmann's Reservations in Signing This Report," *Conclusions and Recommendations*, 165. Ernest Horn also refused to sign Beard's *Conclusions* because of the Commission's criticism of standardized testing. See James E. Schul, "Ensuing Dog Fight: the AHA Commission on the Social Studies' Testing Controversy," *Journal of Educational Administration and History*, 45:1 (Nov. 2013): 1–27.
86. See C. A. Bowers, *The Progressive Educator and the Depression: The Radical Years* (New York: Random House, 1969), 11–45; Lawrence Cremin, *The Transformation of the School: Progressivism in American Education, 1876–1957* (New York: Vintage, 1961), 225–234; Diane Ravitch, *Left Back: A Century of Failed School Reform* (New York: Simon and Schuster, 2000), 208–221; Herbart Kliebard, *The Struggle for the American Curriculum, 1893–1958* (New York: Routledge, 1995), 158– 171; Ronald W. Evans, *The Social Studies Wars: What Should We Teach the Children?* (New York: Teachers College, 2004), 50–59.
87. Paul Hanna, a professor of education at Stanford University, did develop an influential new approach to elementary social studies known as "expanding environments" in the 1930s, based on concentric circles of the students' concrete world. This framework became a commonly used organization for the K–3 social studies curriculum until the 1980s. Historians disagree about the extent to which Hanna's popular approach was influenced by the rhetoric of the social frontier group. See Ravitch, *Left Back*; 256–258; Anne-Lise Halvorsen, *A History of Elementary Social Studies* (New York: Peter Lang, 2013); Jared Stallones, *Paul Robert Hanna: A Life of Expanding Communities* (Washington, DC: Hoover Press, 2002).

Chapter 4

1. See Benjamin Alpers, *Dictatorships, Democracy and American Public Culture: Envisioning the Totalitarian Enemy, 1920s–1950s* (Chapel Hill: University of North Carolina Press, 2003), 15–93; Purcell, Jr., *The Crisis of Democratic Theory*, 117–138; Pells, *Radical Visions and American Dreams*, 292.
2. The concerns among American socialists over the Moscow trials were largely overrun by Stalin's welcomed announcement in 1934 that Russia had entered the League of Nations and had signed a mutual security pact with France, where fascists and socialists were battling for control of the national legislature. By the late 1930s, France was one of the last remaining democracies in Europe. Portugal, Spain, Italy, Greece Turkey, Poland, Czechoslovakia, and Belgium had all fallen to dictators. In 1935, the Seventh World Congress of the Communist International issued an official call for a Popular Front (or United Front) against

fascism, which announced an alliance among Communists, socialists, labor unions, liberals, and moderates against the external threat of fascism.

3. Phillip W. L. Cox, "Fascism, Liberalism, and Individuality in Europe," *Junior-Senior High School Clearing House*, 10 (Oct. 1935): 85–89.
4. Isaac Kandel, "Education in Nazi Germany," *The Annals of the American Academy of Political and Social Science*, 182 (Nov. 1935): 153, 163.
5. Thomas Woody, "Principles of Totalitarian Education," Proceedings of the American Philosophical Society: Symposium on the Totalitarian State, 82 (Feb. 1940): 41, 45, 47, 53, 49.
6. Harold Rugg, *Changing Governments and Changing Cultures: Democracy versus Dictatorship: The World Struggle* (New York: Ginn and Company, 1937), 676, 6.
7. Leon Trotsky, "Question and Answer," in *The Social Frontier: A Critical Reader*, ed. Eugene F. Provenzo, Jr. (New York: Peter Lang, 2011), 222, 228, 229, 230.
8. John Dewey, "Trotsky Inquiry," in *The Later Works*, vol. 11, 333.
9. Les K. Adler and Thomas G. Paterson, "Red Fascism: The Merger of Nazi Germany and Soviet Russia in the American Image of Totalitarianism, 1930s–1950s," *American Historical Review*, 75(4), 1046–1064.
10. John Dewey, *Freedom and Culture* (New York: Putnam's, 1939), 93–94.
11. Quoted in Robert Westbrook, *John Dewey and American Democracy* (Ithaca, NY: Cornell University Press, 1991), 479.
12. Quoted in David Hollinger, *Science, Jews, and Secular Culture: Studies in Mid-Twentieth Century American Intellectual History* (Princeton, NJ: Princeton University Press, 1996), 160.
13. Quoted in G. L. Gutek, "George Counts and Social Issues," in *Addressing Social Issues in the Classroom and Beyond: The Pedagogical Efforts of Pioneers in the Field*, eds., Samuel Totten and Jon Pedersen (Charlotte, NC: IAP, 2007), 43.
14. George Counts, *The Prospects of American Democracy* (New York: John Day, 1938): 143, 146, 357.
15. George Counts, "A Liberal Looks at Life," *Frontiers of Democracy*, VII (May 1941): 231, 232.
16. D. J. Dallin, "America, Russia, and the Communist Party in the Postwar World by Review of John L. Childs & George S. Counts," *The Russian Review*, 3 (Autumn 1943): 109, 110.
17. Fox, *Reinhold Niebuhr*, 190.
18. Quoted in Gary, *The Nervous Liberals*, 94.
19. Norman Holmes Pearson, "The Nazi-Soviet Pact and the End of a Dream," in Daniel Aaron, ed., *America in Crisis* (New York: Alfred A. Knopf, 1952), 344.
20. Quoted in Ronald Steel, *Walter Lippman and the American Century* (Boston: Little Brown & Co, 1980), 235.
21. Quoted in Feuer, "American Travelers to the Soviet Union," 148.
22. See Morton White, *Social Thought in America*; James Kloppenberg, *Uncertain Victory: Social Democracy and Progressivism in European and American Thought*, 1870–1920 (New York: Oxford University Press, 1986).
23. Counts, Dare the Schools, 16.
24. Beard, *The Nature of the Social Sciences*, 173.
25. Rugg, *Foundations for American Education*, xviii; Rugg, "The American Scholar Faces a Social Crisis," 95.

26. Geoffrey O'Connell, *Naturalism in American Education* (New York: Benziger Brothers, 1938), 247, 242.
27. Albert F. Kaiser, "Naturalism and Education," *The Sign*, 13 (March 1934): 492.
28. Louis J. A. Mercier, Preface to *Naturalism in American Education*, viii.
29. Counts and Kilpatrick quoted in Earl Marlott, "Does America Believe in Thinking?" *The Phi Delta Kappan*, 17 (Jan. 1935): 105.
30. William Heard Kilpatrick, "The New Adult Education" in *Educational Frontier*, 52.
31. Bruce Raup, *Education and Organized Interests in America*, 185.
32. Phillip W. L. Cox, "What Might Happen If . . ." *Junior-Senior High School Clearing House*, 9 (April 1935): 486, 491.
33. Cox, "What Might Happen If . . . ," 256.
34. I. Donsky, "Truth and Modern Dictatorship," *Philosophy*, 35 (July 1934): 280.
35. Boyd Bode, *Progressive Education at the Crossroads* (New York: Newsome & Co., 1938), 58, 39.
36. The battle over Rugg's textbooks is one of the most studied episodes in the history of American education. Historians have cast the controversy in the context of ongoing battles over the content of textbooks, backlashes against student-centered progressive education and the social studies, and the censorship of American schools. See Naida Tushnet Bagenstos, "Social Reconstruction: The Controversy over the Textbooks of Harold Rugg," *Theory & Research in Social Education*, 5 (Summer 1977): 22–38; Peter F. Carbone, *The Social and Educational Thought of Harold Rugg* (Durham, NC: Duke University Press, 1977); Charles Dorn, "Treason in the Textbooks: Reinterpreting the Harold Rugg Textbook Controversy in the Context of Wartime Schooling," *Paedagogica Historica*, 44 (Aug. 2008): 457–479; Ronald W. Evans, *This Happened in America: Harold Rugg and Censure of the Social Studies*. (Charlotte, NC: Information Age Publishing, 2007) and *The Social Studies Wars: What Should We Teach the Children?* (New York: Teachers College Press, 2004), 75–84; *Andrew Hartman, Education and the Cold War: The Battle for the American School* (New York: Palgrave Macmillan, 2008), 49–52; Adam Laats, *The Other School Reformers: Conservative Activism in American Education* (Cambridge, MA: Harvard University Press, 2015), 73–122; Joseph Moreau, *Schoolbook Nation: Conflicts over American History Textbooks from the Civil War to the Present* (Ann Arbor: University of Michigan Press, 2003), 219–263; Jonathan Zimmerman, *Whose America? Culture Wars in the Public Schools* (Cambridge, MA: Harvard University Press, 2002), 64–80.
37. American Council for Democracy and Intellectual Freedom, Committee on Textbooks, The Textbooks of Harold Rugg (New York: Author, 1942).
38 Harold Rugg, *An Introduction to Problems of American Life* (New York: Ginn and Company, 1931), 596.
39. Dorn, "Treason in the Textbooks," 473.
40. Quoted in Dorn, "Treason in the Textbooks," 469.
41. Quoted in Laats, *The Other School Reformers*, 116.
42. William Heard Kilpatrick, "Freedom to Develop Social Intelligence" in *The Social Frontier: A Critical Reader*, ed. Eugene F. Provenzo, Jr. (New York: Peter Lang, 2011), 166.
43 Quoted in Evans, *This Happened in America*, 154, 155, 162, 187.
44. Quoted in Laats, *The Other School Reformers*, 92, 100, 114.

45. Quoted in Laats, *The Other School Reformers*, 96.
46. Harold Rugg, "This Has Happened Before," in *The Social Frontier: A Critical Reader*, ed. Eugene F. Provenzo, Jr. (New York: Peter Lang, 2011), 249, 254.
47. Newlon, "Teachers and Politics—1940," 247, 249, 250.
48. Quoted in Bowers, *Progressive Educator and the Depression*, 195.
49. Robert Hutchins, "The Crisis in Contemporary Grammar, Rhetoric, and Mr. Dewey," in *The Social Frontier: A Critical Reader*, ed. Eugene F. Provenzo, Jr. (New York: Peter Lang, 2011), 207; Robert Maynard Hutchins, *Education for Freedom* (Baton Rouge: Louisiana State University Press, 1943), 35.
50. Mortimer Adler, "The Chicago School," *Harper's Magazine*, 183 (Sept. 1941): 388, 387. Similar attacks on the new student-centered, functional, progressive curriculum came from Teachers College professors Isaac Kandel and William Bagley. Although they did not dismiss naturalistic philosophy, like Adler they lamented the loss of the rigorous liberal arts curriculum established by the Committee of Ten. See Ravitch, *Left Back*, 284–298.
51. John Dewey, "The Higher Learning in America," in *The Social Frontier: A Critical Reader*, ed. Eugene F. Provenzo, Jr. (New York: Peter Lang, 2011), 209.
52. Jerome Nathanson, Preface, in *The Authoritarian Attempt to Capture Education: Papers from the 2nd Conference on the Scientific Spirit and Democratic Faith*, ed., Jerome Nathanson (New York: King's Crown Press, 1945), vii, vi. For more on Dewey's debates with Catholics, see McGreevy, *Catholicism and American Freedom*, 138–141, 174–176, 182–183.
53. Charles W. Morris, "The Teaching of Dogmatic Religion in a Democratic Society," in *The Authoritarian Attempt*, 142.
54. John Dewey, "Democratic Faith and Education," in *The Authoritarian Attempt*, 8, 9.
55. Quoted in Zoe Burkholder, "'A War of Ideas': The Rise of Conservative Teachers in Wartime New York City, 1938–1946." *History of Education Quarterly*, 55 (2015): 221.
56. Donsky, "Truth and Modern Dictatorship," 280.
57. Thomas Fallace, "John Dewey's Interdisciplinary Vision(s) for the Social Studies," *Social Studies Research and Practice*, 11 (2016): 177–189 and "The Origins of Classroom Deliberation: Democratic Education in the Shadow of Authoritarianism, 1938–1960," *Harvard Educational Review*, 86 (Fall 2016): 506–526.
58. William Biddle, "Propaganda and the Curriculum," *Curriculum Journal*, 9 (Nov. 1938): 306.
59. Malbone W. Graham, "Analyzing Propaganda," Proceedings of the Annual Meeting—National Education Association of the United States (1939): 428.
60. One account claimed that "five hundred schools scattered throughout the nation" were using the materials from the IPA. See Ernest Hollis, "An Antidote for Propaganda," *School and Society*, 50 (Oct. 1937): 453.
61. Sproule, *Propaganda and Democracy*, 129–177.
62. Sproule, *Propaganda and Democracy*, 135.
63. To aid teachers, the Institute had also published Violet Edwards's *Group Leader's Guide to Propaganda Analysis*. Miller taught a class on the topic at Teachers College. See Sarah Welles Talbot, "Propaganda Analysis in the High School," *Sociology and Social Research*, 28 (Spring 1944): 290–295; Robert. S. Lewis, "Building Pupils' Defenses through a Unit on Propaganda," *The*

Clearing House, 13 (Sept. 1938): 22–24; Minnie C. Squire, "We Read Behind the Lines," *The English Journal*, 29 (Sept. 1940): 556–563.

64. William Biddle, *Teaching Resistance to Propaganda: National Council for the Social Studies Seventh Yearbook* (Washington, DC: NCSS, 1937).
65. Sam Rosenkranz, "Literature and Indoctrination," *The English Journal*, 28 (Sept. 1939): 539–544; Helen I. Davis, "Propaganda Enters the English Classroom," *The English Journal,* 28 (Jan. 1939): 26–31; W. C. Armstrong and Lavergne Wood, "Analyzing Propaganda," Social Education, 4 (1940): 331–337; William Jewett, "Detecting and Analyzing Propaganda," *The English Journal,* 13 (Feb. 1940): 22–24.
66. Howard Cummings, "Teaching Propaganda," *The Clearing House,* 13 (March 1939): 397.
67. Talbot, "Propaganda Analysis," 295.
68. Biddle, "Propaganda and the Curriculum," 308.
69. Armstrong and Wood, "Analyzing Propaganda," 337.
70. Bruce Lannes Smith, "Propaganda Analysis and the Science of Democracy," *The Public Opinion Quarterly* (June 1941): 250.
71. Wayland Osborn, "An Experiment in Teaching Resistance to Propaganda," *The Journal of Experimental Education* (Sept. 1939): 17.
72. Clyde Miller, "Some Comments on Propaganda Analysis and the Science of Democracy," *The Public Opinion Quarterly*, 5 (Winter 1941): 657–665; Cummings, "Teaching Propaganda," 397.
73. Quoted in Sproule, *Propaganda and Democracy,* 162.
74. Quoted in Sproule, *Propaganda and Democracy*, 174, 176.
75. Margaret Mead, "The Problem of Minorities," in *The Social Frontier: A Critical Reader,* ed. Eugene F. Provenzo, Jr. (New York: Peter Lang, 2011), 238–244.
76. Norman Foerster, "Education Leads the Way," *The American Review*, 1 (Sept. 1933): 403.
77. Carroll H. Woody, "Propaganda and Education," *The Annals of American Academy of Political Science*, 179 (May 1939): 228, 230, 233, 237.
78. William Heard Kilpatrick, "Propaganda and Indoctrination," *The American Teacher*, 23 (Nov. 1939): 20.
79. Smith, "Propaganda Analysis," 257, 259.
80. "The New York Meeting of the American Anthropological Association," *Science*, 89 (1939): 29–30.
81. John Dewey, "Racial Prejudice and Friction (1922)," in *John Dewey: The Middle Works, vol. 13 of The Collected Works of John Dewey*, ed. Jo Ann Boydston (Carbondale: Southern Illinois University Press, 1976), 242–254; William Heard Kilpatrick, "Conflict Areas in American Intercultural Life," *The Journal of Educational Sociology*, 16 (Feb. 1943): 340–344. For the views of progressive educators on race, see Ronald K. Goodenow, "The Progressive Educator, Race and Ethnicity in the Depression Years: An Overview," *History of Education Quarterly*, 15 (Dec. 1975): 365–394; Goodenow, "Racial and Ethnic Tolerance in John Dewey's Educational and Social Thought: The Depression Years," *Educational Theory*, 27 (Jan. 1977): 48–64; Goodenow, "The Southern Progressive Educator on Race and Pluralism: The Case of William Heard Kilpatrick," *History of Education Quarterly*, 21 (July 1981): 147–170.
82. Lewis Terman, "Personal Reactions of the Committee: Lewis Terman," in *Intelligence: Its Nature and Nurture, Part 1: Comparative and Critical*

Exposition, The Thirty-Ninth Yearbook of the National Society for the Study of Education, ed., Guy Montrose Wipple (Bloomington, IL: Public School Publishing Company), 462.

83. Ruth Benedict, *Race: Science and Politics* (New York: Viking, 1940), 154.
84. Donald P. Cottrell, "The Educator Studies His Task in the War Situation," *Teachers College Record,* 44 (Jan. 1943): 234.
85. Carter V. Good, "Educational Issues of 1942 and the Task Ahead," *School and Society* (March 27, 1943): 386.
86. W.E.B. Du Bois, "A Chronicle of Race Relations," *Phylon,* 2 (1941): 173.
87. Charles H. Wesley, "Education for Citizenship in a Democracy," *The Journal of Negro Education,* 10 (Jan. 1941): 78.
88. Quoted in Walter G. Daniel and Marion T. Wright, "The Role of Educational Agencies in Maintaining Morale Among Negroes," *The Journal of Negro Education,* 12 (Summer 1943): 491; italics in original.
89. Charles H. Thompson, "Negro Morale and World War II," *The Journal of Negro Education*, 11 (Jan. 1942): 1.
90. Zoe Burkholder, *Color in the Classroom: How American Schools Taught Race, 1900–1954* (New York: Oxford University Press, 2011); Diana Selig, *Americans All: The Cultural Gifts Movement* (Cambridge, MA: Harvard University Press, 2008); Anne-Lise Halvorsen and Jeffrey Mirel, "Intercultural Education in Detroit, 1943–1954," *Paedagogica Historica*, 49 (June 2013): 361–381; Chara Bohan, "'A Rebellious Jersey Girl': Rachel Davis DuBois, Intercultural Education Pioneer," in *Addressing Social Issues in the Classroom and Beyond: The Pedagogical Efforts of Pioneers in the Field*, eds., Samuel Totten and Jon Pedersen (Charlotte, NC: Information Age Publishing, 2007), 99–115; Nicholas V. Montalto, *A History of the Intercultural Education Movement*, 1924–1941 (New York: Garland, 1982); DuBois quoted in Selig, Americans All, 245.
91. Elazar Barkan, *The Retreat of Scientific Racism: Changing Concepts of Race in Britain and the United States between the World Wars* (Cambridge: Cambridge University Press, 1992), 76–95; Lee D. Baker, *From Savage to Negro: Anthropology and the Construction of Race, 1896–1954*. Berkeley: University of California Press, 1998), 101–108, 120–125, 161–163.
92. Benedict, *Race: Science and Politics; Ashley Montagu, Man's Most Dangerous Myth: The Fallacy of Race* (New York: Columbia University Press, 1942). See also Gunnar Dahlberg, *Race, Reason, and Rubbish: A Primer of Race Biology* (New York: Columbia University Press, 1942).
93. Ruth Benedict, "American Melting Pot, 1942 Model," in *Americans All: Studies in Intercultural Education*, ed., M. Edman (Washington, DC: Department of Supervisors and Directors of Instruction, NEA, 1941), 18.
94. Quoted in Burkholder, *Color in the Classroom*, 18.
95. Mead, "The Problem of Minorities," 239.
96. Quoted in Michael Klarman, *From Jim Crow to Civil Rights: The Supreme Court and the Struggle for Racial Equality* (New York: Oxford University Press, 2004), 299.
97. Harvard Committee, *General Education in a Free Society* (Cambridge, MA: Harvard University Press, 1946), 144.
98. Gerstle, *American Crucible*, 195, 205.

Chapter 5

1. Quoted in Benjamin Alpers, *Dictatorships, Democracy and American Public Culture*, 74. See also Les K. Adler and Thomas G. Paterson, "Red Fascism: The Merger of Nazi Germany and Soviet Russia." Contrast Hoover's conflation of fascism and communism with the analysis of Maurice Parmalee, professor of anthropology at City University of New York, who placed the three on a continuum. See Parmalee, "Liberal Democracy, Fascism and Bolshevism," *The Annals of the American Academy of Political and Social Science* (July 1935): 47–54.
2. Quoted in Alpers, *Dictatorships, Democracy and American Public Culture*, 144. For Hook's career battling communists in academia, see Julian Nemeth, "The Case for Clearing House: Sidney Hook and the Ethics of Academic Freedom during the McCarthy Era," *History of Education Quarterly*, 57 (Aug. 2017): 399–426.
3. Purcell, Jr. *The Crisis of Democratic Theory;* Richard H. Pells, *The Liberal Mind in a Conservative Age: American Intellectuals in the 1940s and 1950s* (New York: Harper and Row, 1985); Robert Booth Fowler, *Believing Skeptics: American Political Intellectuals, 1945–1964* (Westport, CT: Greenwood Press, 1978); Stephen J. Whitfield, *The Culture of the Cold War* (Baltimore, MD: Johns Hopkins, 1991), chapter 3.
4. Schlesinger, *The Vital Center*, 250.
5. Floyd Allport, "The Scientific Spirit and the Common Man," in Nathanson, ed., *The Authoritarian Attempt*, 53.
6. Sidney Hook, *Reason, Social Myths, and Democracy* (New York: John Day, 1940), 295.
7. Hook, *Reason, Social Myths and Democracy*, 278, 283. See also Benjamin Ginzburg, "Science under Communism," *The New Republic* (Jan. 6, 1932): 207–209.
8. Robert Merton, "Note on Science and Democracy," *Journal of Legal and Political Sociology*, 1 (1942): 116, 117.
9. Harvard Committee, *General Education in a Free Society*, 65, 50, 108.
10. Harvard Committee, *General Education*, 51, 77, 78, 105.
11. Harvard Committee, *General Education*, 249; Jamie Cohen-Cole, *The Open Mind: Cold War Politics and the Science of Human Nature* (Chicago: University of Chicago Press, 2014), 32.
12. James Conant, *The American High School Today* (New York: Macmillan, 1957), 5.
13. On Conant see Hartman, *Education and the Cold War*, 179–183; Louis Menand, *American Studies* (New York: Farrar, Straus and Giroux, 2002), 91–111.
14. Historian Charles Dorn argues that during World War II schools "resisted efforts to be placed solely in service of the nation's war machine" and "maintained a sturdy commitment to fostering civic mindedness in a society." In contrast, Gerald Giordano argues: "Conservatives revolutionized the schools during World War II." I see the wartime reforms as being more moderate. By taking a broader chronological and cultural view, my account argues that civic education during and after the war rejected the ideological approach of interwar progressive educators, yet retained progressives' commitment to critical and scientific thinking. Thus, interwar progressive education was refashioned during

the war; it was not completely purged by conservatives, nor did it serve as a form of resistance to conservatism. Dorn, *American Education, Democracy and the Second World War* (New York: Palgrave Macmillan, 2007), 3; Giordano, *Wartime Schools: How World War II Changed American Education* (New York: Peter Lang, 2007), xix.

15. Francis O. Wilcox, "Teaching Political Science in a World at War," *The American Political Science Review*, 35(2) (1941): 327.
16. Eugene O. Golub, "Is Ideology Dying?" *Challenge*, 8 (May 1960): 56. See also George Sabine, "Beyond Ideology," *The Philosophical Review*, 57 (Jan. 1948): 1–26.
17. Daniel Bell, *The End of Ideology: On the Exhaustion of Political Ideas in the Fifties* (New York: New Press, 1960), 370, 373, 110.
18. Schlesinger, *The Vital Center*, 245.
19. As Boorstin pointed out, Europeans "look to ideology to help them choose among alternatives"; Americans, in contrast, are "reared with a feeling for the unity of history and an unprecedented belief in the normality of our kind of life to our place on earth." Daniel J. Boorstin, *The Genius of American Politics* (Chicago: University of Chicago Press, 1953), 32. Assuming that "the Bolshevik Revolution represents the most serious threat in modern history to the future of free institutions," Hartz hoped to discover why American never developed the tactics of "European socialists," who were "dominated by ideology." He argued that it was due to America's lack of a feudal past, making the nation exceptional in the modern world. Louis Hartz, *The Liberal Tradition in America: An Interpretation of Political Thought since the Revolution* (New York: Harcourt Brace, 1954), 302, 10.
20. Richard Hofstadter, *The Age of Reform: From Bryan to F.D.R.* (New York: Vintage Books, 1955), 16; quoted in David Hollinger, *Science, Jews, and Secular Culture*, 160.
21. Schlesinger, *The Vital Center*, 42.
22. Richard Burkes, "A Conception of Ideology for Historians," *Journal of the History of Ideas*, 10 (April 1949): 196–197.
23. Reinhold Niebuhr, *The Children of Light and the Children of Darkness: A Vindication of Democracy and a Critique of its Traditional Defense* (Chicago: University of Chicago Press, 1944), 17, xxxii.
24. Perry Miller, "Review of Faith and History by Reinhold Niebuhr," *The Nation* (Aug. 6, 1949): 138.
25. See Walter A. Jackson, *Gunnar Myrdal and America's Conscience: Social Engineering and Racial Liberalism, 1938–1987* (Chapel Hill, NC: The University of North Carolina Press, 1990).
26. Arthur Bestor, *Educational Wastelands: The Retreat from Learning in our Public Schools* (Chicago: University of Illinois Press, 1953), 83. See Burton Weltman, "Reconsidering Arthur Bestor and the Cold War in Social Education," *Theory and Research in Social Education*, 28 (Winter 2000): 11–39.
27. Frederic Lilge, "Reason and Ideology," *Harvard Educational Review*, 22 (Fall 1952): 252; Lilge, "Politicizing of Educational History," *Ethics*, 66 (April 1956): 193.
28. Everett J. Kircher, "Philosophy of Education—Directive Doctrine or Liberal Discipline?" *Educational Theory*, 5 (Oct. 1955): 229, 221.
29. Isaac Kandel, "A Controversy Ended," *Educational Forum*, 22 (Jan. 1958): 177.

30. Allan Nevins, "American History for Americans," *The New York Times Magazine* (May 3, 1942): 28. On the controversy surrounding this article, see Anne-Lise Halvorsen, "'Don't Know Much About History': The *New York Times* 1943 Survey of U.S. History and the Controversy It Generated," *Teachers College Record*, 114 (2012): 1–32
31. Robert Hutchins, *Education for Freedom* (Baton Rouge: Louisiana State University Press, 1943), 14.
32. Quoted in Laats, *The Other School Reformers*, 165.
33. Quoted in Laats, *The Other School Reformers*, 139, 135, 149; Mortimer Smith, *And Madly Teach* (Chicago: University of Chicago Press, 1949), 7.
34. Hartman, *Education and the Cold War*, 140.
35. David Ciepley, *Liberalism in the Shadow of Totalitarianism* (Cambridge, MA: Harvard University Press, 2006); Jamie Cohen-Cole, *The Open Mind*; Andrew Jewett, *Science, Democracy, and the American University: From the Civil War to the Cold War* (New York: Cambridge University Press, 2012).
36. The Education Policies Commission and the American Association of School Administrators, *Educators and the Defense of American Democracy* (Washington, DC: NEA, 1940), 2; Francis O. Wilcox, "Teaching Political Science in a World at War," 333.
37. Erling Hunt (Ed.), *Citizens for a New World: Fourteenth Yearbook, National Council for the Social Studies* (Washington, DC: NEA, 1944); Jesse Newlon, *Education for Democracy in Our Time* (New York: McGraw-Hill, 1939); John Mahoney, *For Us the Living: An Approach to Civic Education* (New York: Harper and Brothers, 1945); The Educational Policies Commission, NEA, and the American Association of School Administrators, *The Unique Function of Education in a Democracy* (Washington, DC: NEA, 1937); *The Structure and Administration of Education in American Democracy* (Washington, DC: NEA, 1938); *Education and Economic Well Being in a Democracy* (Washington, DC: NEA, 1940); Robert Ulich, *Fundamentals of Democratic Education* (New York: American Book Company, 1940).
38. Charles Beard, "The Essentials of Democracy," *Journal of the National Education Association*, 26 (Oct. 1939): 195–196; Boyd Bode, *Democracy as a Way of Life* (New York: Macmillan, 1937); George S. Counts, *The Schools Can Teach Democracy* (New York: John Day, 1939) and *The Education of Free Men in a Democracy* (Washington, DC: NEA, 1941); William Heard Kilpatrick, *Group Education for a Democracy* (New York: Association Press, 1940).
39. Educational Policies Commission, NEA, and the American Association of School Administrators, *Learning the Ways of Democracy* (Washington, DC: NEA, 1940), 460.
40. Harvard Committee, *General Education*, 116.
41. William O. Stanley, "What We Learn from Problem-Solving," *Progressive Education*, 26 (April 1949): 174.
42. R. Bruce Raup, George E. Axtelle, Kenneth D. Benne, and B. Othanel Smith, *The Improvement of Practical Intelligence: The Central Task of Education* (New York: Harper and Brothers, 1950), 49, 101. The book was originally published in 1943 as *The Discipline of Practical Judgment in a Democratic Society*, which was the 28th Yearbook of the National Society of College Teachers of Education.
43. Raup et al., *The Improvement of Practical Intelligence*, 256.

44. Kenneth D. Benne, *A Conception of Authority: An Introductory Study* (New York: Russell and Russell, 1944), i, 160, 165.
45. Veronica Rothenbush, "A Plan for Teaching Pupils How to Think: Achieving Freedom Through Education," *The Clearing House*, 17 (Feb. 1943): 331.
46. R. Roderick Palmer, "Education and Indoctrination," *Peabody Journal of Education*, 34 (Jan. 1957): 228.
47. Robert Henry Thouless, *How to Think Clearly: The Technique of Applying Logic Instead of Emotion* (New York: Simon and Schuster, 1939).
48. John Childs, "Education and Authority," *Religious Education*, 33 (1938): 153.
49. Willis Moore, "Indoctrination versus Education," *Bulletin of the American Association of University Professors*, 38 (Summer 1952): 221–222, 224.
50. Raup et al., *The Improvement of Practical Intelligence*, viii.
51. Committee on Social Studies, *The Social Studies in Secondary Education* (Washington, DC: Government Printing Office, 1916), 11.
52. Edgar Wesley, *Teaching Social Studies in High Schools*, 3rd ed. (Boston: D.C. Heath and Co., 1950), 482.
53. Maurice Moffatt, *Social Studies Instruction: Organization, Teaching and Supervision of the Social Studies in Secondary Schools* (New York: Prentice Hall, 1950), 84.
54. John Dewey, *How We Think* (Mineola, NY: Dover Publishing, 1910), 72. Dewey's 1933 revised version of the text revised the five steps to be less distinct and less linear.
55. James I. Quillen and Lavone A. Hanna, *Education for Social Competence: The Social Studies in the Secondary School*, revised edition (Chicago: Scott Foresman and Company, 1961; originally published in 1948), 156. For the role of Dewey's *How We Think* in popularizing the scientific method in science education, see John Rudolph, "Epistemology for the Masses: The Origins of 'The Scientific Method' in American Schools," *History of Education Quarterly*, 45 (Fall 2005): 341–376.
56. Stanley, "What We Learn from Problem Solving," 175.
57. Frederick Meyer, "Truth Measured by its Consequences," *Phi Delta Kappan*, 35 (June 1954): 384; italics in original.
58. Alan Griffin, *A Philosophical Approach to the Subject Matter Preparation of Teachers of History* (Unpublished Dissertation, Columbus: Ohio State University 1942), 45, 61, 70, 97.
59. Maurice P. Hunt and Lawrence E. Metcalf, *Teaching High School Social Studies: Problems in Reflective Thinking and Social Understanding* (New York: Harper & Row, 1955), 6, 9, 10, 44, 61.
60. See James W. Fraser, *Preparing Americas Teacher's: A History* (New York: Teachers College Press, 2007).
61. Donald Oliver, "The Selection of Content in the Social Studies," *Harvard Educational Review*, 27 (1957): 281, 286, 293.
62. Erling M. Hunt, "Recent Programs for Improving Citizenship Education," in *Education for Citizenship*, 123.
63. Oliver and Shaver, *Teaching Public Issues*, 16. Interestingly, Oliver and Shaver critiqued Dewey's "pragmatic position" to values because it allegedly failed to deal with "extreme violations of important social values, which may be justified rationally" such as "the Soviet treatment of the kulaks" and "Hitler's extermination of the Jews," 33.

64. Stanley E. Diamond, "The Detroit Citizenship Study," *Phi Delta Kappan*, 33 (Dec. 1951): 174.
65. Roy A. Price, "Citizenship Studies at Syracuse," *The Phi Delta Kappan*, 33 (Dec. 1951): 181.
66. Earl E. Edgar, "Kansas Study of Education for Citizenship," *Phi Delta Kappan*, 33 (Dec. 1951): 178.
67. See Ronald Evans and David Warren Saxe, *Handbook on Teaching Social Issues* (Washington, DC: National Council for the Social Studies, 1996); Evans, *The Social Studies Wars: What Should We Teach the Children?* (New York: Teachers College Press, 2004); Walter Parker, ed., *Educating the Democratic Mind* (Albany: State University of New York Press, 1996).
68. Counts wrote: "In a recent paper Professor Dewey has in my judgment, correctly diagnosed our troubles: 'the schools like the nation,' he says, 'are in need of a central purpose which will create new enthusiasm and devotion, and which will unify and guide all intellectual plans.'" Counts, *Dare the Schools*, 33.
69. Chester McArthur Destler, "Some Observations on Contemporary Historical Theory," *American Historical Review*, 55 (April 1950): 525, 504, 515, 517. For Dewey's response to the Destler essay, see Thomas Fallace, "John Dewey on History Education and the Historical Method," *Education and Culture*, 26 (2010): 20–35. See also Sidney Ratner, "Dewey's Contribution to Historical Theory," in *John Dewey: Philosopher of Science and Freedom: A Symposium*, ed., Sidney Hook (New York: The Dial Press, 1950), 134–152; Burleigh Taylor Wilkins, "Pragmatism as a Theory of Historical Knowledge: John Dewey on the Nature of Historical Inquiry," *American Historical Review* 64 (July 1959): 878–890; Thomas Neill, "Dewey's Ambivalent Attitude towards History," in *John Dewey: His Thought and Influence*, ed., John Edward Blewett (New York: Fordham University Press, 1960): 145–160; Ernest Austin, Jr., "Dewey's Consistent Attitude toward History," *Educational Theory*, 15 (1965): 198–204; Joseph Blau, "John Dewey's Theory of History," *Journal of Philosophy*, 57 (Feb. 1960): 89–100.
70. Wilkins, "Pragmatism as a Theory," 880.
71. Neill, "Dewey's Ambivalent Attitude," 137.
72. Lewis S. Fuerer, "Dialectical Materialism and Soviet Science," *Philosophy of Science*, 16 (April 1949): 112, 113.
73. Cited in Hartman, *Education and the Cold War*, 94, 97.
74. Mortimer Smith, *The Diminished Mind: A Study of Planned Mediocrity in Our Public Schools* (Chicago: Henry Regenry Co, 1954), 18.
75. Richard Hofstadter, *Anti-Intellectualism in American Life* (New York: Vintage Book, 1962), 373.

Chapter 6

1. Quoted in Susan Carruthers, *Cold War Captives: Imprisonment, Escape, and Brainwashing* (Berkeley: University of California Press, 2009), 175.
2. Quoted in E. Merrill Root, *Brainwashing in the High School: An Examination of Eleven American History Textbooks* (New York: The Devlin-Adair Company, 1958), 5.
3. Quoted in Carruthers, *Cold War Captives*, 210.
4. Edward Hunter, *Brainwashing: The Story of the Men Who Defied It* (New York: Bookmailer, 1956), 309. See also Hunter, *Brainwashing in Red China* (New

York: Vanguard, 1951); Joost Meerloo, *The Rape of the Mind: The Psychology of Mind Control, Menticide, and Brainwashing* (Cleveland, OH: World, 1956); William Sargent, *Battle for the Mind: A Physiology of Conversion and 'Brainwashing'* (Baltimore, MD: Penguin Books, 1957); William White, *The Captives of Korea: An Unofficial White Paper* (New York: Scribner's, 1957); Albert D. Biderman, "The Image of Brainwashing," *Public Opinion Quarterly*, 26 (Winter 1962): 547–563.

5. Gary Gerstle, *Liberty and Coercion: The Paradox of American Government* (Princeton, NJ: Princeton University Press, 2015), 252.
6. Arthur Bestor, *Restoration of Learning: A Program for Redeeming the Unfulfilled Promise of American Education* (New York: Alfred A. Knopf, 1955), xii.
7. Diane Ravitch, *The Troubled Crusade: American Education, 1945–1980* (New York: Basic Books, 1983), 81–113; Stuart J. Foster, *Red Alert! Educators Confront the Red Scare in American Public Schools, 1947–1954* (New York: Peter Lang, 2000).
8. James T. Patterson, *Grand Expectations: The United States, 1945–1974* (New York: Oxford University Press, 1996), 61–81; Kenneth Jackson, *Crabgrass Frontier: The Suburbanization of the United States* (New York: Oxford, 1985), 190–271; Margaret Peacock, *Innocent Weapons: The Soviet and American Politics of Childhood in the Cold War* (Chapel Hill: University of North Carolina Press, 2014), 17–41.
9. Quoted in Lizabeth Cohen, *A Consumer's Republic: The Politics of Mass Consumption* (New York: Vintage, 2004), 125.
10. Angus and Mirel, *The Failed Promise*, 203, 204, 206. See also Jergen Herbst, *The Once and Future School: Three Hundred and Fifty Years of American Secondary Education* (New York: Routledge, 1996); Arthur Powell, Eleanor Farrar, and David Cohen, *The Shopping Mall High School: Winners and Losers in the Educational Marketplace* (Boston: Houghton Mifflin, 1985); Robert Hampel, *The Last Little Citadel: American High Schools Since 1940* (Boston: Houghton Mifflin, 1987); William Wraga, *Democracy's High School* (Lanham, MD: University Press of America, 1994).
11. Angus and Mirel, *The Failed Promise*, 204, 206.
12. See Ken Smith, *Mental Hygiene: Classroom Films, 1945–1970* (New York: Blast Books, 1999); Devin Orgeron, Marsha Orgeron, and Dan Streible, eds., *Learning with the Lights Off: Educational Film in the United States* (New York: Oxford University Press, 2012); Kelly Ritter, *Re-Framing the Subject: Postwar Instructional Film and Class-Conscious Literacies* (Pittsburgh, PA: University of Pittsburgh Press, 2015).
13. Wendy Wall, *Inventing the American Way: The Politics of Consensus from the New Deal to the Civil Rights Movement* (New York: Oxford University Press, 2008); Benjamin Looker, *A Nation of Neighborhoods: Imagining Cities, Communities, and Democracy in Postwar America* (Chicago: University of Chicago Press, 2015); Whitfield, *The Culture of the Cold War*, 52–76; Robert Westbrook, *Why We Fought: Forging American Obligation in World War II* (Washington, DC: Smithsonian Books, 2004), 1–67.
14. Quoted in Frances FitzGerald, *America Revised: History Textbooks in the Twentieth Century* (New York: Little Brown, 1979), 121.
15. Quoted in Wall, *Inventing the American Way*, 3.
16. William Wythe, *The Organization Man* (New York: Simon and Schuster, 1956);

David Riesman, *The Lonely Crowd* (New Haven, CT: Yale University Press, 1950); Galbraith and McCarthy quoted in Pells, *The Liberal Mind*, 165, 294.

17. Quoted in Christopher J. Philips, *The New Math: A Political History* (Chicago: University of Chicago Press, 2015), 33.
18. Quoted in Matthew W. Dunne, *A Cold War State of Mind: Brainwashing and Postwar American Society* (Boston: University of Massachusetts Press, 2013), 114. See also David Seed, *Brainwashing: The Fictions of Mind Control: A Study of Novels and Films since World War II* (Kent, OH: Kent State University Press, 2004); Timothy Melley, *Empire of Conspiracy: The Culture of Paranoia in Postwar America* (Ithaca, NY: Cornell University Press, 2000).
19. Gregor Ziemer, *Education for Death: The Making of a Nazi* (New York: Oxford University Press, 1941), 7, 107–108, 196.
20. George S. Counts and Nucia Lodge, *The Country of the Blind: The Soviet System of Mind Control* (New York: Houghton Mifflin, 1949), ix, xv, 245, xv. For more on Kasenkina's story see Carruthers, *Cold War Captives*, 2–66.
21. George S. Counts, *The Challenge of Soviet Education* (New York: McGraw Hill, 1957), 295.
22. Counts, *Soviet Challenge*, 307.
23. Robert F. Gleckner, "1984 or 1948?" *College English*, 18 (Nov. 1956): 97.
24. Root, *Brainwashing in the High School*, 10, 11, 14
25. Marie Jahoda, "The Migration of Psychoanalysis: Its Impact on American Psychology," in *The Intellectual Migration: Europe and America, 1930–1960*, eds., Donald Fleming and Bernard Bailyn (Cambridge, MA: Belknap Press, 1969), 420–445.
26. Quoted in Alpers, *Dictators, Democracy, and American Public Culture*, 265.
27. Erik Erikson, *Childhood and Society* (New York: Norton and Company, 1950), 326. Erikson's eight stages of human development, each of which was based on the Freudian resolution of an identity crisis, would become an influential framework for educators for the next half-century.
28. Hannah Arendt, "Total Domination [from *The Origins of Totalitarianism*]," in *The Portable Hannah Arendt*, ed., Peter R. Baehr, (New York: Penguin, 2000), 132.
29. Schlesinger, *The Vital Center*, 250.
30. Theodore Adorno, Else Frenkel-Brunswik, Daniel Levinson, and R. Nevitt Sanford, *The Authoritarian Personality*, Abridged Version (New York: Norton, 1982), 10. Originally published in 1950.
31. Adorno et al., *The Authoritarian Personality*, 4.
32. See Richard Christie and Peggy Cook, "A Guide to Published Literature Relating to the Authoritarian Personality through 1956," *The Journal of Psychology* 45(2) (1958): 171–199; Howard Gabennesch, "Authoritarianism as World View," *American Journal of Sociology*, 77 (March 1972): 857–875.
33. Adorno et al., *The Authoritarian Personality*, 9, xi, 104, 1.
34. Sol Cohen, "The Mental Hygiene Movement, the Development of Personality and the School: The Medicalization of American Education," *History of Education Quarterly*, 23 (Summer 1983): 123–149; Stephen Petrina, "The Medicalization of Education: A Historiographical Synthesis," *History of Education Quarterly*, 46 (Winter 2006): 503–531; Catherine Gavin Loss, "Public Schools, Private Lives: American Education and Psychological Authority, 1945–1975," doctoral dissertation, University of Virginia, 2005.

35. Wilfred Overholser, "Mental Hygiene," *Proceedings of the American Philosophical Society*, 90 (Sept. 1946): 259; T. L. Engle, "Wartime Mental Hygiene," *The Clearing House*, 16 (May 1942): 532–533; John D. M. Griffin and William Line, "Trends in Mental Hygiene," *Review of Educational Research*, 16 (Dec. 1946): 394–400; William U. Snyder, "Recent Investigations of Mental Hygiene in the Schools," *Educational Research Bulletin*, 24 (Oct. 1945): 178–185.
36. George S. Stevenson, "Trends in Mental Hygiene: An Interpretation," *Review of Educational Research*, 10 (Dec. 1940): 407.
37. Theodore Meltzer, "Mental Hygiene," *The Journal of Higher Education*, 16 (March 1945): 136.
38. Nicholas Hobbs, "Group Therapy in Preventative Mental Hygiene," *Teachers College Record*, 50 (March 1948): 170.
39. Griffin and Line, "Trends in Mental Hygiene," 399.
40. Smith, *Diminished Mind*, 19.
41. Harvard Committee, *Education in a Free Society*, 168.
42. H. H. Cummings, W. Gaumnitz, A. T. Hamilton, J. D. Hull, J. R. Ludington, B. Mallory, and L. Miller, *A Look Ahead in Secondary Education, Bulletin No. 4* (Washington, DC: Department of the Interior, Bureau of Education, 1954), 4, 5.
43. Rugg, *Foundations*, 639.
44. Harold Rugg, *Citizenship and Civic Affairs: Community and National Life, Book One* (New York: Ginn and Company, 1940), viii–ix.
45. Ralph W. Tyler, *Basic Principles of Curriculum and Instruction* (Chicago: University of Chicago, 1949). On Tyler's controversial influence see Herbert Kliebard, "The Tyler Rationale," *The School Review*, 78 (Feb. 1970): 259–272; George A. Antonelli, "Ralph Tyler: The Man and His Work," *Peabody Journal of Education*, 50 (Oct. 1972): 68–74; Ronald Tyrell, "An Appraisal of the Tyler Rationale," *The School Review*, 83 (Nov. 1974): 151–162.
46. Quoted in J. Eunice (Ed.), *Social Studies in the Senior High School: Programs for Grades Ten, Eleven, and Twelve* (Washington, DC: National Council for the Social Studies, 1953), 80.
47. Eunice, *Social Studies in the Senior High School*, 89.
48. See Thomas Fallace, "The Effects of Life Adjustment Education on the U.S. History Curriculum, 1948–1957," *The History Teacher*, 44 (Fall 2011): 569–589.
49. George Peabody College for Teachers, Division of Surveys and Field Services, *Trends in the Production of Curriculum Guides: A Survey of Courses of Study Published in 1951 through 1953* (Nashville, TN: George Peabody College for Teachers, 1955), 35, 6.
50. Edwin Carr, "The Social Studies in the Curriculum, " in The High School Curriculum, ed. H.R. Douglass (New York: Ronald Press Company, 1956), 438-444, 438.
51. Curriculum *guides* were designed and distributed by local and state curriculum developers and represented the *intended* curriculum, not necessarily what was being implemented in schools; they were prescriptive. *Curriculum programs* were reports of what had already been implemented in some particular schools; they were descriptive. In other words, unlike the curriculum guides, the programs reflected ideas that had in fact been implemented in schools. Both the guides and programs reflected similar characteristics, but we must be careful not

to conflate them lest we confuse what was proposed with was actually adopted at the ground level.

52. Alabama Department of Education Division of Instruction, *Course of Study and Guide for Teachers Grades 1–12* (Montgomery, AL: Department of Education, 1950), 192.
53. Bestor, *Educational Wastelands*, 82.
54. Mortimer Smith, *The Diminished Mind: A Study of Planned Mediocrity in our Schools* (Chicago: Henry Regnery Company, 1954), 24.
55. Quoted in Ravitch, *The Troubled Crusade*, 72.
56. Hofstadter, *Anti-Intellectualism in American Life*, 345.
57. See William G. Wraga, "From Slogan to Anathema: Historical Representations of Life Adjustment Education," *American Journal of Education*, 116 (2009): 185–209; Dorothy Broder, *Life Adjustment Education: An Historical Study of a Program of the United States Office of Education, 1945–1954*, 1977, doctoral dissertation, Teachers College, Columbia University. Wraga and Broder argue that the impact of life adjustment education was minimal, but my previous research documents the extent to which at least its rhetoric was widely adopted across the United States. The only historians somewhat sympathetic to life adjustment were Daniel Tanner and Laurel N. Tanner, *History of the School Curriculum* (New York: Macmillan, 1990), 249.
58. On Brameld, see William B. Stanley, *Curriculum for Utopia: Social Reconstructionism and Critical Pedagogy in the Postmodern Era* (Albany, NY: SUNY Press, 1992), 16–21, 32–44; Pells, *Radical Visions & American Dreams*, 130–131, 301–302; Hartman, *Education and the Cold War*, 140–156; Karen Riley, "Imagining the Future: Theodore Brameld on the Frontiers of Multicultural Education," in *Addressing Social Issues in the Classroom and Beyond*, edited by Samuel Totten and Jon Pedersen (Charlotte, NC: Information Age Publishing, 2007), 201–220.
59. Theodore Brameld, *Design for America* (New York: Hinds, Hayden, and Eldredge, Inc., 1945).
60. Theodore Brameld, *Patterns of Educational Philosophy: A Democratic Interpretation* (New York: World Book Company, 1950), 537, 552, 558, 589, 599. Brameld's four-philosophy scheme (essentialism, perennialism, progressivism, reconstructionism) was hugely influential in helping teacher educators to clarify the major educational philosophies for the next half-century. Open virtually any introductory education textbook today and you will see some version of Brameld's four-philosophy scheme. Prospective teachers are often asked to write an education philosophy that draws on or aligns with one of Brameld's four philosophies. Interestingly, only two of the terms, *essentialism* and *progressivism*, actually align with terminology employed by the historical actors themselves. Historian William Reese traced references to *progressive* education back to the 19th century, and Teachers College Professors William Bagley and Isaac Kandel coined the term *essentialism* as an alternative to progressive education in the late 1930s. The other two, *reconstructionism* and *perennialism*, were apparently coined by Brameld in *Patterns of Educational Philosophy*. See William J. Reese, "The Origins of Progressive Education," *History of Education Quarterly*, 41 (Spring 2001): 1–24; J. Wesley Null, "William C. Bagley and the Founding of Essentialism: An Untold Story in American Educational History," *Teachers College Record*, 109 (2007): 1013–1055.

61. Smith, *Diminished Mind*, 73, 58.
62. Theodore Brameld, *Education for the Emerging Age: A Mid-Century Appraisal* (New York: Harper and Brothers, 1950), 90; quoted in Hartman, *Education and the Cold War*, 145.
63. Lilge, "Reason and Ideology," 247, 256. For another negative review see Melvin Rader, "Review of Patterns of Educational Philosophy by Theodore Brameld," *The Journal of Philosophy*, 48 (July 1951): 482–483.

Chapter 7

1. Jerome Bruner, *The Process of Education* (Cambridge, MA: Harvard University Press, 1960), 75.
2. Quoted in Hartman, *Education and the Cold War*, 176.
3. George S. Counts, *Khrushchev and the Central Committee Speak on Education* (Pittsburgh: University of Pittsburgh Press, 1959), 14–15.
4. Quoted in Peacock, *Innocent Weapons*, 62.
5. See Fallace, "Did the Social Studies Really Replace History in American Secondary Schools?"; Oliver M. Keels, "The Collegiate Influence on the Early Social Studies Curriculum: A Reassessment of the Role of Historians," *Theory and Research in Social Education*, 8 (Summer 1980): 105–120.
6. See Larry Cuban, *How Teachers Taught: Constancy and Change in American Classrooms, 1880–1990,* 2nd ed. (New York: Teachers College Press, 1993); David B. Tyack and Larry Cuban, *Tinkering Toward Utopia: A Century of School Reform* (Cambridge, MA: Harvard University Press, 1995); Linda McNeil, *Contradictions of Control: School Structure and School Knowledge* (New York: Routledge, 1986); David Labaree, *Someone Has to Fail: The Zero-Sum Game of Public Schooling* (Cambridge, MA: Harvard University Press, 2010); John Goodlad, *A Place Called School* (New York: McGraw-Hill, 2004).
7. See Cremin, *The Transformation of the School*; Bowers, *The Progressive Educator and the Depression*; Ravitch, *The Troubled Crusade*; Ravitch, *Left Back*; E. D. Hirsch, *Cultural Literacy: What Every American Needs to Know* (Boston: Houghton Mifflin, 1987); Hirsch, *The Schools We Need: And Why We Don't Have Them* (New York: Anchor Books, 1999).
8. Quoted in Barbara Slater Stern, "Donald Oliver: The Search for Democratic Community," in *Addressing Social Issues in the Classroom and Beyond*, ed. Samuel Totten and Jon Pedersen (Charlotte, NC: Information Age Publishing, 2007), 281.
9. For analysis of course enrollments between 1916 and 1958, see Fallace, "Did the Social Studies Really Replace History?"; Barry Franklin, *Building the American Community: The School Curriculum and the Search for Social Control* (Philadelphia: Falmer Press, 1986); Michael C. Johanek and John L. Puckett, *Leonard Covello and the Making of Benjamin Franklin High School: Education as if Citizenship Mattered* (Philadelphia: Temple University Press, 2007), 149–224; Course enrollments are reported in Harry Moore, *Status of Certain Social Studies in High Schools, Bulletin 1922, No. 45* (Washington, DC: Department of the Interior, Bureau of Education, 1923); Walter Monroe and I. O. Foster, *The Status of the Social Sciences in the High Schools of the North Central Association* (Urbana, IL: Bureau of Educational Research, College of Education, University of Illinois, 1922); William Kimmel, *Instruction in*

the Social Studies: Bulletin No. 17, National Survey of Secondary Education (Washington, DC: U.S. Government Printing Office, 1933); *Offerings and Enrollments in High-School Subjects, 1948–1949* (Washington, DC: Federal Security Agency, U.S. Office of Education, 1949).

10. Lucile Lurry and Elsie Alberty, *Developing a High School Core Program* (New York: Macmillan, 1957), 4–5.
11. H. G. Rickover, *Education and Freedom* (New York: Dutton, 1959), 35, 38.
12. Nicholas DeWitt, *Soviet Professional Manpower* (Washington, DC: National Science Foundation, 1955), 39.
13. Wayne J. Urban, *More Than Science and Sputnik: The National Defense Act of 1958* (Tuscaloosa: University of Alabama Press, 2010).
14. Cohen-Cole, *The Open Mind*, 127–157; Burton Weltman, "The Message and the Medium: Roots/Routes of Jerome Bruner's Postmodernism," *Theory and Research in Social Education*, 29 (Spring 1999), 160–178.
15. Jewett, *Science, Democracy, and the American University*, 302–334; see also Hollinger, *Science, Jews, and Secular Culture*, 155–174; David Haney, *The Americanization of Social Science: Intellectuals and Public Responsibility in the Postwar United States* (Philadelphia: Temple University Press, 2008); Nils Gilman, *Mandarins of the Future: Modernization Theory in Cold War America* (Baltimore, MD: Johns Hopkins, 2003), 1–70.
16. B. F. Skinner, "The Science of Learning and the Art of Teaching," *Harvard Educational Review*, 24 (Spring 1954): 96. Skinner placed quotation marks around these terms to underscore their unscientific nature.
17. Jamie Cohen-Cole, *The Open Mind*, 125, 70; quoted in Cohen-Cole, 149.
18. Jerome Bruner, *Toward a Theory of Instruction* (Cambridge, MA: Belknap, 1966), 72.
19. See Fallace, "John Dewey's Interdisciplinary Vision(s) for the Social Studies,"177–189.
20. Additional critiques of progressive education include Robert Hutchins, *The Conflict of Education in a Democratic Society* (New York: Harper and Brothers, 1953); Albert Lynd, *Quackery in the Public Schools* (New York: Grosset and Dunlap, 1953); Kitty Jones and Robert Olivier, *Progressive Education is REDucation* (Boston: Meador Publishing Company, 1956); Paul Woodring, *Let's Talk Sense About Our Schools* (New York: McGraw-Hill, 1953).
21. Bestor, *Educational Wastelands*, 19, 14. For more on Bestor see Weltman, "Reconsidering Arthur Bestor," 11–39.
22. See Joseph Schwab, "John Dewey: The Creature as Creative," *The Journal of General Education* 7 (Jan. 1953): 109–121; Schwab, "The Impossible Role of the Teachers in Progressive Education," *School Review*, 67 (Summer 1959): 139–159.
23. Joseph J. Schwab, "The Nature of Scientific Knowledge as Related to Liberal Education," *The Journal of General Education*, 3 (July 1949): 265.
24. Joseph J. Schwab, "Science and Civic Discourse: The Uses of Diversity," *The Journal of General Education*, 9 (April 1956): 133; see also Schwab, "The Teaching of Science as Enquiry," in *The Teaching of Science*, eds., Joseph Schwab and Paul F. Brandwein (Cambridge, MA: Harvard University Press, 1960), 3–103.
25. Joseph J. Schwab, "The Structure of the Disciplines: Meanings and Significance," in *The Structure of Knowledge and the Curriculum*, eds., Joseph J. Schwab,

Gordon W. Ford, and Lawrence Pungo (Chicago: Rand McNally, 1964), 13, 15, 29.

26. Sales figures come from the publisher, Harvard University Press. See harvardpress.typepad.com/hup_publicity/2013/03/the-process-of-education-jerome-bruner-1960.html
27. Edwin Fenton, *Teaching the New Social Studies in Secondary Schools: An Inductive Approach* (New York: Holt, Rinehart, and Winston, Inc., 1966), 81.
28. Bruner, *Process of Education*, xi, vii, 20. As Bruner explained elsewhere: "The structure of any domain of knowledge may be characterized in three ways each affecting the ability of any learner to master it: the mode of representation in which it is put, its economy, and its effective power. Mode, economy, and power vary in relation to different ages, to different 'styles' among learners, and different subject matters." *Towards a Theory of Instruction*, 44.
29. Bruner and Zacharias quoted in Ronald Evans, *The Hope for American School Reform: The Cold War Pursuit of Inquiry Learning in Social Studies* (New York: Palgrave Macmillan, 2011), 64, 54, 64.
30. Schwab, "The Impossible Role of Teachers," 159.
31. Bruner, *Process of Education*, 10.
32. Quoted in Evans, *The Hope for American School Reform*, 51.
33. Thomas Fallace, "From the German Schoolmaster's Psychology to the Psychology of the Child: Evolving Rationales for the Teaching of History in American Schools in the 1890s," *The Journal of the Gilded Age and Progressive Era*, 10 (April 2011): 161–186.
34. Quoted in John Rudolph, *Scientists in the Classroom: The Cold War Reconstruction of American Science Education* (New York: Palgrave Macmillan, 2002), 111.
35. Gerstle, *Liberty and Coercion*, 266–270; Ravitch, *The Troubled Crusade*, 12–15; Louis Menand, *The Marketplace of Ideas: Reform and Resistance in the American University* (New York: Norton, 2010), 63–70.
36. Richard H. Brown, of the Amherst Project on history as discovery, is quoted in Fenton, *Teaching the New Social Studies in Secondary Schools*, 443. See also Donald Gross and Judith Murphy, *The Revolution in the School* (New York: Harcourt, Brace and World, Inc., 1966).
37. Phillips, *The New Math*, 94, 122.
38. Evans, *The Hope for American School Reform*, 107–136.
39. Edwin Fenton, *32 Problems in World History: Source Readings and Interpretations* (Fair Lawn, NJ: Scott Foresman and Co., 1964), 14.
40. Edwin Fenton, *Developing a New Curriculum: A Rationale for the Holt Social Studies Curriculum* (New York: Holt, Rinehart, and Winston, Inc., 1967), 2, 4.
41. For a recent appreciation of Fenton see Bruce VanSledright, *The Challenge of Rethinking History Education: On Practices, Theories, and Policies* (New York: Routledge, 2011).
42. Quoted in Stern, "Donald Oliver: Search for Democratic Community," 275.
43. Bruner, "Man: A Course in Study," in *Toward a Theory of Instruction*, 73–101; Peter B. Dow, *Schoolhouse Politics: Lessons from the Sputnik Era* (Cambridge, MA: Harvard University Press, 1991), 33–138; Dow, "MACOS: The Study of Human Behavior as One Road to Survival," *The Phi Delta Kappan*, 57 (Oct. 1975): pp. 79–81; Harry F. Wolcott, "The Middlemen of MACOS," *Anthropology & Education Quarterly*, 38 (June 2007): 195–206.

44. Rudolph, *Scientists in the Classroom*, 199.
45. Quoted in Charles E. Silberman, *Crisis in the Classroom: The Remaking of American Education* (New York: Vintage Books, 1970), 171.
46. FitzGerald, *America Revised*, 190.
47. See Evans, *The Hope for American School Reform*, 174–220; Evans, *The Tragedy of American School Reform: How Curriculum Politics and Entrenched Dilemmas Have Diverted Us from Democracy* (New York: Palgrave Macmillan, 2011), 185–208. Fenton was an exception. He did author a text aimed specifically at struggling readers.
48. Menand, *The Marketplace of Ideas*, 104, 62.
49. Quoted in FitzGerald, *America Revised*, 185.
50. Shirley Engle, "Decision Making: The Heart of Social Studies Instruction," *Social Education*, 24 (Nov. 1960): 301.
51. James P. Shaver, "A Critical View of the Social Studies Profession," *Social Education*, 41(April 1977): 305.
52. Quoted in Evans, *The Tragedy of American School Reform*, 91.
53. Quoted in Phillips, *The New Math*, 124, 136.
54. Quoted in Dow, *Schoolhouse Politics*, 197, 207, 208.
55. George Weber, "The Case Against Man: A Course in Study," *The Phi Delta Kappan*, 57 (Oct. 1975): 81.
56. Byron G. Massialas and C. Benjamin Cox, *Inquiry in Social Studies* (New York: McGraw-Hill, 1966), 90–91, 330, 331. See also Hullfish and Smith, *Reflective Thinking*, which also drew heavily on Dewey's *How We Think* and insisted that "education is a front-line activity in the warfare of competing ideologies," 15; Fenton, *Teaching the New Social Studies*, also included excerpts from *How We Think*, 117–124.
57. Byron G. Massialas, Nancy F. Sprague, and Joseph B. Hurst, *Social Issues through Inquiry: Coping in an Age of Crises* (Englewood Cliffs, NJ: Prentice Hall, 1975).

Chapter 8

1. Lawrence Kohlberg, "My Personal Search for Universal Morality," in L. Kuhmerker (Ed.), *The Kohlberg Legacy for the Helping Professions* (Birmingham, AL: Doxa Books, 1991), 11–13.
2. Lawrence Kohlberg, "The Moral Atmosphere of the School," in *Moral Education . . . It Comes with the Territory*, eds. David Purpel and Kevin Ryan (Berkeley, CA: McCutchan Publishing Corp., 1976), 202.
3. Evans, *The Social Studies Wars*, 134–135; Hazel Whitman Hertzberg, *Social Studies Reform 1880–1980* (Boulder, CO: SSEC Publications, 1981), 121–126.
4. Thomas Kuhn, *The Structure of Scientific Revolutions*, 2nd ed. (University of Chicago Press, 1970); Hayden White, *Metahistory: The Historical Imagination in Nineteenth-Century Europe* (Baltimore, MD: Johns Hopkins University Press, 1975); Clifford Geertz, *The Interpretation of Cultures* (New York: Basic Books, 1973); Richard Rorty, *Philosophy and the Mirror of Nature* (Princeton, NJ: Princeton University Press, 2009).
5. A. S. Neill, *Summerhill: A Radical Approach to Child Rearing* (New York: Hart, 1960); Paulo Freire, *Pedagogy of the Oppressed* (New York: Herder, 1972); Rachel Carson, *Silent Spring* (New York: Houghton Mifflin, 1962); Michael

Harrington, *The Other America: Poverty in the United States* (New York: Simon and Schuster, 1962).

6. Daniel T. Rodgers, *Age of Fracture* (Cambridge, MA: Belknap Press, 2011).
7. Louis Menand, *Marketplace of Ideas*, 80.
8. Quoted in Kendi, *Stamped from the Beginning*, 428.
9. James Coleman, "The Concept of Educational Opportunity," *Harvard Educational Review*, 38 (Winter 1968): 7–22.
10. *Social Education*, 33 (April 1969).
11. "An Interview with Gunnar Myrdal," *Phi Delta Kappan*, 49 (May 1968): 491.
12. William F. Connell, "Moral Education: Aims and Methods in China, the U.S.S.R., the U.S., and England," in *Moral Education . . . It Comes with the Territory*, eds. David Purpel and Kevin Ryan (Berkeley, CA: McCutchan Publishing Corp., 1976), 33.
13. Israel Scheffler, "The Moral Content of Education" in *Moral Education . . . It Comes with the Territory*, eds. David Purpel and Kevin Ryan (Berkeley, CA: McCutchan Publishing Corp., 1976), 23.
14. Fenton, *Teaching the New Social Studies*, 44.
15. Gerald Marker and Howard Mehlinger, "Social Studies," in *The Handbook of Research on Curriculum*, ed. Philip W. Jackson (New York: Macmillan, 1992), 830–851.
16. David R. Krathwohl, Benjamin S. Bloom, and Bertram B. Masia, *Taxonomy of Educational Objectives: Handbook II: The Affective Domain* (New York: David McKay Company, Inc., 1964), 23.
17. Krathwohl et al., *Taxonomy of Educational Objectives*, 184.
18. Benjamin Bloom and David R. Krathwohl, *Taxonomy of Educational Objectives: Handbook I: The Cognitive Domain* (New York: David McKay Company, Inc., 1956).
19. Lawrence Kohlberg, "The Cognitive Developmental Approach to Moral Education," in *Moral Education . . . It Comes with the Territory*, ed. David Purpel and Kevin Ryan (Berkeley: McCutchan Publishing Corp., 1976), 20, 24.
20. Lawrence Kohlberg, "Stage and Sequence: The Cognitive-Developmental Approach to Socialization," in *Handbook of Socialization Theory and Research*, ed., David A. Goslin (Chicago: Rand McNally College Publishing Company, 1969), 376, 414.
21. Lawrence Kohlberg, "Educating for a Just Society," in *Moral Development, Moral Education, and Kohlberg: Basic Issues in Philosophy, Psychology, Religion, and Education*, ed. Brenda Munsey (Birmingham, AL: Religious Education Press, 1980), 466.
22. Kohlberg, "Educating for a Just Society," 457; Kohlberg, *Meaning and Measurement in Moral Development: Heinz Werner Memorial Lecture* (Worcester, MA: Clark University Press, 1976).
23. Kohlberg, "Stage and Sequence," 393.
24. Kohlberg, "The Cognitive Developmental Approach,"185–186.
25. Kohlberg, "The Cognitive Developmental Approach," 189.
26. See James Rest, "Developmental Psychology as a Guide to Value Education: A Review of 'Kohlbergian' Programs," in Munsey (Ed.), *Moral Development, Moral Education, and Kohlberg*, 252–274.

27. Gilman, *Mandarins of the Future*, 203–241.
28. William J. Bennett, "The Teacher, the Curriculum, and Values Education Development," *New Directions for Higher Education*, 31 (1980): 27; George Sher and William J. Bennett, "Moral Education and Indoctrination," *The Journal of Philosophy* 79, no. 11 (1982): 665.
29. G. S. Wright, *Subject Offerings and Enrollments in Public Secondary Schools* (Washington, DC: Government Printing Office, 1965); National Center for Educational Statistics, *A Trend Study of High School Offerings and Enrollments: 1972–73 and 1981–82* (Washington, DC: Government Printing Office, 1984), 57.
30. Powell, Farrar, and Cohen, *The Shopping Mall High School.*
31. Philip A. Cusiak, *The Egalitarian Ideal and the American High School: Studies of Three Schools* (New York: Longman, 1983), 122.
32. Scott Baker, "Desegregation, Minimum Competency Testing, and the Origins of Accountability: North Carolina and the Nation," *History of Education Quarterly*, 55 (Spring 2015): 33–57.
33. The National Commission on Educational Excellence, *A Nation at Risk: The Imperative for Educational Reform: A Report to the Nation and the Secretary of Education* (Washington, DC: Government Printing Office, 1983); E. D. Hirsch, "Cultural Literacy," *American Scholar*, 52 (Spring 1983): 159–169.
34. National Commission on Educational Excellence, *A Nation at Risk*, 6, 13, 9.
35. National Commission on Educational Excellence, *A Nation at Risk*, 9, 10.
36. National Commission on Educational Excellence, *A Nation at Risk*, 10.
37. Hirsch, "Cultural Literacy," 159.
38. Hirsch, "Cultural Literacy," 161, 162.
39. Hirsch, "Cultural Literacy," 168.
40. See Hirsch, *Cultural Literacy*; E. D. Hirsch, Joseph Kett, James Trefil, *The New Dictionary of Cultural Literacy: What Every American Needs to Know* (New York: Houghton Mifflin, 2002).
41. David Berliner and Bruce J. Biddle, *The Manufactured Crisis: Myths, Fraud, and the Attack on America's Public Schools* (New York: Basic Books, 1996).
42. Those who continued to develop rationales for classroom deliberation include Shirley Engle and Anna S. Ochoa, *Education for Democratic Citizenship: Decision Making in the Social Studies* (New York: Teachers College Press, 1988); Walter Parker, *Teaching Democracy: Unity and Diversity in Public Life* (New York: Teachers College Press, 2003); Diana Hess, *Controversy in the Classroom: Democratic Power of Discussion* (New York: Routledge, 2009).
43. See Johann Neem, *Democracy's School: The Rise of Public Education in America* (Baltimore, MD: Johns Hopkins, 2017).

Bibliography

Collected Papers in Print

Bulletins. (1916–1980). Bureau of Education, Department of the Interior. Washington, DC: U.S. Government Printing Office.

The Correspondence of John Dewey, Vols. 1–3. (2005). Third edition CD-ROM. Edited by Larry Hickman. Carbondale, IL: Center for Dewey Studies, Southern Illinois University.

John Dewey: Critical Assessments: Vol. II: Political and Social Practice. (1992). Edited by J. E. Tiles. New York: Routledge.

The Early Works of The Collected Works of John Dewey. (1969–1972). Edited by Jo Ann Boydston. Carbondale, IL: Southern Illinois University Press.

The Middle Works of The Collected Works of John Dewey. (1976–1983). Edited by Jo Ann Boydston. Carbondale, IL: Southern Illinois University Press.

The Later Works of The Collected Works of John Dewey. (1981–1990). Edited by Jo Ann Boydston. Carbondale, IL: Southern Illinois University Press.

Forgotten Heroes of American Education: The Great Tradition of Teaching Teachers. (2006). Edited by J. Wesley Null and Diane Ravitch. Greenwich, CT: Information Age Publishing.

The Portable Hannah Arendt. (2000). Edited by Peter R. Baehr. New York: Penguin.

The Social Frontier: A Critical Reader. (2011). Edited by Eugene Provenzo, Jr. New York, NY: Peter Lang.

War and the Intellectuals: Essays by Randolph Bourne, 1915–1919. (1964). Edited by C. Resek. New York, NY: Harper and Row.

Periodicals

American Economic Review	*Journal of General Education*
American Journal of Education	*Journal of Higher Education*
American Political Science Review	*Journal of the History of Ideas*
The American Review	*Journal of Negro History*
American School Board Journal	*Nation*
American Speech	*New Republic*
The Clearing House	*New York Times*
Commentary	*Peabody Journal of Education*
The Common School Journal	*Phi Delta Kappan*
Dial	*Philosophy*
Educational Research Bulletin	*Phylon*
Educational Review	*Political Science Journal*
Elementary School Journal	*Public Opinion Quarterly*
The English Journal	*Review of Educational Research*
Foreign Affairs	*Russian Review*
Harper's Magazine	*School and Home Education*
Harvard Educational Review	*School and Society*
High School Journal	*Science*
Historical Outlook	*Scientific Monthly*
International Journal of Ethics	*Social Education*
Journal of Education	*Social Frontier*
Journal of Educational Psychology	*Teachers College Record*

Primary Sources

Adams, H. B. (1883). The Germanic origin of New England towns. *Johns Hopkins University Studies in Historical and Political Science*, 1, 5–78.

Adams, J. (1897). *The Herbartian psychology applied to education*. New York, NY: D.C. Heath.

Adorno, T., Frenkel-Brunswik, E., Levinson, D., & Nevitt Sanford, R. (1982). *The authoritarian personality* (Abridged). New York, NY: Norton.

Alabama Department of Education Division of Instruction. (1950). *Course of study and guide for teachers grades 1–12*. Montgomery, AL: Montgomery Department of Education.

Alexander, T. (1919). *The Prussian elementary schools*. New York, NY: Macmillan.

American Council for Democracy and Intellectual Freedom, Committee on Textbooks. (1942). *The textbooks of Harold Rugg*. New York, NY: ACDIF.

American Historical Association. (1899). *The study of history in schools: Report to the American Historical Association by the Committee of Seven.* New York, NY: AHA.

Bagley, W. C., & Rugg, H. O. (1916). *The content of American history as taught in the seventh and eighth grades: An analysis of typical school textbooks.* Urbana, IL: University of Illinois.

Barnard, H. (1860). Public instruction in Prussia. *American Journal of Education, 8,* 431.

Beard, C. (1916, May). "Politics and Education," *Teachers College Record, 17,* 225.

Beard, C., & Beard, M. (1927). *The rise of American civilization.* New York, NY: Macmillan.

Beard, C., & Beard, M. (1934). *Conclusions and recommendations of the Commission: Report of the Commission on Social Studies of the American Historical Association.* New York, NY: Scribner's and Sons.

Beard, C., & Beard, M. (1934). *The nature of the social sciences (part VII): Report of the Commission on Social Studies of the American Historical Association.* New York, NY: Scribner's and Sons.

Bell, D. (1960). *The end of ideology: On the exhaustion of political ideas in the fifties.* New York, NY: New Press.

Benedict, R. (1940). *Race: Science and politics.* New York, NY: Viking.

Benne, K. B. (1944). *A conception of authority: An introductory study.* New York, NY: Russell & Russell.

Bennett, W. J. (1980). The teacher, the curriculum, and values education development. *New Directions for Higher Education, 31,* 27–34.

Bennion, M. (1917). *Citizenship: An introduction to social ethics.* Yonkers-on Hudson, NY: World Book.

Berliner, D., & Biddle, B. J. (1996). *The manufactured crisis: Myths, fraud, and the attack on America's public schools.* New York, NY: Basic Books.

Bestor, A. (1953). *Educational wastelands: The retreat from learning in our public schools.* Chicago, IL: University of Illinois Press.

Bestor, A. (1955). *Restoration of learning: A program for redeeming the unfulfilled promise of American education.* New York, NY: Knopf.

Biddle, W. (1937). *Teaching resistance to propaganda: National Council for the Social Studies seventh yearbook.* Washington, DC: NCSS.

Billings, N. (1928). *A determination of generalizations basic to the social studies curriculum.* Baltimore, MD: Warwick and York.

Bloom, B., & Krathwohl, D. R. (1956). *Taxonomy of educational objectives: Handbook I: The cognitive domain.* New York, NY: David McKay.

Bobbitt, J. F. (1918). *The curriculum.* New York, NY: Houghton Mifflin.

Bode, B. (1937). *Democracy as a way of life.* New York, NY: Macmillan.

Bode, B. (1938). *Progressive education at the crossroads.* New York, NY: Newsome & Co.

Boorstin, D. J. (1953). *The genius of American politics.* Chicago, IL: University of Chicago Press.

Bourne, R. (1920). *History of a literary radical and other essays*. New York, NY: B. W. Huebsch.

Brameld, T. (1945). *Design for America*. New York, NY: Hinds, Hayden, and Eldredge.

Brameld, T. (1950). *Education for the emerging age: A mid-century appraisal*. New York, NY: Harper and Brothers.

Brameld, T. (1950). *Patterns of educational philosophy: A democratic interpretation*. New York, NY: World Book.

Brigham, C. C. (1923). *A study of American intelligence*. Princeton, NJ: Princeton University Press.

Broome, E. (1929). *Report of the committee on propaganda in the schools*. Presented at the annual meeting of the National Education Association, July 1929. Washington, DC: NEA.

Bruner, J. (1960). *The process of education*. Cambridge, MA: Harvard University Press.

Bruner, J. (1966). *Toward a theory of instruction*. Cambridge, MA: Belknap.

Carson, R. (1962). *Silent spring*. New York, NY: Houghton Mifflin.

Charters, W. W. (1923). *Curriculum construction*. New York, NY: Macmillan.

Childs, J. (1931). *Education and the philosophy of experimentalism*. New York, NY: The Century Company.

Conant, J. (1957). *The American high school today*. New York, NY: Macmillan.

Connell, W. F. (1976). Moral education: Aims and methods in China, the U.S.S.R., the U.S., and England. In D. Purpel & K. Ryan (Eds.), *Moral education . . . it comes with the territory* (pp. 702–706). Berkeley, CA: McCutchan.

Counts, G. S. (1922). *The selective character of American secondary education*. Chicago, IL: University of Chicago Press.

Counts, G. S. (1927). *The social composition of school boards*. Chicago: University of Chicago Press.

Counts, G. S. (1930). *A Ford crosses Soviet Russia*. Boston, MA: The Stratford Co.

Counts, G. S. (1931). *The Soviet challenge to America*. New York, NY: John Day.

Counts, G. S. (1932). *Dare the schools build a new social order*? New York, NY: John Day.

Counts, G. S. (1938). *The prospects of American democracy*. New York, NY: John Day.

Counts, G. S. (1939). *The schools can teach democracy*. New York, NY: John Day.

Counts, G. S. (1941). *The education of free men in a democracy*. Washington DC: NEA.

Counts, G. S. (1957). *The challenge of Soviet education*. New York, NY: McGraw Hill.

Counts, G. S. (1959). *Khrushchev and the central committee speak on education*. Pittsburgh, PA: University of Pittsburgh Press.

Counts, G. S., & Lodge, N. (1949). *The country of the blind: The Soviet system of mind control*. New York, NY: Houghton Mifflin.

Creel, G. (1920). *How we advertised America: The first telling of the amazing story of the committee of public information that carried the gospel of Americanism to every corner of the globe*. New York, NY: Harper and Brothers.

Cubberley, E. P. (1909). *Changing conceptions of education*. New York, NY: Houghton Mifflin.

Dahlberg, G. (1942). *Race, reason, and rubbish: A primer of race biology*. New York, NY: Columbia University Press.

De Garmo, C. (1889). *The essentials of methods: A discussion of the essential forms of right methods of teaching observation, generalization, application*. Boston, MA: D.C. Heath.

Dewey, J. (1910). *How we think*. Mineola, NY: Dover.

Dewey, J. (1915). *German philosophy and politics*. New York, NY: Henry Holt.

Dewey, J. (1929). *Impressions of Soviet Russia and the revolutionary world*. New York, NY: New Republic.

Dewey, J. (1939). *Freedom and culture*. New York, NY: Putnam's.

Dewey, J. (1997). *Democracy and education: An introduction to the philosophy of education*. New York, NY: New Press. First published in 1916.

DeWitt, N. (1955). *Soviet professional manpower*. Washington, DC: National Science Foundation.

Dixon, R. (1916). *Americanization*. New York, NY: Macmillan.

Dodd, C I. (1898). *Introduction to the Herbartian principles of teaching*. New York, NY: Macmillan.

Dow, P. B. (1991). *Schoolhouse politics: Lessons from the* Sputnik *era*. Cambridge, MA: Harvard University Press.

Education Policies Commission and the American Association of School Administrators. (1937). *The unique function of education in a democracy.* Washington, DC: NEA.

Education Policies Commission and the American Association of School Administrators. (1938). *The structure and administration of education in American democracy*. Washington, DC: NEA.

Education Policies Commission and the American Association of School Administrators. (1940). *Education and economic well being in a democracy*. Washington, DC: NEA.

Education Policies Commission and the American Association of School Administrators. (1940). *Educators and the defense of American democracy*. Washington, DC: NEA.

Educational Policies Commission, National Education Association, and the American Association of School Administrators. (1940). *Learning the ways of democracy.* Washington, DC: NEA.

Engle S., & Ochoa, A. S. (1988). *Education for democratic citizenship: Decision making in the social studies*. New York, NY: Teachers College Press.

Erikson, E. (1950). *Childhood and society.* New York, NY: Norton.

Fenton, E. (1964). *32 problems in world history: Source readings and interpretations*. Fair Lawn, NJ: Scott Foresman and Co.

Fenton, E. (1966). *Teaching the new social studies in secondary schools: An inductive approach*. New York, NY: Holt, Rinehart, and Winston.

Fenton, E. (1967). *Developing a new curriculum: A rationale for the Holt social studies curriculum*. New York, NY: Holt, Rinehart, and Winston.

Finney, R. L. (1922). *Causes and cures for social unrest: An appeal to the middle class*. New York, NY: Macmillan.

Freire, P. (1972). *Pedagogy of the oppressed*. (Trans. Myra Bergman Ramos.) New York, NY: Herder.

Friedel, V. H. (1918). *The German school as war nursery*. New York, NY: Macmillan.

Geertz, C. (1973). *The interpretation of cultures*. New York, NY: Basic Books.

Griffin, A. (1942). *A philosophical approach to the subject matter preparation of teachers of history*. Doctoral dissertation, The Ohio State University, Columbus.

Gross, D., & Murphy, J. (1966). *The revolution in the school*. New York, NY: Harcourt, Brace and World.

Hall, G. S. (Ed.). (1883). *Methods of history*. Boston, MA: D.C. Heath.

Harper, S. N. (1929). *Civic training in Soviet Russia*. Chicago, IL: University of Chicago Press.

Harrington, M. (1962). *The other America: Poverty in the United States*. New York, NY: Simon and Schuster.

Hartz, L. (1954). *The liberal tradition in America: An interpretation of political thought since the revolution*. New York, NY: Harcourt Brace.

Harvard Committee. (1946). *General education in a free society*. Cambridge, MA: Harvard University Press.

Hess, D. (2009). *Controversy in the classroom: Democratic power of discussion*. New York, NY: Routledge.

Hirsch, E. D. (1983). Cultural literacy. *American Scholar, 52*, 159–169.

Hirsch, E. D. (1987). *Cultural literacy: What every American needs to know*. Boston, MA: Houghton Mifflin.

Hirsch, E. D., Kett, J., & Trefil, J. (2002). *The new dictionary of cultural literacy: What every American needs to know*. New York, NY: Houghton Mifflin.

Hofstadter, R. (1955). *The age of reform: From Bryan to F.D.R.* New York, NY: Vintage Books.

Hofstadter, R. (1962). *Anti-intellectualism in American life*. New York, NY: Vintage Books.

Hook, S. (1940). *Reason, social myths, and democracy*. New York, NY: John Day.

Hullfish, G. H., & Smith, P. G. (1961). *Reflective thinking: The method of education*. New York, NY: Dodd, Mead, and Co.

Hunt, E. (Ed.). (1944). *Citizens for a new world: Fourteenth yearbook, National Council for the Social Studies*. Washington, DC: NEA.

Hunt, M. P., & Metcalf, L. E. (1955). *Teaching high school social studies: Problems in reflective thinking and social understanding*. New York, NY: Harper & Row.

Hunter, E. (1951). *Brainwashing in Red China*. New York, NY: Vanguard.

Hunter, E. (1956). *Brainwashing: The story of the men who defied it*. New York, NY: Bookmailer.

Hutchins, R. (1943). *Education for freedom*. Baton Rouge, LA: Louisiana State University Press.

Hutchins, R. (1953). *The conflict of education in a democratic society*. New York, NY: Harper and Brothers.

James, W. (1909). *The meaning of truth, a sequel to pragmatism*. New York, NY: Longman, Green, & Co.

Jones, K., & Olivier, R. (1956). *Progressive education is REDucation*. Boston, MA: Meador Publishing Co.

Kilpatrick, W. H. (Ed.). (1933). *The educational frontier*. New York, NY: D. Appleton-Century Co.

Kilpatrick, W. H. (1940). *Group education for a democracy*. New York, NY: Association Press.

King, B. (1937). *Changing man: The education system of the U.S.S.R.* New York, NY: Viking.

Kohlberg, L. (1969). Stage and sequence: The cognitive-developmental approach to socialization. In D. A. Goslin (Ed.), *Handbook of socialization theory and research* (pp. 347–480). Chicago, IL: Rand McNally College Publishing Co.

Kohlberg, L. (1976). The cognitive developmental approach to moral education. In D. Purpel & K. Ryan (Eds.), *Moral education . . . it comes with the territory* (pp. 176–195). Berkeley, CA: McCutchan.

Kohlberg, L. (1976). *Meaning and measurement in moral development*. Heinz Werner Memorial Lecture. Worcester, MA: Clark University Press.

Kohlberg, L. (1976). The moral atmosphere of the school. In D. Purpel & K. Ryan (Eds.), *Moral education . . . it comes with the territory* (pp. 196–220). Berkeley, CA: McCutchan.

Kohlberg, L. (1980). Educating for a just society. In B. Munsey (Ed.), *Moral development, moral education, and Kohlberg: Basic issues in philosophy, psychology, religion, and education* (pp. 455–471). Birmingham, AL: Religious Education Press.

Kohlberg, L. (1991). My personal search for universal morality. In L. Kuhmerker (Ed.), *The Kohlberg legacy for the helping professions* (pp. 11–17). Birmingham, AL: Doxa Books.

Krathwohl, D. R., Bloom, B. S., & Masia, B. B. (1964). *Taxonomy of educational objectives: Handbook II: The affective domain*. New York, NY: David McKay.

Kuhn, T. (1970). *The structure of scientific revolutions*. Chicago, IL: University of Chicago Press.

Lasswell, H. (1927). *Propaganda technique in the World War*. New York, NY: Peter Smith.

Lasswell, H. (1971). *A pre-view of policy sciences*. New York, NY: American Elsevier.

Lippman, W. (1922). *Public opinion*. New York, NY: Harcourt, Brace, and Co.

Lumley, F. E. (1933). *The propaganda menace*. New York, NY: The Century Company.

Lurry, L., & Alberty, E. (1957). *Developing a high school core program*. New York, NY: Macmillan.

Lynd, A. (1953). *Quackery in the public schools*. New York, NY: Grosset and Dunlap.

Mahoney, J. (1945). *For us the living: An approach to civic education.* New York, NY: Harper and Brothers.

Marker, G., & Mehlinger, H. (1992). Social studies. In P. W. Jackson (Ed.), *The handbook of research on curriculum* (pp. 830–851). New York, NY: Macmillan.

Massialas, B. G., & C. B. Cox. (1966). *Inquiry in social studies.* New York, NY: McGraw-Hill.

Massialas, B. G., Sprague N. F., & Hurst, J. B. (1975). *Social issues through inquiry: Coping in an age of crises.* Englewood Cliffs, NJ: Prentice Hall.

Meerloo, J. (1956). *The rape of the mind: The psychology of mind control, menticide, and brainwashing.* Cleveland, OH: World.

Moffatt, M. (1950). *Social studies instruction: Organization, teaching and supervision of the social studies in secondary schools.* New York, NY: Prentice Hall.

Montagu, A. (1942). *Man's most dangerous myth: The fallacy of race.* New York, NY: Columbia University Press.

Montague, C. E. (1922). *Disenchantment.* New York, NY: Brentano's.

Myers, P.V.N. (1906). *A short history of medieval and modern times.* New York, NY: Ginn and Company.

Nathanson, J. (Ed.). (1945). *The authoritarian attempt to capture education: Papers from the 2nd conference on the scientific spirit and democratic faith.* New York, NY: King's Crown Press.

National Commission on Educational Excellence. (1983). *A nation at risk: The imperative for educational reform: A report to the nation and the Secretary of Education.* Washington, DC: Government Printing Office.

National Education Association. (1894). *Report of the Committee of Ten on secondary school studies with the reports arranged by the committees.* New York, NY: NEA.

Nearing, S. (1924). *Education in Soviet Russia.* New York, NY: International Publishers.

Neill, A. S. (1960). *Summerhill: A radical approach to child rearing.* New York, NY: Hart.

Newlon, J. (1939). *Education for democracy in our time.* New York, NY: McGraw-Hill.

Niebuhr, R. (1944). *The children of light and the children of darkness: A vindication of democracy and a critique of its traditional defense.* Chicago, IL: University of Chicago Press.

O'Connell, G. (1938). *Naturalism in American education.* New York, NY: Benziger Brothers.

Ohlinger, G. (1919). *The German conspiracy in American education.* New York, NY: George H. Doran.

Oliver, D., & Shaver, J. (1966). *Teaching public issues in the high school.* Boston, MA: Houghton Mifflin.

Palmer, R. R. (1957, January). Education and indoctrination. *Peabody Journal of Education, 34,* 228.

Parker, W. (2003). *Teaching democracy: Unity and diversity in public life*. New York, NY: Teachers College Press.

Pearson, N. H. (1952). The Nazi-Soviet pact and the end of a dream. In D. Aaron (Ed.), *America in crisis* (pp. 327–348). New York, NY: Knopf.

Pinkevitch, A. (1929). *The new education in the Soviet Republic*. New York, NY: John Day.

Purpel, D., & Ryan, K. (Eds.). (1976). *Moral education . . . it comes with the territory*. Berkeley, CA: McCutchan.

Quillen, J. I., & Hanna, L. A. (1961). *Education for social competence: The social studies in the secondary school*, revised ed. Chicago, IL: Scott Foresman. Originally published 1948.

Raup, R. B. (1936). *Education and organized interest in America*. New York, NY: Putnam's.

Raup, R. B., Axtelle, G. E., Benne, K. D., & Othanel Smith, B. (1950). *The improvement of practical intelligence: The central task of education*. New York, NY: Harper and Brothers.

Raushenbush, S. (1928). *High power propaganda*. New York, NY: New Republic.

Raushenbush, S. (1932). *The power fight*. New York, NY: New Republic.

Rest, J. (1980). Developmental psychology as a guide to value education: A review of "Kohlbergian" programs. In B. Munsey (Ed.), *Moral development, moral education, and Kohlberg: Basic issues in philosophy, psychology, religion, and education* (pp. 252–274). Birmingham, AL: Religious Education Press.

Rickover, H. G. (1959). *Education and freedom*. New York, NY: Dutton.

Riesman, D. (1950). *The lonely crowd*. New Haven, CT: Yale University Press,

Ripley, W. Z. (1899). *The races of Europe: A sociological study*. New York, NY: D. Appleton and Co.

Robinson, J. H. (1912). *The new history: Essay illustrating the modern American outlook*. New York, NY: Macmillan.

Root, E. M. (1958). *Brainwashing in the high school: An examination of eleven American history textbooks*. New York, NY: Devlin-Adair.

Rorty, R. (2009). *Philosophy and the mirror of nature*. Princeton, NJ: Princeton University Press.

Rugg, H. (1931). *An introduction to problems of American life*. New York, NY: Ginn and Company.

Rugg, H. (1937). *Changing governments and changing cultures: Democracy versus dictatorship: The world struggle*. New York, NY: Ginn and Company.

Rugg, H. (1940). *Citizenship and civic affairs: Community and national life*, Vol. 1. New York, NY: Ginn and Company.

Rugg, H. (1946). *Foundations for American education*. New York, NY: World Book.

Sargent, W. (1957). *Battle for the mind: A physiology of conversion and "brainwashing."* Baltimore, MD: Penguin.

Scheffler, I. (1976). The moral content of education. In D. Purpel & K. Ryan (Eds.), *Moral education . . . it comes with the territory* (pp. 20–29). Berkeley, CA: McCutchan.

Schlesinger, A. M., Jr. (1949). *The vital center: The politics of freedom*. New York, NY: Riverside Press.

Schwab, J. J. (1960). The teaching of science as enquiry. In J. Schwab & P. F. Brandwein (Eds.), *The teaching of science* (pp. 3–103). Cambridge, MA: Harvard University Press.

Schwab, J. J. (1964). The structure of the disciplines: Meanings and significance. In J. J. Schwab, G. W. Ford, & L. Pungo (Eds.), *The structure of knowledge and the curriculum* (pp. 13–29). Chicago, IL: Rand McNally.

Scott, J. F. (1926). *The menace of nationalism in education*. London, UK: G. Allen and Unwin.

Sher, G., & Bennett, W. J. (1982). Moral education and indoctrination. *The Journal of Philosophy*, *79*(11), 665–667.

Silberman, C. E. (1970). *Crisis in the classroom: The remaking of American education*. New York, NY: Vintage Books.

Sinclair, U. (1923). *The goose-step: A study of American education*. New York, NY: AMS Press.

Sinclair, U. (1924). *The goslings: A study of American education*. New York, NY: AMS Press.

Smith, M. (1949). *And madly teach*. Chicago, IL: University of Chicago Press.

Smith, M. (1954). *The diminished mind: A study of planned mediocrity in our public schools*. Chicago, IL: Henry Regenry Co.

Soper, W. (1929, November). What species propaganda? *The Elementary School Journal*, *30*, 224.

Stevenson, G. S. (1940, December). Trends in mental hygiene: An interpretation. *Review of Educational Research*, *10*, 407.

Stowe, C. E. (1839). *Common schools and teachers' seminaries*. Boston, MA: Marsh, Capen, Lyon, and Webb.

Thompson, C. D. (1932). *Confessions of the power trust*. New York, NY: E.P. Dutton.

Thouless, R. H. (1939). *How to think clearly: The technique of applying logic instead of emotion*. New York, NY: Simon and Schuster.

Trow, W. C. (Ed.). (1934). *Character education in Soviet Russia*. Ann Arbor, MI: University of Michigan Press.

Tyler, R. W. (1949). *Basic principles of curriculum and instruction*. Chicago, IL: University of Chicago.

Ulich, R. (1940). *Fundamentals of democratic education*. New York, NY: American Book Company.

Veblen, T. (1915). *Imperial Germany and the industrial revolution*. New York, NY: Macmillan.

Washburne, C. (1936). Indoctrination versus education. *Teachers College Record*, *2*, 213.

Wesley, E. (1950). *Teaching social studies in high schools*, 3rd ed. Boston, MA: D.C. Heath.

White, H. (1975). *Metahistory: The historical imagination in nineteenth-century Europe*. Baltimore, MD: Johns Hopkins University Press.

White, W. (1957). *The captives of Korea: An unofficial white paper*. New York, NY: Scribner's.

Wilson, L. W. (1928). *The new schools of new Russia*. New York, NY: Vanguard.

Woodring, P. (1953). *Let's talk sense about our schools*. New York, NY: McGraw-Hill.

Wythe, W. (1956.) *The organization man*. New York, NY: Simon and Schuster.

Ziemer, G. (1941). *Education for death: The making of a Nazi*. New York, NY: Oxford University Press.

Secondary Sources

Adler, L. K., & Paterson, T. G. (1970). Red fascism: The merger of Nazi Germany and Soviet Russia in the American image of totalitarianism, 1930s–1950s. *American Historical Review*, *75*, 1046–1064.

Alpers, B. (2003). *Dictatorships, democracy and American public culture: Envisioning the totalitarian enemy, 1920s–1950s*. Chapel Hill, NC: University of North Carolina Press.

Angus, D., & Mirel, J. E. (1999). *The failed promise of the American high school, 1890–1995*. New York, NY: Teachers College Press.

Auerbach, J. (2015). *Weapons of democracy: Propaganda, progressivism, and American public opinion*. Baltimore, MD: Johns Hopkins University Press.

Axelrod, A. (2009). *Selling the war: The making of American propaganda*. New York, NY: St. Martin's Press.

Bagenstos, N. T. (1977, Summer). Social reconstruction: The controversy over the textbooks of Harold Rugg. *Theory & Research in Social Education*, *5*, 22–38.

Baker, L. D. (1998). *From savage to negro: Anthropology and the construction of race, 1896–1954*. Berkeley, CA: University of California Press.

Baker, S. (2015, Spring). Desegregation, minimum competency testing, and the origins of accountability: North Carolina and the nation. *History of Education Quarterly*, *55*, 33–57.

Barkan, E. (1992). *The retreat of scientific racism: Changing concepts of race in Britain and the United States between the world wars*. Cambridge, UK: Cambridge University Press.

Barton, K. C. (2009, Fall). Home geography and the development of elementary social education, 1890–1930. *Theory and Research in Social Education*, *37*, 484–514.

Blakey, G. (2015). *Historians on the home front: American propagandists for the Great War*. Lexington, KY: University of Kentucky Press.

Bohan, C. (2007). "A rebellious Jersey girl": Rachel Davis DuBois, intercultural education pioneer. In S. Totten & J. Pedersen (Eds.), *Addressing social issues in the classroom and beyond: The pedagogical efforts of pioneers in the field* (pp. 99–115). Charlotte, NC: Information Age Publishing.

Bowers, C. A. (1969). *The progressive educator and the depression: The radical years*. New York, NY: Random House.

Broder, D. (n.d.) *Life adjustment education: An historical study of a program of the United States Office of Education, 1945–1954*. (Unpublished doctoral dissertation). Teachers College, Columbia University, New York.

Burkholder, Z. (2011). *Color in the classroom: How American schools taught race, 1900–1954*. New York, NY: Oxford University Press.

Burkholder, Z. (2015). "A war of ideas": The rise of conservative teachers in wartime New York City, 1938–1946. *History of Education Quarterly*, *55*, 218–243.

Capozzola, C. (2008). *Uncle Sam wants you: World War I and the making of the modern American citizen*. New York, NY: Oxford.

Carbone, P. F. (1977). *The social and educational thought of Harold Rugg*. Durham, NC: Duke University Press.

Carruthers, S. (2009). *Cold War captives: Imprisonment, escape, and brainwashing*. Berkeley, CA: University of California Press.

Ciepley, D. (2006). *Liberalism in the shadow of totalitarianism*. Cambridge, MA: Harvard University Press.

Cohen, L. (2004). *A consumer's republic: The politics of mass consumption*. New York, NY: Vintage.

Cohen, S. (1983, Summer). The mental hygiene movement, the development of personality and the school: The medicalization of American education. *History of Education Quarterly*, *23*, 123–149.

Cohen-Cole, J. (2014). *The open mind: Cold War politics and the science of human nature*. Chicago, IL: University of Chicago Press.

Collins, R. F. (2012, Spring). This is your propaganda, kids: Building a war myth for World War I children. *Journalism History*, *38*, 13–22.

Coughlan, N. (1975). *Young John Dewey: An essay in American intellectual history*. Chicago, IL: University of Chicago Press.

Cravens, H. (1978). *The triumph of evolution: American scientists and the heredity-environment controversy, 1900–1941*. Philadelphia, PA: University of Pennsylvania Press.

Cremin, L. (1961). *The transformation of the school: Progressivism in American education, 1876–1957*. New York, NY: Vintage.

Cuban, L. (1993). *How teachers taught: Constancy and change in American classrooms, 1880–1990*, 2nd ed. New York, NY: Teachers College Press.

Cusiak, P. A. (1983). *The egalitarian ideal and the American high school: Studies of three schools*. New York, NY: Longman.

Diggins, J. (1966, January). Flirtation with fascism: American pragmatic liberals and Mussolini's Italy. *American Historical Review*, *71*, 487–506.

Diggins, J. (1972). *Mussolini and fascism: The view from America*. Princeton, NJ: Princeton University Press.

Donson, A. (2010). *Youth in the fatherless land: Pedagogy, nationalism, and authority in Germany, 1914–1918*. Cambridge, MA: Harvard University Press.

Dorn, C. (2007). *American education, democracy and the Second World War*. New York, NY: Palgrave Macmillan.

Dorn, C. (2008, August). Treason in the textbooks: Reinterpreting the Harold

Rugg textbook controversy in the context of wartime schooling. *Paedagogica Historica, 44*, 457–479.

Dunne, M. W. (2013). *A Cold War state of mind: Brainwashing and postwar American society*. Boston, MA: University of Massachusetts Press.

Dykhuizen, G. (1973). *The life and mind of John Dewey*. Carbondale, IL: University of Chicago Press.

Evans, R. W. (2004). *The social studies wars: What should we teach the children?* New York, NY: Teachers College.

Evans, R. W. (2007). *This happened in America: Harold Rugg and censure of the social studies*. Charlotte, NC: Information Age Publishing.

Evans, R. W. (2011). *The hope for American school reform: The Cold War pursuit of inquiry learning in social studies*. New York, NY: Palgrave Macmillan.

Evans, R. W. (2011). *The tragedy of American school reform: How curriculum politics and entrenched dilemmas have diverted us from democracy*. New York, NY: Palgrave Macmillan.

Evans, R., & Saxe, D. W. (1996). *Handbook on teaching social issues*. Washington, DC: National Council for the Social Studies.

Fallace, T. (2008). Did the social studies really replace history in American secondary schools? *Teachers College Record, 110*, 2245–2270.

Fallace, T. (2011, April). From the German schoolmaster's psychology to the psychology of the child: Evolving rationales for the teaching of history in American schools in the 1890s. *The Journal of the Gilded Age and Progressive Era, 10*, 161–186.

Fallace, T. (2011, Fall). The effects of life adjustment education on the U.S. history curriculum, 1948–1957. *The History Teacher, 44*, 569–589.

Fallace, T. (2015). *Race and the origins of progressive education 1880–1929*. New York, NY: Teachers College Press.

Fallace, T. (2016). John Dewey's interdisciplinary vision(s) for the social studies. *Social Studies Research and Practice, 11*, 177–189.

Fallace, T. (2016, Fall). The origins of classroom deliberation: Democratic education in the shadow of authoritarianism, 1938–1960. *Harvard Educational Review, 86*, 506–526.

Feuer, L. (1962, Summer) American travelers to the Soviet Union, 1917–32: Formation of a component of New Deal ideology. *American Quarterly, 14*, 119–149.

Filene, P. (1967). *Americans and the Soviet experiment, 1917–1933*. Cambridge, MA: Harvard University Press.

FitzGerald, F. (1979). *America revised: History textbooks in the twentieth century*. New York, NY: Little, Brown.

Foster, S. J. (2000). *Red alert!: Educators confront the red scare in American public schools, 1947–1954*. New York, NY: Peter Lang.

Fowler, R. B. (1978). *Believing skeptics: American political intellectuals, 1945–1964*. Westport, CT: Greenwood Press.

Franklin, B. (1986). *Building the American community: The school curriculum and the search for social control*. Philadelphia, PA: The Falmer Press.

Fraser, J. W. (2007). *Preparing America's teacher's: A history*. New York, NY: Teachers College Press.

Gagnon, P. (Ed.). (1989). *Historical literacy: The case for history in American education*. Boston, MA: Houghton Mifflin.

Gardner, H. (1987). *The mind's new science: A history of the cognitive revolution*. New York, NY: Basic Books.

Gary, B. (1999). *The nervous liberals: Propaganda anxieties from World War I to the Cold War*. New York, NY: Columbia University Press.

Gerstle, G. (2001). *American crucible: Race and nation in the twentieth century*. Princeton, NJ: Princeton University Press.

Gerstle, G. (2015). *Liberty and coercion: The paradox of American government*. Princeton, NJ: Princeton University Press.

Gilman, N. (2003). *Mandarins of the future: Modernization theory in Cold War America*. Baltimore, MD: Johns Hopkins University Press.

Giordano, G. (2007). *Wartime schools: How World War II changed American education*. New York, NY: Peter Lang.

Goodenow, R. K. (1975, December). The progressive educator, race and ethnicity in the depression years: An overview. *History of Education Quarterly*, *15*, 365–394.

Goodenow, R. K. (1977, January). Racial and ethnic tolerance in John Dewey's educational and social thought: The depression years. *Educational Theory*, *27*, 48–64.

Goodenow, R. K. (1981, July). The southern progressive educator on race and pluralism: The case of William Heard Kilpatrick. *History of Education Quarterly*, *21*, 147–170.

Goodlad, J. (2004). *A place called school*. New York, NY: McGraw-Hill.

Graham, P. A. (1967). *Progressive education from Arcady to academe: A history of the progressive Education Association, 1919–1955*. New York, NY: Teachers College Press.

Grant, M. (1916). *The passing of the great race*. New York, NY: Charles Scribner's Sons.

Green, A. (2013). *Education and state formation: Europe, East Asia and the U.S.A.* New York, NY: Palgrave Macmillan.

Gutek, G. H. (1984). *George S. Counts and American civilization: The educator as social theorist*. Macon, GA: Mercer University Press.

Gutek, G. H. (2007). George Counts and social issues. In S. Totten & J. Pedersen (Eds.), *Addressing social issues in the classroom and beyond: The pedagogical efforts of pioneers in the field* (pp. 31–48). Charlotte, NC: IAP.

Halvorsen, A.-L. (2013). *A history of elementary social studies*. New York, NY: Peter Lang.

Halvorsen, A.-L., & Mirel, J. (2013, June). Intercultural education in Detroit, 1943–1954. *Paedagogica Historica*, *49*, 361–381.

Hampel, R. (1987). *The last little citadel: American high schools since 1940*. Boston, MA: Houghton Mifflin.

Haney, D. (2008). *The Americanization of social science: Intellectuals and public responsibility in the postwar United States*. Philadelphia, PA: Temple University Press.

Hartman, A. (2008). *Education and the Cold War: The battle for the American school*. New York, NY: Palgrave Macmillan.

Herbst, J. (1965). *The German historical school in American scholarship: A study in the transfer of culture*. Ithaca, NY: Cornell University Press.

Herbst, J. (1996). *The once and future school: Three hundred and fifty years of American secondary education*. New York, NY: Routledge.

Herbst, J. (2002, Fall). Nineteenth century schools between community and the state: The case of Prussia and United States. *History of Education Quarterly*, *42*, 317–341.

Hertzberg, H. W. (1981). *Social studies reform 1880–1980*. Boulder, CO: SSEC Publications.

Hirsch, E. D. (1999). *The schools we need: And why we don't have them*. New York, NY: Anchor Books.

Hollinger, D. (1995). *Post-ethnic America: Beyond multiculturalism*. New York, NY: Basic Books.

Hollinger, D. (1996). *Science, Jews, and secular culture: Studies in mid-twentieth century American intellectual history*. Princeton, NJ: Princeton University Press.

Holmes, L. E. (1991). *The Kremlin and the schoolhouse: Reforming education in Soviet Russia 1911–1931*. Bloomington, IN: Indiana University Press.

Jackson, K. (1985). *Crabgrass frontier: The suburbanization of the United States*. New York, NY: Oxford.

Jackson, W. A. (1990). *Gunnar Myrdal and America's conscience: Social engineering and racial liberalism, 1938–1987*. Chapel Hill, NC: University of North Carolina Press.

Jahoda, M. (1969). The migration of psychoanalysis: Its impact on American psychology. In D. Fleming & B. Bailyn (Eds.), *The intellectual migration: Europe and America, 1930–1960* (pp. 420–445). Cambridge, MA: Belknap Press.

Jewett, A. (2012). *Science, democracy, and the American university: From the Civil War to the Cold War*. New York, NY: Cambridge University Press.

Johanek, M. C., & Puckett, J. L. (2007). *Leonard Covello and the making of Benjamin Franklin High School: Education as if citizenship mattered*. Philadelphia, PA: Temple University Press.

Keels, O. M. (1980, Summer). The collegiate influence on the early social studies curriculum: A reassessment of the role of historians. *Theory and Research in Social Education*, *8*, 105–120.

Kennedy, D. M. (1980). *Over here: The First World War and American society*. New York, NY: Oxford University Press.

Kingsbury, C. M. (2010). *For home and country: World War I propaganda on the home front*. Lincoln, NE: University of Nebraska Press.

Klarman, M. (2004). *From Jim Crow to civil rights: The Supreme Court and the struggle for racial equality*. New York, NY: Oxford University Press.

Kliebard, H. (1995). *The struggle for the American curriculum, 1893–1958*. New York, NY: Routledge.

Kloppenberg, J. (1986). *Uncertain victory: Social democracy and progressivism in European and American thought, 1870–1920*. New York, NY: Oxford University Press.

Krug, E. (1972). *The American high school, volume 2, 1920–1941*. Madison, WI: University of Wisconsin Press.

Laats, A. (2015). *The other school reformers: Conservative activism in American education*. Cambridge, MA: Harvard University Press.

Labaree, D. (2010). *Someone has to fail: The zero-sum game of public schooling*. Cambridge, MA: Harvard University Press.

Lagemann, E. C. (1992, February). Prophesy or profession? George S. Counts and the social study of education. *American Journal of Education*, *100*, 137–155.

Lasch, C. (1962). *The American liberals and the Russian Revolution*. New York, NY: McGraw-Hill.

Looker, B. (2015). *A nation of neighborhoods: Imagining cities, communities, and democracy in postwar America*. Chicago, IL: University of Chicago Press.

Loss, C. G. (2005). *Public schools, private lives: American education and psychological authority, 1945–1975*. (Unpublished doctoral dissertation). University of Virginia.

McGreevy, J. T. (2003). *Catholicism and American freedom: A history*. New York, NY: Norton.

McMurry, D. (1946). *Herbartian contributions to history instruction in American schools*. New York, NY: Teachers College Press.

McNeil, L. (1986). *Contradictions of control: School structure and school knowledge*. New York, NY: Routledge.

Mehaffy, G. L. (1987, Winter). Social studies in World War One: A period of transition. *Theory and Research in Social Education*, *15*, 23–32.

Melley, T. (2000). *Empire of conspiracy: The culture of paranoia in postwar America*. Ithaca, NY: Cornell University Press.

Menand, L. (2001). *The metaphysical club: A story of ideas in America*. New York, NY: Farrar, Strauss, and Giroux.

Menand, L. (2010). *The marketplace of ideas: Reform and resistance in the American university*. New York, NY: Norton.

Mirel, J. E. (2010). *Patriotic pluralism: Americanization education and European immigrants*. Cambridge, MA: Harvard University Press.

Montalto, N. V. (1982). *A history of the intercultural education movement, 1924–1941*. New York, NY: Garland.

Moreau, J. (2003). *Schoolbook nation: Conflicts over American history textbooks from the Civil War to the present*. Ann Arbor, MI: University of Michigan Press.

Myrdal, G. (1944). *An American dilemma: The negro problem and modern democracy*. New York: Harper.

Nash, G. B., Crabtree, C., & Dunn, R. E. (1997). *History on trial: Culture wars and teaching the past*. New York, NY: Vintage.

Neem, J. (2017). *Democracy's school: The rise of public education in America*. Baltimore, MD: Johns Hopkins University Press.

Neill, T. (1960). Dewey's ambivalent attitude towards history. In J. E. Blewett (Ed.), *John Dewey: His thought and influence*. New York, NY: Fordham University Press.

Nemeth, J. (2017, August). The case for clearing house: Sidney Hook and the ethics of academic freedom during the McCarthy era. *History of Education Quarterly*, *57*, 399–426.

Novick, P. (1987). *That noble dream: The objectivity question and the American historical profession*. New York, NY: Cambridge University Press.

Null, J. W. (2007). William C. Bagley and the founding of essentialism: An untold story in American educational history. *Teachers College Record*, *109*, 1013–1055.

Orgeron, D., Orgeron, M., & Streible, D. (Eds.). (2012). *Learning with the lights off: Educational film in the United States*. New York, NY: Oxford University Press.

Orrill, R., & Shapiro, L. (2005). From bold beginnings to an uncertain future: The discipline of history and history education. *The American Historical Review*, *110*, 727–751.

Parker, W. (Ed.). (1996). *Educating the democratic mind*. Albany, NY: State University of New York Press.

Patterson, J. T. (1996). *Grand expectations: The United States, 1945–1974*. New York, NY: Oxford University Press.

Peacock, M. (2014). *Innocent weapons: The Soviet and American politics of childhood in the Cold War*. Chapel Hill, NC: University of North Carolina Press.

Pells, R. H. (1973). *Radical visions and American dreams: Culture and social thought in the depression years*. Urbana, IL: University of Illinois Press.

Pells, R. H. (1985). *The liberal mind in a conservative age: American intellectuals in the 1940s and 1950s*. New York, NY: Harper and Row.

Petrina, S. (2006, Winter). The medicalization of education: A historiographical synthesis. *History of Education Quarterly*, *46*, 503–531.

Philips, C. J. (2015). *The new math: A political history*. Chicago, IL: University of Chicago Press.

Powell, A., Farrar, E., & Cohen, D. (1985). *The shopping mall high school: Winners and losers in the educational marketplace*. Boston, MA: Houghton Mifflin.

Purcell, E. A., Jr. (1973). *The crisis of democratic theory: Scientific naturalism and the problem of value*. Lexington, KY: University of Kentucky Press.

Ratner, S. (1950). Dewey's contribution to historical theory. In S. Hook (Ed.), *John Dewey: Philosopher of science and freedom: A symposium* (pp. 134–152). New York, NY: The Dial Press.

Ravitch, D. (1983). *The troubled crusade: American education, 1945–1980*. New York, NY: Basic Books.

Ravitch, D. (1987). Tot sociology, or what happened to history in grade schools. *American Scholar*, *56*, 343–354.

Ravitch, D. (1998). Who prepares our history teachers? Who should prepare our history teachers? *The History Teacher*, *31*(3), 495–503.

Ravitch, D. (2000). *Left back: A century of failed school reform*. New York, NY: Simon and Schuster.

Ravitch, D., & Finn, C. (1987). *What do our 17-year-olds know? A report on the first national assessment of history and literature*. New York, NY: Harper and Row.

Reese, W. J. (2001, Spring). The origins of progressive education. *History of Education Quarterly*, *41*, 1–24.

Riley, K. (2007). Imagining the future: Theodore Brameld on the frontiers of multicultural education. In S. Totten & J. Pedersen (Eds.), *Addressing social issues in the classroom and beyond* (pp. 201–220). Charlotte, NC: Information Age Publishing.

Ritter, K. (2015). *Re-framing the subject: Postwar instructional film and class-conscious literacies*. Pittsburgh, PA: University of Pittsburgh Press.

Rochester, S. I. (1977). *American liberal disillusionment in the wake of World War I*. University Park, PA: Pennsylvania State University Press.

Rodgers, D. T. (1998). *Atlantic crossings: Social politics in a progressive age*. Cambridge, MA: Harvard University Press.

Rodgers, D. T. (2011). *Age of fracture*. Cambridge, MA: Belknap Press, 2011.

Ross, S. H. (2009). *Propaganda for war: How the United States was conditioned to fight the Great War of 1914–1918*. San Diego, CA: Progressive Press.

Rudolph, J. (2002). *Scientists in the classroom: The Cold War reconstruction of American science education*. New York, NY: Palgrave Macmillan.

Rudolph, J. (2005, Fall). Epistemology for the masses: The origins of "the scientific method" in American schools. *History of Education Quarterly*, *45*, 341–376.

Seed, D. (2004). *Brainwashing: The fictions of mind control: A study of novels and films since World War II*. Kent, OH: Kent State University Press.

Selig, D. (2008). *Americans all: The cultural gifts movement*. Cambridge, MA: Harvard University Press.

Smith, K. (1999). *Mental hygiene: Classroom films, 1945–1970*. New York, NY: Blast Books.

Smith, M. C. (1994). *Social science in the crucible: The American debate over objectivity and purpose, 1918–1914*. Durham, NC: Duke University Press.

Sproule, M. J. (1997). *Propaganda and democracy: The American experience of media and mass persuasion*. New York, NY: Cambridge University Press.

Stallones, J. (2002). *Paul Robert Hanna: A life of expanding communities*. Washington, DC: Hoover Press.

Stanley, W. B. (1992). *Curriculum for utopia: Social reconstructionism and critical pedagogy in the postmodern era*. Albany, NY: State University of New York Press.

Steel, R. (1980). *Walter Lippman and the American century*. Boston, MA: Little, Brown & Co.

Tanner, D., & Tanner, L. N. (1990). *History of the school curriculum*. New York, NY: Macmillan.

Todd, L. P. (1945). *Wartime relations of the federal government and public schools, 1917–1918*. New York, NY: Teachers College, Columbia University.

Tyack D. B., & Cuban, L. (1995). *Tinkering toward utopia: A century of school reform*. Cambridge, MA: Harvard University Press.

Ulich, R. (1935). *A sequence of educational influences: Traced through unpublished writings of Pestalozzi, Froebel, Diesterweg, Horace Mann, and Henry Barnard*. Cambridge, MA: Harvard University Press.

Urban, W. J. (2010). *More than science and Sputnik: The National Defense Act of 1958*. Tuscaloosa, AL: University of Alabama Press.

Vaughn, S. (n.d.) *Holding fast the inner lines: Democracy, nationalism, and the committee on public information*. Chapel Hill, NC: University of North Carolina Press.

Valkanova, Y. (2009, May). The passion for educating the "new man": Debates about pre-schooling in Soviet Russia. *History of Education Quarterly*, *49*, 211–221.

VanSledright, B. (2011). *The challenge of rethinking history education: On practices, theories, and policies*. New York, NY: Routledge.

Wall, W. (2008). *Inventing the American way: The politics of consensus from the New Deal to the Civil Rights Movement*. New York, NY: Oxford University Press.

Weltman, B. (1999, Spring). The message and the medium: Roots/routes of Jerome Bruner's postmodernism. *Theory and Research in Social Education*, *29*, 160–178.

Weltman, B. (2000, Winter). Reconsidering Arthur Bestor and the Cold War in social education. *Theory and Research in Social Education*, *28*, 11–39.

Westbrook, R. (1991). *John Dewey and American democracy*. Ithaca, NY: Cornell University Press.

Westbrook, R. (2004). *Why we fought: Forging American obligation in World War II*. Washington, DC: Smithsonian Books.

White, M. (1947). *Social thought in America: The revolt against formalism*. New York, NY: Oxford.

Whitfield, S. J. (1991). *The culture of the Cold War*. Baltimore, MD: Johns Hopkins University Press.

Wraga, W. (1994). *Democracy's high school*. Lanham, MD: University Press of America.

Wraga, W. (2009). From slogan to anathema: Historical representations of life adjustment education. *American Journal of Education*, *116*, 185–209.

Zimmerman, J. (2002). *Whose America? Culture wars in the public schools*. Cambridge, MA: Harvard University Press.

Index

Note: Page numbers followed by "n" indicate numbered endnotes.

About the Author

Thomas D. Fallace is a professor of education at William Paterson University of New Jersey. He is author of *The Emergence of Holocaust Education in American Schools* (2008), *Dewey and the Dilemma of Race: An Intellectual History, 1895–1922* (2011), and *Race and the Origins of Progressive Education, 1890–1929* (2015). He lives in Montclair, New Jersey, with his wife and two sons.